THE
DOMELINERS

THE DOMELINERS

By Patrick C. Dorin

A Pictorial History of the Penthouse Trains

SUPERIOR PUBLISHING COMPANY-SEATTLE

to by W. Frank Clodfelter)

SUPERIOR PUBLISHING COMPANY SEATTLE, WASHINGTON

LIBRARY OF CONGRESS CATALOGUE CARD NUMBER 73–79356

FIRST EDITION

PRINTED IN THE UNITED STATES OF AMERICA

DEDICATION

TO THE MEMORY
OF MY WIFE'S MOTHER,
SENIA MARIE FOLEY,
I DEDICATE THIS BOOK.

ACKNOWLEDGMENTS

A large number of people lent freely of their time and resources to this writer during the search for data and materials for this book. For their time, assistance and encouragement, the author wishes to gratefully acknowledge the following people:

Mr. Albert P. Salisbury of Superior Publishing Company for his encouragement and work with layout through to the final publication of this book.

My wife, Karen, who gave much of her time checking materials and the manuscript for errors, Sy Dykhouse for the various Railroad Company Route Maps and the following railroad photographers: Bob Lorenz, George Cockle, Jim Scribbins, Louis A. Marre, Lloyd Lewis, James Morin, Harold K. Vollrath, J.W. Swanberg, Ted Shrady, William S. Kuba, Paul Stringham, William A. Raia, John H. Kuehl, William Warden, Chapman S. Root, W. Frank Clodfelter, Carl H. Smith, Dick Steinheimer, Mrs. Alice L. Sharp of the Historical Society of Colorado, H.W. Pontin and other staff members of Rail Photo Service, and David J. Overhouse for his excellent photo printing and photography.

A special note of thanks must go to the following operating, mechanical and public relations men of the following companies: Alaska Railroad – B.G. Bailey; AMTRAK – E.E. Edel; Auto-Train – R.A. Goldstein; Auto-Liner – W.W. Kratville; Baltimore & Ohio – William F. Howes, Jr.; Burlington Northern – Peter A. Briggs; Canadian National – R.A. Boden; Canadian Pacific – O.S.A. LaVallee; Chesapeake and Ohio Railway Company; Denver & Rio Grande Western – Alexis McKinney; General Motors Corporation – Joseph McKeon; Illinois Central – Robert W. O'Brien; Louisville & Nashville – Edison H. Thomas; Milwaukee Road – Marc Green; Missouri Pacific – M.F. Hengel, Harry Hammer; Norfolk & Western – R.W. Pendergast; Pullman Standard – John Sward, John J. McHugh, John Kniola; Rock Island – E.J. Wojtas; Sikorsky Aircraft Division of United Aircraft Company – Paul Burton; Santa Fe – Bill Burk; Seaboard Coast Line – Don Martin; Southern Railway – William F. Geeslin; Southern Pacific – R.A. Sederholm; Union Pacific – Edwin C. Schafer; Western Pacific Railroad Company.

Without the complete and unselfish cooperation of the above men and women, this book would not have been possible. Should an acknowledgment have been left out inadvertently, this writer trusts it will be found in its appropriate place within the book.

TABLE OF CONTENTS

Introduction

Perhaps one of the greatest, if not the greatest, sets of passenger trains ever to be sired by the design engineers were the "DOMELINERS." These trains equipped with cars with penthouses on top cris-crossed the United States and Canada, and gave passengers the greatest travel thrill available anywhere on any type of transportation. Stop for a moment. Imagine you are in the lead dome of the Denver Zephyr heading west. The sun is just coming up behind you, the great and glorious Rocky Mountains are literally rising up out of the Great Plains before you. The sun shines on the snow-capped peaks west of Denver. The beauty is so immense, that if you traveled on No. 1 (now No. 5) a thousand times, you cannot tear your eyes away from the wondrous spectacle before you. Everyone in the Dome is completely quiet and, for a moment, it seems as though the whole world has stopped still.

Businessmen have told this writer that shortly after viewing the scene described above, they were able to make decisions regarding problems that had been plaguing them for a long time. There is no doubt about it, a trip on a Domeliner is unforgettable.

This, then, is the story of those unique passenger trains that operated over every major railroad line in the west. Each chapter contains a brief history of the trains involved along with an explanation of the train operation, the dome equipment, both interior and exterior, route maps and time tables. The time period covered extends from 1891 and the design of the first dome car through to the Domeliners operated by AMTRAK in 1972. The "Domeliners" were, and are, a fabulous way to travel.

The railroads and companies that owned and/or operated domeliners on a regular basis in the United States and Canada are as follows:

- Alaska Railroad
- AMTRAK
- Atlantic Coast Line
- Auto-Train
- Baltimore & Ohio
- Burlington Northern
- Burlington Route
- Canadian National
- Canadian Pacific
- Central of Georgia
- Chesapeake and Ohio
- Chicago & North Western
- Denver & Rio Grande Western
- Great Northern
- Illinois Central
- Louisville and Nashville
- Milwaukee Road
- Missouri Pacific
- Norfolk and Western
- Northern Pacific
- Penn Central
- Pennsylvania
- Pullman Company
- Richmond, Fredericksburg and Potomac
- Rock Island
- Santa Fe
- Seaboard Coast Line
- Southern
- Southern Pacific
- Spokane, Portland & Seattle
- Union Pacific
- Wabash
- Western Pacific

Patrick C. Dorin

At Ashland, Wisconsin
August 1, 1972

PROBABLY FEW PEOPLE REALIZED it when the DeWitt Clinton was built in 1831, but the top seats of the stage coaches on flanged wheels were great places to observe the country side provided one could dodge the smoke and sparks from the steam locomotive. These coaches were the first rail passenger cars to provide seats "up top," although they were probably not built for the specific purpose of observation. (Bob Lorenz)

CHAPTER 1

A History of Observation

The Dome Car is essentially a special type of an observation car, and the railroads have been building and operating such equipment since the earliest companies were constructed. In fact, ever since the passenger car evolved from the wagon and stage coach design into the basic tube design in the late 1830's and 1840's, there has been at least one car in every prominent train that has been designed particularly for relaxation and observation. At first, this car was known as the "Smoker" and was usually no different from the other coaches. However, as time went on and enclosed vestibules were invented changes began to take place in passenger car design.

The open end coaches were a natural design for observation cars. Both passengers and railroad men noted the view that could be had from the rear platform of the last car of the train. With enclosed vestibules, came the first cars to be designed with an observation platform. Nearly every railroad in the United States began operating such cars and by 1900 every primary and secondary main line (and many branches, too) had such equipment operating over them.

By the mid-1920's, observation cars were being turned out with enclosed Sun Rooms and abbreviated platforms; and finally by 1930 Solarium Cars without any platform at all were rolling out of the Car Builders' shops. These cars were built from standard designs with large windows enclosing the rear Sun Rooms, and could be operated mid-train if desired.

Along with the depression, the 1930's brought more changes to the Observation Cars as the new streamliners were being built with tear drop ends. The 1940's brought another development that seemed almost like a step backward. The Observation Cars were being built with squared off ends similar in many respects to the Solarium Cars of the 1930's. The last such cars to be built were the 1956 Denver Zephyr Dome Parlor Observation Lounges.

However, the ultimate in Observation Car design is the Milwaukee Road Skytop Observation Sleeper Lounges and Parlor Cars built in 1948 and 1949. These cars literally provided the traveling public with dome car viewing and no Observation Car built before or since their construction could match them.

The rear Observation Cars, which were built with just about every car type imaginable (coach, parlor, sleeper, diner, lounge, etc.), were not the only types of such cars to be designed. For example, in the 1920's, the Union Pacific operated a car that resembled a gondola fitted with safety railings and seats for mountain viewing. In 1921, the Milwaukee Road constructed two open air Observation Cars – fitted with a roof – for service on the Olympian between Harlowton, Montana, and Avery, Idaho.

The Soo Line and the Canadian Pacific Summer Season Mountaineer and Soo-Dominion carried such an Open Observation between Calgary and Vancouver during the period June 1st to September 15th. This was the last oper-

A TYPICAL EXAMPLE of the standard open-end observation car of the 1920's and 1930's is portrayed by Circus Car No. 46, the Baraboo. It is easy to see how designers eventually enclosed the rear end of the car. (Rail Photo Service)

ation of such a car and it was not discontinued until the mid-1950's – the arrival of the Dome Cars for the Canadian and the Dominion.

The original idea for a Dome Observatory was born in Canada in the 19th Century. According to the May 2, 1891, issue of *Scientific American*, an inventor by the name of Mr. T.J. McBride constructed a special form of a car (with three domes) known as "McBride's Observatory Sleeper." The car was designed to eliminate the hazards, dust, cinders and tempest of the open observation car. The upper berths of the car furnished the seats for dome observation of the passing scenery. The top of the domes were 15 feet above the rail, which prevented the eastern railroads from operating such a car which happens to be still true today. However, McBride proposed that by using only the side seats of the domes, the extreme height could be reduced for use on such railroads. McBride's Observatory Sleeper was constructed and patented in Winnipeg, Manitoba. His idea was well ahead of its time and the innovation was not to be used again by a steam railroad until 1902, again in Canada.

Meanwhile, the electric railways were also looking at the idea of a raised section for viewing scenery. The March 25, 1893, supplement issue of *Scientific American* reported that Mr. B.C. Riblet, the Chief Engineer of the Spokane and Coeur d' Alene Railroad and Navigation Company designed a new style of electric car. The car was 40 feet long and had a raised observation section to accommodate both passengers and motorman. The car had a total capacity of 60 persons and the section beneath the dome was reserved for freight and express. The article did not state if the car was actually built, but the idea was alive in 1893.

In 1902, the Canadian Pacific took a close look at McBride's car and came up with their own design with two domes. This dome car was an open end car without vestibules. The Canadian Pacific built eight such cars and operated them in the western Provinces until 1908 when they were withdrawn from service. The idea of Dome Cars was then to lie dormant until the Second World War.

The steward's compartment was located to the right of the stairway leading to the dome. This area contained a refrigerator, an intertrain phone, space for cigars and cigarettes and a locker. Beverage lockers were also located beneath and beside the stairs.

The dining car also contained facilities for storing large quantities of fresh and frozen foods, etc. Eleven refrigerators provided a total of 111 cubic feet of storage space, or more than that supplied by 15 standard sized household refrigerators. It was a great car to dine in. According to the Union Pacific, the car was retired in February, 1961.

The Sleeping Car

The sleeping car contained three compartments, each with two lower berths; two drawing rooms, each with two upper and one lower berth and eight duplex roomettes. All beds in the car ran lengthwise of the train.

The compartments were on the lower level of the car and one of the berths converted to a sofa for day use.

The two drawing rooms were located at the forward end of the car and could be used en suite if desired. In addition to the berths, each room contained two upholstered lounge chairs, even when all three berths were made up. The lower berth converted into a sofa for day time use. There was a lavatory and toilet room opposite the entrance of each room. The two rooms also included overhead baggage space and a wardrobe.

OVERHEAD VIEW OF THE "Train of Tomorrow" during its stop at the Hanging Bridge. The reader should note the shape of the domes and compare them with the domes built by Pullman Standard at later times. (State Historical Society of Colorado)

THE GENERAL MOTORS "Train of Tomorrow" stopping at the Hanging Bridge in the Royal Gorge on the Rio Grande Railroad during its tour of the USA in 1947. (State Historical Society of Colorado)

AFTER A NATION WIDE TOUR and exhibition at the Chicago Railroad Fair, the Train of Tomorrow was sold to the Union Pacific Railroad. At that time, the entire train was repainted in the UP yellow and grey and sent on a tour of the system. This photo shows the train after purchase running as train No. 104 during its tour. During the summer of 1950, the UP assigned the four cars to the Portland–Seattle passenger train pool service. (Union Pacific)

The duplex roomettes were built so that the level of one was two steps above the aisle and the adjoining one was level with the aisle. In the aisle level roomettes, the bed pulled out at floor level or pushed in - drawer like - under the floor of the adjoining roomette when not in use. The beds in the other roomettes pulled down from the wall at one end. All of the beds were fully made up. Each roomette contained one built in easy sofa chair. Opposite this there was a high level recess for luggage, a wash stand and a toilet.

All of the rooms were decorated in a combination of colors, carpeting and draperies that was different from all of the others. For example, the color scheme in one of the drawing rooms was as follows: The carpet was Araby silver grey. The ceiling and an 18" width at the top of the walls was a blue-green. The walls were a light warm grey. The drapes were a Cape Cod rose with floral reds and greens on white. The sofa and one chair were covered in needle point green, while the other chair was needle point egg plant color. The wood portion of the chairs was bleached walnut. This sleeping car, Dream Cloud, was the only dome sleeper constructed by Pullman-Standard.

The Observation Lounge Car

The dome observation car brought up the rear of the four car domeliner. There were four areas in the car with seating for 68 people. More than half of the chairs in the car were movable to permit varied seating for different groups.

The rear observation room provided seating for 18 passengers, most of it movable. The carpeting was Araby peach. The walls were covered to the window line with rich red Velvean leather with a satin stainless steel moulding and trim. Drapes with a Persian tree design on a light background concealed all of the wall columns between the extra wide windows. This gave the impression of complete glass encirclement. The upper walls were grey and the ceiling was a light ivory in color. Lounge seating was upholstered in turquoise and in grey super needlepoint. This room also contained a desk to the right of the stairway leading to the dome.

The lower section beneath the Astra Dome contained an intimate cocktail lounge seating 10 passengers. The bar in this section had plywood paneling stained just off natural with a dark top and a metal and picture glass back bar and front trim. The chairs were covered with honey colored leather. The tables had a formica top with a special design on each.

The front lounge section seated 16 passengers. The seats were upholstered in chartreuse nylon with bolster rolls of rose nylon. Light drapes carried a tropical motif. The walls were painted silver grey with carpeting to match. This room was lighted by circular ceiling fixtures.

The Astra Dome of this car, as in all others, seated 24 people in seats upholstered in a turquoise fabric. The walls and upper structure of the dome was painted in a gray tan. The carpeting was Araby peach. The dome observation lounge car was a restful piece of equipment, but the design was not duplicated for dome lounge cars built since this first dome observation lounge. The closest cars in interior design were the Union Pacific dome lounge cars. But even these were quickly and quietly modified for mid-train use. According to the Union Pacific, this car was retired March, 1965.

The Exhibition Tour.

After the train had been completed, and tested, General Motors operated the train on its first press run on May 26th and 27th, 1947 over the Monon Railroad between Chicago and French Lick, Indiana. The train hosted over 100 travel and industrial writers for the press and radio commentators. On May 28th, the train was formally dedicated and then placed on public exhibition for Chicagoans until June 2nd. On that date the train departed Chicago for a tour that took it to such cities as Detroit, Pittsburgh, Baltimore, Washington, D.C., Jacksonville, Indianapolis, Denver, Portland, Los Angeles, Dallas, St. Louis and many other cities. The train was very popular with the public if the number of people viewing the train is a true indication. For example, in one 150 hour period, 150,000 visitors inspected the train.

After the tour was completed, the train spent time at the Chicago Railroad Fair – and it was expected that after that a Class I Railroad would purchase the train. And this in fact did happen in early 1950, the train was purchased by the Union Pacific.

UNION PACIFIC DOME SLEEPER, Dream Cloud, was operated as a parlor car in the Seattle–Portland service, and rarely functioned in sleeping car service. The car had a sleeping capacity of 20 people, or 44 passengers in parlor car service. The car contained 3 compartments, 2 drawing rooms and 8 duplex roomettes. Although the car served as a prototype for dome sleepers on other railroads, the Union Pacific did not purchase any additional dome sleepers for operation over its lines. (Union Pacific)

TRAIN OF TOMORROW DOME COACH in the UP scheme after purchase by that railroad. The car was later numbered 7010, was 85 feet long and had a total seating capacity of 72 passengers. (Union Pacific)

TRAIN OF TOMORROW DOME DINING CAR, Sky View, after repainting by the Union Pacific Railroad. This car served as a prototype for the dome diners purchased in 1955. Sky View was later numbered 8010 and had a seating capacity of 52 people including 18 in the dome. (Union Pacific)

Union Pacific Ownership and Operation

When the Union Pacific purchased the Train of Tomorrow in early 1950, they refurbished and repainted the entire train and, of course, sent it on another tour. This time the tour stayed primarily on UP rails. When this was completed, the company sent her to the Pacific Northwest and the pool service operated by the Northern Pacific, Great Northern and Union Pacific between Seattle and Portland.

On June 18, 1950, the Union Pacific placed the four Train of Tomorrow cars in service on trains 457 and 458 between Portland and Seattle. The train departed Portland daily at 8:00 AM and arrived at Seattle at 11:59 AM. The consist of the train included a varied number of baggage, mail and express cars, five or six 48 seat coaches, a straight parlor car, the Chicago–Seattle sleeper (from the City of Portland) and the four Astra Dome cars. The consist of the south bound run was virtually identical. The train departed Seattle at 4:45 PM in the early 1950's and thus provided one day travelers over four and one half hours in Seattle. (In later years, the schedules were modified extensively. For example, by the mid-1960's; when the Train of Tomorrow finally faded away; No. 457 departed Portland at 9:30 AM, arriving Seattle at 1:30 PM. No. 458 departed Seattle at 5:00 PM arriving Portland at 9:15 PM. Running times remained virtually the same for the 182 mile run over the years.)

The four Astra dome cars were nifty ways to travel the Pacific Coast Route. The cars were gradually removed from service until 1962 when the Union Pacific began operating the equipment off of train No. 105, the City of Portland, on train No. 457 and 458. The Train of Tomorrow equipment was retired during the years of 1961 through 1965.

It may seem to some that revenue service for the train was rather short. For at least one of the cars, the Dome Diner "Sky View", it was only about a decade. However, the train was an astounding success. According to General Motors, it was the "Idea" train. It fostered an idea, the dome, for easy and pleasurable viewing. In fact, besides the act of transporting a person(s) from one place to another, trains are best for viewing. How else can you travel and see the USA and Canada for real at the same time. When you drive, your eyes had better be on the road. Over 50,000 deaths annually show that someone did not have his eyes on the road. When you fly, you are up above the weather and the clouds, and you are limited as to what you can see in any detail. Although the view can be pretty nice up there. (Now with the jumbo jets people don't even look to the ground.) Bus travel is functional, but one cannot really do any serious viewing "up and down or all around". Only in a "Domeliner" can you do that. The Train of Tomorrow "Idea" spread to several types of passenger train equipment – all off shoots from the four original cars – and to dozens of railroads. It helped three car builders sell passenger cars until the late 1950's, and it helped General Motors sell passenger engines to pull those domeliners. Yes, the Train of Tomorrow was a success in terms of what it sired, and the rest of this book is about those trains.

THE TRAIN OF TOMORROW DOME observation lounge car, Moon Glow, is probably one of the most unique cars of this type ever built. It just has "that look to it." The car was later numbered 9015 and had a total seating capacity of 68 passengers. (Union Pacific)

A CUT-A-WAY VIEW of the Union Pacific – General Motors Train of Tomorrow dome observation lounge car. Note that the arrangement of the seats in the observation room face the windows, a practice that was seldom followed in almost all observation cars. While this car was in service in the Portland–Seattle pool train operations, it was open to only parlor or sleeping car passengers. (Union Pacific)

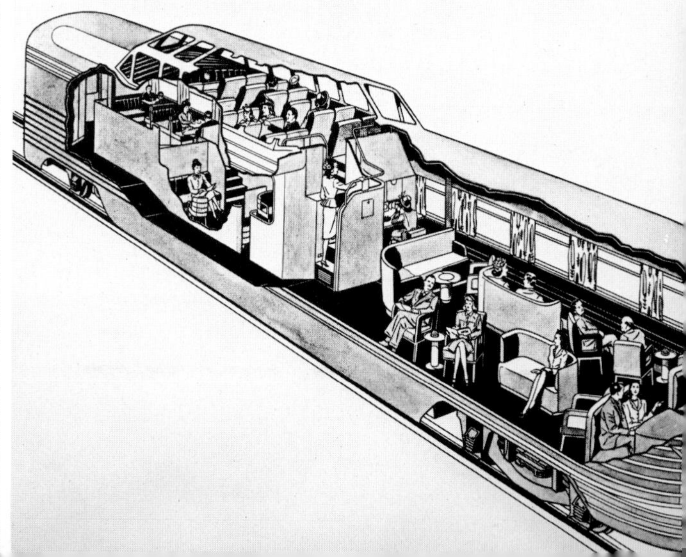

INTERIOR OF THE DOME DINING SECTION of the Union Pacific – General Motors Train of Tomorrow dining car. (Union Pacific)

Seattle, San Francisco and Los Angeles

	No. 402 9-58 Shasta	No. 408 -11-52 Cascade Daily	**Table Y** (*Pacific Standard Time*)		No. 51- 12-457 Cascade Daily	No. 57- 10-401 Shasta	
.....	**11.45**	**12.30**	Lv **Seattle**	Ar	**1.00**	6.30	.....
.....	1.15	**1.26**	" Tacoma	"	**12.01**	4.15	.....
.....	6.05	**4.30**	Ar **Portland**	Lv	9.00	**11.45**	.....
....	7.45	**4.45**	Lv **Portland** (So. Pac.)	Ar	8.15	**11.25**	....
....	8.57	**5.57**	" Salem	Lv	7.02	**10.11**	....
....	10.14	**7.14**	" Eugene	"	5.55	**9.04**	....
....	**2.35**	**11.40**	" Klamath Falls	"	1.35	**4.40**	....
....	**9.08**	6.40	Ar **Davis**	Lv	**6.30**	9.40	....
⊙	♦ **9.40**	♦ 7.15	Ar **Sacramento** (Bus)	Lv	♦ **5.55**	♦ 9.00	✱ ....
....	'**9.57**	7.35	Lv **Martinez** (So. Pac.)	Ar	**5.35**	8.45	....
....	**10.40**	8.20	Ar Oakland (16th St.)	Lv	**4.35**	8.00	....
....	**11.20**	9.00	Ar **San Francisco** (3rd Townsend)	Lv	**3.55**	7.20	....
.....	**10.35**	8.23	Lv **Martinez**	Ar	**5.00**	5.30	.....
.....	2.40	11.59	" Fresno	"	**1.35**	1.15	.....
.....	10.40	**7.15**	Ar **Los Angeles**	Lv	6.30	**6.15**	.....

PORTLAND, TACOMA AND SEATTLE

	401 Daily	459 Daily	407 Daily	457 Daily	**Table Z** All Trains Daily		460 Daily	408 Daily	458 Daily	402 Daily	
.....	**11.45**	**1.30**	**5.30**	9.00	Lv **Portland**..Ore..	Ar	**12.10**	**4.30**	**9.15**	6.05	.....
.....	12.11	**1.49**	**5.49**	9.21	" Vancouver Wash.	Ar	11.48	**4.08**	**8.43**	5.30	.....
.....	1.17	**2.28**	**6.29**	10.01	" ▲ Kelso-Longview	Lv	11.04	**3.24**	**8 04**	4.38	.....
.....	2.19	**3.12**	**7.11**	10.43	" Chehalis..... "	"	10.19	**2.39**	**7.18**	3.20	.....
.....	2.30	**3.23**	**7.21**	10.53	Ar Centralia..... "	"	10.14	**2.32**	**7.11**	3.00	.....
.....	4.15	**4.31**	**8.29**	12.01	Ar **Tacoma**..... "	Lv	9.06	**1.26**	**6.02**	1.15	.....
.....	5.05	**4.35**	**8.33**	12.05	Lv **Tacoma**..... "	Ar	8.02	**1.22**	**5.57**	12.55	.....
.....	°6.30	°**5.30**	°**9.30**	▪1.00	Ar **Seattle**...... "	Lv	°8.10	°12.30	▪**5.00**	°1145	.....

"SUN VALLEY IDAHO"

ideal for

Spring and Fall Conventions

This is the place where business *is* a pleasure, thanks to the tonic effect of the mountainside setting . . . excellent hotel accommodations . . . superb food and service . . . and the many pleasurable ways you can spend your free time. Golf, fishing, swimming, tennis, riding, bowling, trapshooting and ski-lift riding tell part of the story.

For a copy of our convention folder, address Mr. Winston McCrea, Mgr., Sun Valley, Idaho or Union Pacific Railroad, Room 2650, Omaha 2, Nebraska.

Equipment for Tables Y and Z

NORTHBOUND

NO. 457—DAILY *Domeliner*

Dome Lounge ⊗..........Portland to Seattle.
Parlor Car..............Portland to Seattle (R. R. Owned).
Astra Dome Room— Parlor Car..........Portland to Seattle (R. R. Owned)—**8 Duplex Rmtte.,** 3 Compartments, 2 Drawing-rooms.
Streamlined Sleeping Cars..Chicago to Seattle—6 Roomettes, 4 Double Bedrooms, 6 Sections (No. 105 to Portland).
San Francisco to Seattle—10 Roomettes, 6 Double Bdrms.(1 car); 4 Compartments, 4 Double Bdrms., 2 Drawing-rooms (1 car) (S.P. No. 12 to Portland).
Reclining Seat Coaches....Portland to Seattle (not reserved).
Dining Car..............Portland to Seattle.

NO. 407—DAILY

Parlor Car..............Portland to Seattle (R. R. Owned)
Reclining Seat Coaches....Portland to Seattle.
Dining Car..............Serving necessary meals enroute.

NO. 459—DAILY

Reclining Seat Coaches....Portland to Seattle.

NO. 401—DAILY

Streamlined Sleeping Cars. Portland to Seattle—12 Roomettes, 4 Double Bedrooms.

Sleepers open at Portland 9:30 p.m., **at Seattle until 7:30 a.m.**

Reclining Seat Coaches.. .Portland to Seattle.

SOUTHBOUND

NO. 460—DAILY

Streamlined Sleeping Car...Seattle to Chicago—6 Roomettes, 4 Double Bedrooms, 6 Sections (No. 106 from Portland).
Reclining Seat Coaches....Seattle to Portland.

NO. 408—DAILY

Parlor Car..............Seattle to Portland (R. R. Owned).
Streamlined Sleeping Cars. Seattle to San Francisco—10 Roomettes, 6 Double Bdrms. (1 car); 4 Compartments, 4 Double Bdrms., 2 Dr.-rooms (1 car) (S.P. No. 11 south of Portland).
Reclining Seat Coaches....Seattle to Portland.
Dining Car..............Serving necessary meals enroute.

NO. 458—DAILY *Domeliner*

Dome Lounge..........⊗Seattle to Portland.
Parlor Car..............Seattle to Portland (R. R. Owned).
Astra Dome Room— Parlor Car..........Seattle to Portland (R. R. Owned)—**8 Duplex Rmtte.,** 3 Compartments, 2 Drawing-rooms.
Reclining Seat Coaches....Seattle to Portland (not reserved).
Dining Car..............Seattle to Portland.

NO. 402—DAILY

Streamlined Sleeping Cars. Seattle to Portland—12 Roomettes, 4 Double Bedrooms.

Sleepers open at Seattle at 9:30 p.m., at Portland until 7:30 a.m.

Reclining Seat Coaches....Seattle to Portland.

▪ Arrives, departs Seattle Union Depot. ° Arrives, departs Seattle King Street Station.
▲ Rail station is at Kelso. There is bus service between Kelso and Longview every 20 minutes.
⊙ Operates Mondays, Thursdays and Saturdays.
⊗ Observation-Lounge for Parlor and Sleeping Car passengers only.
♦ Via Pacific Greyhound Bus.
✱ Operates Sundays, Wednesdays and Fridays.

CHAPTER 3

The Burlington Zephyrs

Christened in Philadelphia on April 18, 1934, the Pioneer Zephyr began life and started a chain reaction that put Zephyr streamliners on every major line of the Chicago, Burlington and Quincy Railroad System. But the original Zephyr was only a prelude to the Zephyrs that were to be born in 1947, the Zephyr Domeliners.

In 1945, the Burlington was very much impressed with the General Motors scale models of a Dome Observation Car, Dome Sleeper, Dome Diner and Dome Coach. Due to the War new passenger equipment could not be ordered, so the CB&Q rebuilt a streamlined coach with a Dome. The car rolled out of the Aurora shops in June, 1945. Nobody could know at that time that within the next ten years every major railroad in the West, except the Rock Island, Great Western and the Soo Line, would have Dome Cars streaking over their lines.

The first Dome Coach, the Silver Dome, made its first revenue trip on the Twin Cities Zephyr on July 23, 1945. The public immediately fell in love with this innovation in train travel. Meanwhile, the Burlington equipped a second coach with a Dome and placed an order with the Budd Company for Dome Cars for the Twin Cities Zephyrs in 1946.

By 1957, the CB&Q had purchased all of the Dome Cars it would ever place in operation, including the Great Northern and Northern Pacific Domes - all from the Budd Company. The CB&Q operated Dome Cars on a regular basis on the following Zephyrs:

Train	Dates of Service
California Zephyr	1949 to 1970 (See Chapters 4 and 21)
Denver Zephyr	1956 to the Present Time
Morning Twin Zephyr	1947 to 1971
Afternoon Twin Zephyr	1947 to 1971
Kansas City Zephyr	1953 to 1968
American Royal Zephyr	1953 to 1967

Other trains, such as the Ak-Sar-Ben Zephyr and Blackhawk, also carried domes from time to time during the off seasons; especially after Dome Car service was discontinued on such trains as the American Royal Zephyr. Each of the trains listed in the table above will now be covered separately.

The Twin Cities Zephyrs

The Twin Zephyrs entered service in December, 1947 and were the first Vista Dome streamliners in the Nation. Initially each train, which provided both morning and afternoon service between Chicago and St. Paul-Minneapolis, consisted of a Baggage Buffet Lounge Car, three or four Vista Dome Coaches, a Dining Car, and last but not least a Dome Observation Parlor Car. Not only were they spectacular trains as far as equipment was concerned, but the trains were the world's fastest passenger schedules in the 1950's. The trains sped the distance between Chicago and Minneapolis in 6 hours and 45 minutes. In early 1971, the schedule was about 7 hours and 15 minutes.

ROUTE OF THE ZEPHYRS

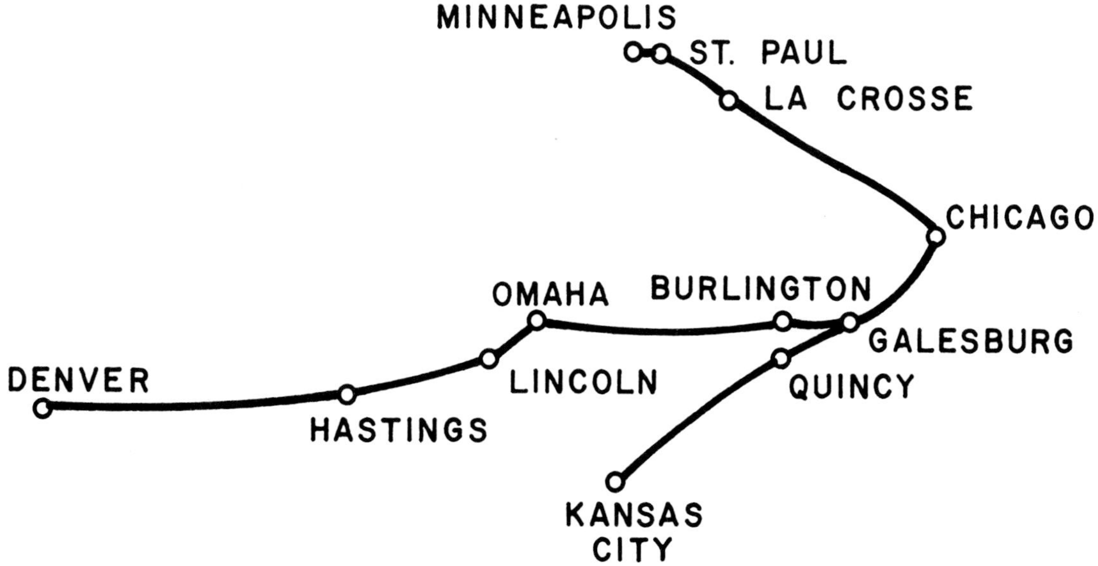

BURLINGTON ROUTE

Drawn By: Sy Dykhouse III

Following page:

THE FIRST ZEPHYR WAS BUILT in 1934, and the first Twin Cities Zephyrs went into operation in 1935. Shortly after, other Zephyrs hit the trail including the streamlined Denver Zephyr in 1936. Yet nine years and a World War would go by before streamliner dome cars would be placed in operation in 1945. The first domeliner passenger trains, the Twin Cities Zephyrs, were placed in service in 1947. From that time until 1956, the CB&Q added dome cars to much of the Zephyr fleet and other streamliners. The Burlington Zephyrs were, and are, *World Famous.* The Twin Cities Zephyr with its typical consist of the 1950's is shown here crossing the Stone Arch Bridge at Minneapolis. (Burlington Northern)

The westbound Morning Twin and the eastbound Afternoon Twin have operated independently throughout their careers. In the early 1960's, the Westbound Afternoon Zephyr was combined with the Empire Builder except during the Summer Season. (The corresponding eastbound combination was the North Coast Limited and Empire Builder.) This arrangement continued until 1966 when the westbound Builder was combined with the North Coast and the Afternoon Twin became a separate train again. By 1968 the eastbound Morning Twin and the Wesbound Afternoon Twin were combined with the already combined transcontinental trains - three trains in one in both directions. The exception to this was Friday and Sunday operation of the Afternoon Twin. This operation continued until AMTRAK.

The combined trains, ever since 1961, must have set some sort of record for the number of Domes regularly operated in one train. During the first part of the decade each Twin was assigned two Dome Coaches, A Diner and a Dome Observation Parlor Car. The independent train (the westbound Morning Twin and the eastbound Afternoon Twin) carried the original Twin Zephyr Dome Parlors with the round end. The Afternoon westbound Twin carried a squared end Dome Parlor Observation because of its head-end operation in the Empire Builder. This car was part of the original Kansas City Zephyr equipment. Parlor Car service continued until 1968 when the Builder, North Coast and westbound Afternoon Twin and eastbound Morning Twin were finally rolled into one train.

In 1971 the independent Twin Zephyrs consisted of a Baggage Buffet Lounge and one or two Dome Coaches and one or two flat top coaches. The combined Zephyrs usually had one Dome Coach and possibly a flat top coach. The passengers had access to the Dining and Lounge facilities provided by the combined Builder and North Coast. The combined train carried six or seven Dome Cars on nearly every trip between Chicago and St. Paul.

Despite the cut backs in service and train consolidations the public still had a choice of twice daily Domeliner train service between Chicago and Minneapolis prior to AMTRAK. As of May 1, 1971 all passenger train service was discontinued between Aurora, Illinois and St. Paul, Minnesota on the Burlington Northern.

The American Royal and Kansas City Zephyrs

Besides the California Zephyr, the next trains to be equipped with Domes were the Kansas City Zephyr and the American Royal Zephyr. These trains were placed in service in 1953 shortly after the opening of the Kansas City Short Cut (The Short Cut was opened in late 1952).

The Kansas City Zephyr began service with a consist of four or five cars as follows: 1 Mail and Baggage, 1 Vista Dome Coach, 1 Dining Car and 1 Vista Dome Parlor. The train sometimes carried one or more flat top coaches. This consist prevailed until 1960, when the Vista Dome Parlor and the Diner were replaced with a flat top Parlor Diner. The Dome Coach remained in the consist regularly at first, and then less and less so as business continued to decline throughout the 1960's. The Kansas City Zephyr, a train that always had to compete with the Santa Fe, finally became part of history when the train was discontinued in 1968.

The American Royal Zephyr was the night schedule between Chicago and Kansas City. In the 1950's the train carried a Vista Dome Buffet Lounge along with flat top coaches and three or four sleepers. The operation continued until

ORIGINAL BURLINGTON ROUTE Twin Cities Zephyr dome coach, the Silver Glade, was constructed by the Budd Company in 1947. This car, and the Silver Bluff, included a lounge room for the train crew; note the single frosted window beneath the dome. These and other TCZ dome coaches often saw service on other Zephyr trains. (Patrick C. Dorin)

CB&Q NO. 22, THE EAST BOUND MORNING TWIN CITIES ZEPHYR races southward along joint Burlington – Milwaukee Road trackage south of St. Paul, Minnesota. (Burlington Northern)

1960, when with declining patronage, the CB&Q discontinued Buffet service to and from Kansas City. Also, the American Royal was combined with the Ak-Sar-Ben between Chicago and Galesburg. The Vista Dome Buffet Lounge then saw service on an "off and on" basis on the Blackhawk and the Ak-Sar-Ben. Also in late 1960 and early 1961, the Ak-Sar-Ben carried a Vista Dome Coach on a regular basis.

From 1961 on, business continued to decline on the American Royal Zephyr, as with all other trains and by 1970 the train had lost all of its equipment except a single coach and one head-end car.

The Denver Zephyr

In 1956, the last Dome Cars ordered by the Burlington Railroad were placed in service on one of the Nation's finest trains, the Denver Zephyr. The Dome Cars were part of a complete set of equipment that completely replaced the original DZ. The new train went into service on October 28, 1956.

The 1956 Vista Dome Denver Zephyr consisted of a Baggage Car, a Flat top leg rest coach, a Dome coach, another Flat top coach, a Dome Buffet Lounge, a Dining Car, three Pullmans and

THE KANSAS CITY ZEPHYR poses for its portrait by the company photographer with its standard operating consist of 2 "E" units and five streamlined cars including one dome coach and one dome parlor observation car. (Burlington Northern)

a Dome Parlor Observation Lounge Car. In 1958, two Slumber-coaches were added to the train.

Originally, the DZ included a Chicago - Colorado Springs section which was handled by the Rio Grande in its Royal Gorge train. Three cars were normally added or cut out of the DZ at Denver. The Colorado Springs section included a Dome Coach, a Slumber-coach and a Sleeper. This operation continued until 1967, when a Continental Lines Bus was substituted for train service between Denver and Colorado Springs.

Aside from seasonal fluctuations of the total consist of the train, the DZ has normally carried a full complement of three domes during its entire career. The only exception to this was during two or three section operation. When this occurred, usually the Dome Buffet Lounge along with an extra Dining Car operated on the second section. A third section has carried the ex-American Royal Dome Lounge but this was not always the case. The Denver Zephyr was one of the few trains in the United States in 1971 that had additional sections when traffic required them. The extra sections were usually put on for foot ball games and skiing in Colorado. The heaviest travel has usually occured on week-ends in the Summer, Fall and Winter months. For this business, the CB&Q even borrowed coaches from their competing Chicago- Denver Railroad, the Union Pacific. The Vista Dome Denver Zephyr remains in 1972 under AMTRAK as one of America's finest trains.

INTERIOR OF THE Vista Dome 27 seat, 1 drawing room parlor car operated on the Kansas City Zephyr. (Burlington Northern)

CB&Q TRAIN NO. 35, the Kansas City Zephyr, rounds the curve south of the Chicago Union Station on its fast daylight run to Kansas City. This photograph was taken on March 8, 1954, about a year after the KCZ was placed in service. (Burlington Northern)

CB&Q NO. 21, THE MORNING TWIN CITIES ZEPHYR, passing Alma, Wisconsin, in the summer of 1967 with two "E" units and seven cars including two dome coaches and one dome parlor car. By 1967, the TCZ's no longer carried the baggage buffet lounge car but still included the dining car, which was listed as a dining-refreshment car in the June 1, 1967, time table. (Bob Lorenz)

CB&Q NO. 22, THE MORNING TWIN CITIES ZEPHYR races eastward en route to Chicago with a seven car consist including five dome cars. There were two parlor dome observation cars, the Silver View and the Silver Vista, built for the TCZ's and each made one round trip per day between Chicago and Minneapolis on their original schedules. (Burlington Northern)

CB&Q TRAIN NO. 35 is shown here roaring westward on the triple track speedway between Chicago and Aurora en route to Kansas City. Notice the standard RPO–Baggage (in place of the usual strealined RPO–Baggage car) painted in the Zephyr color scheme.

THE 1956 DENVER Zephyr Vista Dome coach has fifty seats downstairs with individual stretch-out leg rests. Upstairs, the dome seats 24. (Burlington Northern)

FORMER BURLINGTON dome parlor observation, the Silver Terrace, was originally built for service on the Kansas City Zephyr. This car and its running mate, the Silver Tower, later saw service on the Twin Cities Zephyrs; and on occasion ran substitute and/or extra service on the Denver Zephyr. (Patrick C. Dorin)

FORMER BURLINGTON ROUTE dome coach buffet lounge car, the Silver Patio, was originally constructed for the American Royal Zephyr. The two cars (also the Sliver Garden) later saw service on the Black Hawk and the Ak–Sar–Ben Zephyr. (Ak–Sar–Ben is Nebraska spelled backwards.) The equipment also ran extra service on the Denver Zephyrs. (Patrick C. Dorin)

THE ORIGINAL 10 CAR Denver Zephyr including three dome cars poses for the company photographer shortly after its construction in 1956 by the Budd Company. (Burlington Northern)

THE INTERIOR OF THE buffet lounge section of the dome buffet lounge coach car operated on the American Royal Zephyr. (Burlington Northern)

INTERIOR VIEW of the Budd-built Vista Dome coach operated on the Denver Zephyr. The cars featured leg rest seats, venetian blinds, curtains and individual reading lights over all seats. (Burlington Northern)

INTERIOR OF THE DOME "Chuck Wagon" car showing the table seating arrangement. The car was decorated in a Western and Colorado motif including the dishes, napkins, and place mats. (Burlington Northern)

THE INTERIOR OF THE "Chuck Wagon" showing lunch counter area. The cars served inexpensive meals and were pleasant to ride in. (Burlington Northern)

THE 11 SEAT PARLOR section of the DZ dome parlor was equipped with soft easy chairs, carpeting, drapes and overhead reading lamps. The car also contained a drawing room. (Burlington Northern)

FORMER BURLINGTON ROUTE "Chuck Wagon" dome coffee shop lunch counter dormitory car, the Silver Cup (and Silver Kettle) were constructed by the Budd Company in 1956 for the new Denver Zephyr. (Patrick C. Dorin)

THE DENVER ZEPHYR carried the last dome parlor observation car ever constructed. There were two cars built for the Chicago–Denver service, the Silver Chateau and the Silver Veranda, and both served exclusively on the Denver Zephyr from October, 1956, until April, 1971. This photo shows the Silver Veranda after renumbering by AMTRAK in April, 1972. (John H. Kuehl)

THE COLORADO ROOM was a smart meeting place for travelers aboard the Denver Zephyrs. Located in the dome parlor lounge car beneath the dome, the Colorado Room served a variety of light refreshments. (Burlington Northern)

THE OBSERVATION lounge section of the dome parlor lounge car assigned to the DZ. As one can see, the entire train was decorated in a Rocky Mountain motif. (Burlington Northern)

CB&Q ALCO SWITCH ENGINE NO. 9307 puts the finishing touches, the last five cars, on the assembling of train No. 10, the Denver Zephyr at the Union Station in Denver prior to its departure for Chicago. (Bob Lorenz)

CB&Q TRAIN NO. 17 departing Chicago en route to California with three "F" units and 11 cars. Note the Pennsylvania Railroad coach yards in the background with the numerous heavy weight Pullmans. The photo was taken on April 1, 1949 by the CB&Q photographer. (Burlington Northern)

CB&Q TRAIN NO. 18, the stainless steel California Zephyr completing its 2532 mile run from San Francisco, arrives at Chicago simultaneously with train No. 32, the Empire Builder. (Burlington Northern)

CALIFORNIA ZEPHYRS, NO. 17 and 18 meet in CTC territory on the Rio Grande's Main Line thru the Rockies. (Rio Grande)

IT IS TRAIN TIME at Grand Junction. During the CZ's 10 minute stop, she will change crews, receive water and other servicing and be inspected from the locomotive to the dome observation lounge car on the rear end. (B. F. Cutler, Rail Photo Service)

THE USUAL MOTIVE POWER on the Rio Grande's portion of the CZ run in post Alco "PA" days was four "F" units. However, during the summers traffic often required an extra unit for a total of five to power 17 and 18 over the "Main Line Thru the Rockies." Notice the Krauss-Maffei diesel hydraulic on the east bound freight in the left hand of the photo. The picture was taken at East Portal during the summer of 1963. (Bob Lorenz)

THE CALIFORNIA ZEPHYR was a popular train right up to the end of its "Railroad" operation by the three companies. Here the CZ rolls along the Colorado River near Bond, Colorado on the Rio Grande's Colorado Division with 5 "F" units and 13 cars on June 19, 1969. 1969 was the last full year of operation. (Paul Stringham)

THE CALIFORNIA ZEPHYR is shown here climbing a 1% grade over Rock Creek Bridge in the heart of the Feather River Canyon near Pulger, California on the Western Pacific Railroad. (B. F. Cutler, Rail Photo Service)

THE CALIFORNIA ZEPHYR ROARS OUT of a rock cut (on the right side of the photo) in the heart of Niles Canyon. (David Gray Edwards, Rail Photo Service)

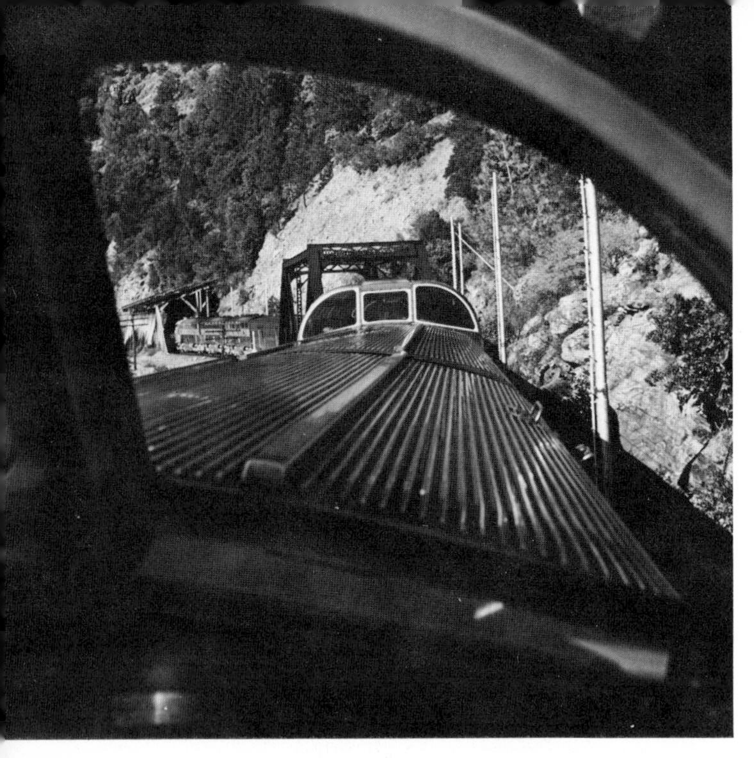

THE WESTERN PACIFIC'S eastbound "California Zephyr" zips through a bridge and then into a snow shed near Pulga, California in the Feather River Canyon. (Dick Steinheimer)

THE CALIFORNIA ZEPHYR rounding Williams Loop showing both levels of track. The upper level is in the lower right corner of the photograph. (B. F. Cutler, Rail Photo Service)

THE TIME IS 1964 and the westbound California Zephyr moves out of a tunnel in the Feather River Canyon behind three "F" units, which was customary power for the Western Pacific. However, today ahead of the CZ baggage car is a dead heading Southern Pacific Pullman and a Western Pacific flexi-van car with two containers of mail. (Dick Steinheimer)

Mls.	WESTBOUND		Daily (1 day for example) CALIFORNIA ZEPHYR 17	
	Burlington Route		PM	
0	**Chicago**	Lv	3.30	Mon
162	Galesburg, Ill.	Lv	5.53	Mon
206	Burlington, Iowa	Lv	6.38	Mon
280	Ottumwa, Iowa	Lv	7.53	Mon
443	Red Oak, Ia.	Lv	x 10.39	Mon
496	Omaha, Nebr.	Lv	11.40	Mon
551	Lincoln, Nebr. (C.T.)	Lv	12.50	Tue
1034	**Denver, Colo.** (M.T.)	Ar	7.40	Tue
	Rio Grande R.R. (Via Moffat Tunnel)			
1034	**Denver**	Lv	8.40	Tue
1163	Bond	Ar	12.28	Tue
1219	Glenwood Springs	Ar	2.00	Tue
1308	Grand Junction, Colo.	Ar	3.40	Tue
1485	Helper, Utah	Ar	7.05	Tue
1560	Provo	Ar	9.05	Tue
1604	**Salt Lake City**	Ar	10.00	Tue
	Western Pacific RR.			
1604	**Salt Lake City, Utah** (M.T.)	Lv	10.15	Tue
1867	Elko, Nev. (P.T.)	Ar	1.25	Wed
2000	Winnemucca	Ar	3.37	Wed
2094	Gerlach, Nev.	Ar	5.10	Wed
2160	Herlong, Calif.	Ar	6.15	Wed
2211	Portola	Ar	7.10	Wed
2251	Keddie	Ar	8.25	Wed
2327	Oroville	Ar	11.00	Wed
2353	Marysville	Ar	11.35	Wed
2393	Sacramento	Ar	12.25	Wed
2438	Stockton	Ar	1.27	Wed
2502	Fremont (Niles)	Ar	2.55	Wed
2525	Oakland (3rd & Washington)	Ar	3.35	Wed
2532	**San Francisco**	Ar	4.15	Wed
			PM	

Mls.	EASTBOUND		Daily (1 day for example) CALIFORNIA ZEPHYR 18	
	Western Pacific R.R.		AM	
0	**San Francisco, Calif.** (P.T.)	Lv	9.45	Sun
7	Oakland (3rd & Washington)	Lv	10.25	Sun
30	Fremont (Niles)	Lv	11.02	Sun
94	Stockton	Lv	12.25	Sun
139	Sacramento	Lv	1.25	Sun
179	Marysville	Lv	2.08	Sun
205	Oroville	Lv	2.40	Sun
281	Keddie	Lv	5.00	Sun
321	Portola	Lv	6.15	Sun
372	Herlong, Calif.	Lv	7.20	Sun
438	Gerlach, Nev.	Lv	8.30	Sun
532	Winnemucca	Lv	9.55	Sun
665	Elko, Nev. (P.T.)	Lv	12.05	Mon
928	**Salt Lake City, Utah** (M.T.)	Ar	5.40	Mon
	Rio Grande R.R. (Via Moffat Tunnel)			
928	**Salt Lake City**	Lv	6.00	Mon
972	Provo	Lv	6.50	Mon
1047	Helper, Utah	Lv	8.46	Mon
1224	Grand Junction, Colo.	Lv	11.58	Mon
1313	Glenwood Springs	Lv	1.40	Mon
1369	Bond	Lv	3.14	Mon
1498	**Denver**	Ar	7.00	Mon
	Burlington Route			
1498	**Denver, Colo.** (M.T.)	Lv	7.15	Mon
1981	Lincoln, Nebr. (C.T.)	Ar	3.35	Tue
2036	Omaha, Nebr.	Ar	4.45	Tue
2252	Ottumwa, Iowa	Ar	8.26	Tue
2326	Burlington, Iowa	Ar	9.42	Tue
2370	Galesburg, Ill.	Ar	10.28	Tue
2532	**Chicago**	Ar	1.00	Tue
			PM	

EQUIPMENT

Tape-recorded music, Controlled radio reception, Hostess Service, Valet Service.

WESTBOUND No. 17

	Car
Vista-Dome Observation-Lounge Chicago to San Francisco 1 drawing room (with shower bath), 3 double bedrooms	CZ-10
Standard Sleeping Cars Chicago to San Francisco	
10 roomettes, 6 double bedrooms	CZ-11
▲16 sections	CZ-12
10 roomettes, 6 double bedrooms	CZ-14
10 roomettes, 6 double bedrooms	CZ-15
6 double bedrooms, 5 compartments	CZ-16
Vista-Dome Buffet-Lounge Chicago to San Francisco Lounge for all passengers; Dome for sleeping car passengers	
Dining Car For all Meals	
Vista-Dome Reclining Chair Coaches (leg rests) Chicago to San Francisco	CZ-20, CZ-21, CZ-22

EASTBOUND No. 18

	Car
Vista-Dome Observation-Lounge San Francisco to Chicago 1 drawing room (with shower bath); 3 double bedrooms	CZ-10
Standard Sleeping Cars San Francisco to Chicago	
10 roomettes, 6 double bedrooms	CZ-11
▲16 sections	CZ-12
10 roomettes, 6 double bedrooms	CZ-14
10 roomettes, 6 double bedrooms	CZ-15
6 double bedrooms, 5 compartments	CZ-16
Vista-Dome Buffet-Lounge San Francisco to Chicago Lounge for all passengers; Dome for sleeping car passengers	
Dining Car For all Meals	
Vista-Dome Reclining Chair Coaches (leg rests) San Francisco to Chicago	CZ-20, CZ-21, CZ-22

Source: CB&Q Time Table
May, 1959

CHAPTER 5

The Empire Builder

The Great Northern Railway's Empire Builder was the company's fleet leader since 1929, and what a fabulous train it was and still is today under AMTRAK.

Over the years, Great Northern constantly up dated and modernized the train. Streamlined coaches arrived in 1937 and it was completely streamlined in 1947. Eight years later, the Great Northern, the Burlington and the Spokane, Portland and Seattle Railways placed in service 16 dome coaches and 6 dome lounge cars – designated Great Domes by the Big G. The 22 domes provided 3 dome coaches and one dome lounge car for each of the five sets of equipment plus one spare dome lounge and dome coach. Twelve dome coaches were owned by the Great Northern while the CB&Q and SP&S owned three and one respectively. Of the dome lounges, the GN owned five while the "Q" owned only one. As the dome lounges did not operate into Portland, the SP&S did not participate in the ownership of those cars.

At the time of purchase, the three companies operated 3 dome coaches and 1 dome lounge on each train. However, by the late 1950's, only two dome coaches operated on 31 and 32 during the off seasons. During this time, the extra domes were either stored at St. Paul or assigned to the Western Star. In fact, in at least two summers, 1960 and 1961, the Star carried a single dome coach on a daily basis between St. Paul and Seattle.

By 1962, however, the public timetables listed 3 dome coaches operating on the Empire Builder on a year around basis. In actual operation this was not always true during the months of November and January through April.

For most of their careers including AMTRAK, the dome lounges operated between Chicago and Seattle. When first placed in service, the cars were reserved exclusively for Pullman passengers. During this time, the dome lounge always ran behind the dining car. With declining patronage during the mid and late 1960's, the GN removed the coffee shop (Ranch Car) car from the consist during the off seasons. This meant that coach passengers no longer had any lounge space with the dome lounge open to Pullman passengers only. Therefore in order to provide lounge space for coach passengers, the GN opened the 34 seat lower lounge of the car to all passengers. The dome itself was still reserved for Pullman patrons. From this time on, the dome lounge operated ahead of the dining car.

While most of the Empire Builder equipment operated a Chicago – Seattle – Chicago circuit, the dome lounge and diner did not. In this case, the lounge and diner were stocked with food and beverages at St. Paul on a daily basis. The eastbound Builder would set out the dome lounge and diner upon its arrival at St. Paul, and pick up the freshly stocked cars before continuing on to Chicago.

The Spokane, Portland & Seattle Railway portion of the Empire Builder carried one dome coach for a Chicago – Portland assignment. the SP&S also painted some of their own equipment in the Empire Builder scheme so that 1 and 2 ran in a solid and matched color scheme, at least in and out of Spokane. The color scheme was broken at Pasco where Northern Pacific's North Coast Limited cars were added.

For the most part, the Empire Builder domes remained with their own train. After the March, 1970 merger date, it was reported that Builder dome coaches have run west on the Denver Zephyr and even made a trip or two to Duluth-Superior. AMTRAK has sent some of the cars far and wide, but most are still serving on the Incomparable EMPIRE BUILDER.

THE GREAT NORTHERN purchased 12 of these beautiful dome coaches in 1955 for operation on the Empire Builder. At the same time, the Burlington purchased three cars and the SP&S one car identical to the GN order. The cars contained 46 leg rest seats and 24 dome seats for a total seating capacity of 70 passengers. All cars were painted with the train name in the letter board. (Budd Company)

AMONG THE MOST BEAUTIFUL lounge cars ever built were the six Empire Builder dome lounge cars in the "View" series constructed by the Budd Company in 1955. During most of their GN career the cars were operated for use of Pullman passengers only. Normally, the cars were operated only on the Empire Builder, but often picked up assignments such as a "Governor's Special" or a "Board of Director's Special." This happened not only on the GN or CB&Q but for other railroads, such as the Duluth, Missabe and Iron Range Railway when they needed a high capacity observatory car for an inspection tour. (Burlington Northern)

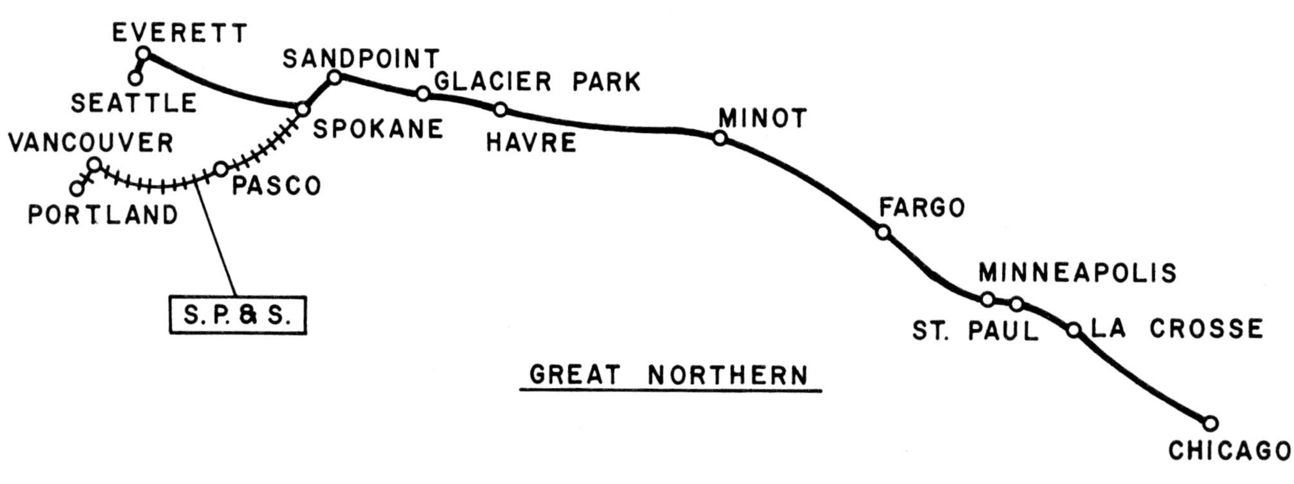

SPOKANE, PORTLAND AND SEATTLE Railway No. 2, the combined Empire Builder and North Coast Limited heads eastward at dusk with 11 cars near Wishram, Washington. (J. W. Swanberg)

THE LOWER LEVEL of the dome lounge seated 34 people in a very attractive seating arrangement. Note the Northwest Indian totems. Prior to AMTRAK operation, the lower level was opened to coach passengers, which for the most of the GN–BN career was open to Pullman passengers only. (Burlington Northern)

GREAT NORTHERN
GREAT NORTHER

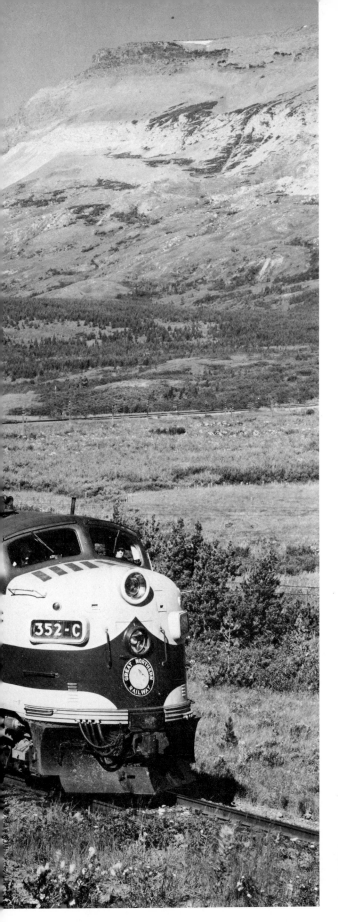

THE GREAT NORTHERN Railway placed the first Empire Builder in service between Chicago and Seattle–Portland in 1929. The train was equipped with the finest of standard Pullmans which remained in service until 1947. The train received streamlined coaches in 1937 and was completely streamlined in 1947.

In 1951, the GN completely re-equipped the Empire Builder, shifting the 1947 equipment to the new "Western Star." 1955 brought the final new equipment additions that the train has received to this date (Fall, 1972), the dome cars. The GN, CB&Q and SP&S railroads purchased 16 dome coaches and 6 dome lounge cars in order to equip each train with 3 dome coaches and 1 dome lounge car. To the Empire Builder, prior to AMTRAK, goes the distinction of being the only train to operate with two different types of dome cars – the short and long dome. The train was truly "incomparable." (Burlington Northern)

INTERIOR OF THE Great Northern Railway dome coach. This equipment featured Northwest Indian Art for the motif. (Budd Company)

THERE WERE 57 SEATS in the dome section of this very distinctive lounge car. The soft sofa seats were angled toward the windows for easy viewing. (Burlington Northern)

THE DOMELINER EMPIRE BUILDER, train No. 32 loads passengers, mail and express at Havre, Montana on a September day in 1964. The new blue color scheme has not yet been thought of. (J. W. Swanberg)

IN 1967 ANOTHER CHANGE CAME to the Empire Builder: a new color scheme known as "Big Sky Blue." Here two SDP units lead a 12 car Empire Builder south of Glacier National Park as No. 31 winds its way westbound over the Montana Division. (Burlington Northern)

BURLINGTON NORTHERN 1ST NO. 25, the Empire Builder, arriving at East Dubuque on the Fourth Subdivision of the Chicago Division en route to Seattle and Portland. The train consist on this dark and dreary December 22, 1970 included 2 dome coaches and a Great Dome lounge car. The train had a total of 10 cars and was powered by two E–8A's. (Dr. J. DeVries)

FORMER CB&Q EMPIRE BUILDER full length dome lounge No. 1395, "River View," in the Burlington Northern green, white and black color scheme. (John H. Kuehl)

BURLINGTON NORTHERN TRAIN NO. 25, the combined Empire Builder/North Coast Limited speeds past the tower at Clyde Yard in Cicero, Illinois on April 17, 1970, with 12 cars including five domes. The first six cars make up the Empire Builder section. Hardly a full year would pass before this train would no longer polish the BN rails between Chicago and St. Paul (John H. Kuehl)

IT IS TRAIN TIME at the Seattle, Washington King Street Station, and 4 Great Northern "F" units lead the eastbound Empire Builder toward a commitment to be in Chicago two days from now. As the domeliner leaves the depot, a number of people watch from the protective railings. They probably wish they were on it. (Dick Steinheimer)

EMPIRE BUILDER

(Trains 31-32)†

Coach Seat Charge On Great Northern
Radio and tape recorded music, Coach Porter Service

	CAR West and North	CAR East and South
Reclining 60-Seat Coach—Chicago to Seattle {Car Reservation Only}	100	200
Following is summer consist—Altered during September.		
Chicago-Seattle—46 Seats Dome Coach . . . . . . {All Seats Reserved}	101	201
Chicago-Seattle—46 Seats Dome Coach . . . . . . {All Seats Reserved}	102	202
St. Paul-Seattle—48 Reclining Seat Coach . . . . . {All Seats Reserved}	103	203
St. Paul-Portland—48 Reclining Seat Coach . . . {All Seats Reserved}	104	204
Chicago-Portland—46 Seats Dome Coach . . . . . {All Seats Reserved}	105	205
Ranch Lounge (Meals—Beverages)—Chicago-Seattle . . . . Lounge for coach passengers	. . .	. . .
Dining Car (Dinner by reservation)—Chicago-Seattle-Portland . . .	. . .	. . .
Sleeping Cars		
Chicago-Seattle—6 Rmt., 5 Dbl. Bdrm., 2 Compt.	314	324
Chicago-Seattle—7 Dup. Rmt., 6 Dbl. Bdrm., 1 Compt.	315	325
Chicago-Portland—6 Rmt., 5 Dbl. Bdm., 2 Compt.	317	327
St. Paul-Seattle—6 Rmt., 5 Dbl. Bdrm, 2 Compt.	316	326
Spokane-Portland—SP&S—6 Roomettes, 3 Bdrm., Buffet Lounge	10	20

GREAT DOME full length lounge (Beverage Service)

Chicago-Seattle—Lower Level—Beverage Service All Passengers.
Upper Level—Pullman Passengers Only.

EMPIRE BUILDER

Detailed Schedules Begin on Page 6, Table 1

West—Read Down | **East**—Read Up

Example by days	**Empire Builder** 31 Daily	Miles	Central Standard Time	**Empire Builder** 32 Daily	Example by days
			Burlington Route		
Mon	**1 15**	0	Lv Chicago . . . . Ar	**2 55**	Wed
Mon	**8 00**	427	Ar St. Paul Lv	8 10	Wed
			Great Northern ★		
Mon	**8 35**	0	Lv St. Paul . . . . Ar	7 10	Wed
Mon	**9 00**	11	Ar Minneapolis Lv	6 35	Wed
Mon	**9 05**	11	Lv Minneapolis . . . . Ar	6 30	Wed
Mon	**10 40**	102	" Willmar Lv	4 30	Wed
Tue	12 27	215	Lv Breckenridge . . . . "	2 20	Wed
Tue	1 17	262	Ar Fargo Lv	1 00	Wed
Tue	1 30	262	Lv Fargo . . . . Ar	12 50	Wed
Tue	3 25	386	Lv New Rockford Lv	**10 50**	Tue
Tue	5 00	495	Ar Minot Lv	**9 05**	Tue
Tue	5 10	495	Lv Minot . . . . Ar	**8 55**	Tue
Tue	7 25	615	Ar Williston Lv	**6 35**	Tue
			Mountain Standard Time		
Tue	6 35	615	Lv Williston . . . . Ar	**5 25**	Tue
Tue	▲ 8 23	721	" Wolf Point Lv	▲ **3 38**	Tue
Tue	▲ 9 10	771	" Glasgow . . . . "	▲ **2 50**	Tue
Tue	▲10 10	836	Lv Malta . . . . "	▲ **1 45**	Tue
Tue	11 35	924	Ar Havre Lv	**12 20**	Tue
Tue	Ⓐ**3 00**	. . . . .	Ar Great Falls Lv	Ⓐ8 30	Tue
Tue	11 50	924	Lv Havre . . . . Ar	**12 05**	Tue
Tue	f**12 50**	985	" Chester Lv	f10 59	Tue
Tue	**1 40**	1028	" Shelby . . . . "	10 17	Tue
Tue	▲ **2 17**	1053	Lv Cut Bank . . . . "	▲ 9 40	Tue
Tue	• **3 25**	1099	Lv Glacier Park Lv	• 8 40	Tue
Tue	• **5 25**	1156	Lv Belton Lv	• 6 50	Tue
Tue	**6 00**	1178	Ar Whitefish Lv	6 10	Tue
Tue	**6 05**	1178	Lv Whitefish . . . . Ar	6 00	Tue
Tue	▲ **8 35**	1295	Lv Libby Lv	▲ 3 30	Tue
Tue	**9 05**	1313	Ar Troy Lv	3 10	Tue
			Pacific Standard Time		
Tue	**8 05**	1313	Lv Troy . . . . Ar	2 10	Tue
Tue	**11 15**	1452	Ar Spokane Lv	**11 10**	Mon
Tue	**11 45**	1452	Lv Spokane . . . . Ar	**10 40**	Mon
Wed	2 01	1574	" Ephrata Lv	**8 25**	Mon
Wed	3 10	1627	Ar Wenatchee Lv	**7 18**	Mon
Wed	3 20	1627	Lv Wenatchee . . . . Ar	**7 10**	Mon
Wed	6 30	1748	Ar Everett Lv	**3 58**	Mon
Wed	6 40	1748	Lv Everett . . . . Ar	**3 58**	Mon
Wed	■ 7 07	1764	Lv Edmonds Lv	♦ **3 31**	Mon
Wed	7 45	1781	Ar Seattle Lv	**3 00**	Mon
Wed	8 57	. . . . .	Ar Tacoma Lv	**12 38**	Mon
	1 Daily	Miles	**Spokane, Portland & Seattle Ry.**	2 Daily	
Tue	**11 40**	0	Lv Spokane . . . . Ar	**9 50**	Mon
Wed	2 30	148	Ar Pasco Lv	**7 10**	Mon
Wed	4 40	273	" Wishram . . . . "	**5 00**	Mon
Wed	6 30	370	" Vancouver, Wash . . . "	**3 22**	Mon
Wed	7 00	380	Ar Portland Lv	**3 00**	Mon

COACH SEAT CHARGE ON GREAT NORTHERN

•—The Empire Builder stops at Glacier Park and Belton, eastern and western rail entrances to Glacier National Park, June 8th thru September 8.

★—Equipment for these trains shown on page 25.

For connections to and from California see Table 15.

Source: GN Time Table
June 30, 1968

CHAPTER 6

The North Coast Limited

The Northern Pacific's North Coast Limited began operation on April 29, 1900 when it made its inaugural run between St. Paul and Seattle. The train was the "talk of the Pacific Northwest" for many years, in fact for 71 years almost to the day. During its history, the NP consistently improved the schedules and the equipment of old No. 1 and 2. At the end of 1946, for example, the NP authorized a 10 million dollar order for 18 "F" units from EMD and 78 streamlined passenger cars from Pullman Standard; all for the North Coast Limited. The Burlington and the Spokane, Portland and Seattle also ordered 10 and 2 light weight cars respectively for operation on the North Coast. In 1954, the NP, CB&Q and SP&S purchased 10 dome coaches and 10 dome sleepers. The coaches seated 46 passengers on the main level and 24 in the dome. The sleeping cars contained 4 roomettes, 4 duplex single rooms (under the dome) and 4 double bedrooms. The twenty cars provided 2 dome coaches and 2 dome sleepers for each set of equipment. In 1957, the NP purchased an additional dome coach and dome sleeper as protection equipment so that each set (five sets) of equipment could always run with a full complement of four domes, while one of the regular coaches or sleepers was in the shops. Initially one dome coach and dome sleeper operated between Chicago and Seattle, and one each between Chicago and Portland. The dome coaches continued to operate in this manner until AMTRAK on the Burlington Northern. For the sleepers, it was somewhat of a different and interesting story.

As everyone knows, the late 1950's brought declines in passenger patronage even on the best of trains during the off seasons. For winter season travel to the Pacific Northwest, two dome sleepers (along with the beautiful observation car) were simply just too much lounge space – especially non-revenue lounge space as domes usually are. In 1959, the Northern Pacific sought a solution to the lack of use for such expensive equipment. The answer came from the Florida service that needs extra cars during the time the north has less need of equipment. The NP and Pullman negotiated a lease arrangement with the Illinois Central and Pennsylvania Railroads and other participating lines for the use of dome sleepers in the operation of the South Wind, City of Miami and for a short time, the Panama Limited, during the heavy winter season travel. This operation continued until the late 1960's. When the dome sleepers returned to the CB&Q and NP during the summers, they went into service between Chicago and Seattle instead of the original Portland run.

In early 1967, another major change took place in the operation of the NP sleeper domes. Five NP and one of the CB&Q cars were rebuilt into dome "Lounge-in-the-Sky" Buffet sleepers. The dome was refitted with 24 seats at tables, and two of the duplex single rooms were removed for the buffet section. Also at that time, the NP discontinued the operation of the 4 double bedroom, 1 compartment observation lounge cars between Chicago and Seattle.

The Vista domes were an asset to the North Coast Limited as it traveled through some of the finest scenery on the North American continent. The dome coaches operated consistently from 1954 through 1971 over their original routes. One dome sleeper operated on a year around basis between Chicago and Seattle, while the second operated on a seasonal basis since the late 1950's. Until AMTRAK, the BN operated the dome lounge sleeper between Chicago and Seattle, while the second dome often ran a St. Paul – Seattle circuit during the summers. The domeliner North Coast Limited was still regarded in 1971 as one of the nation's finest trains.

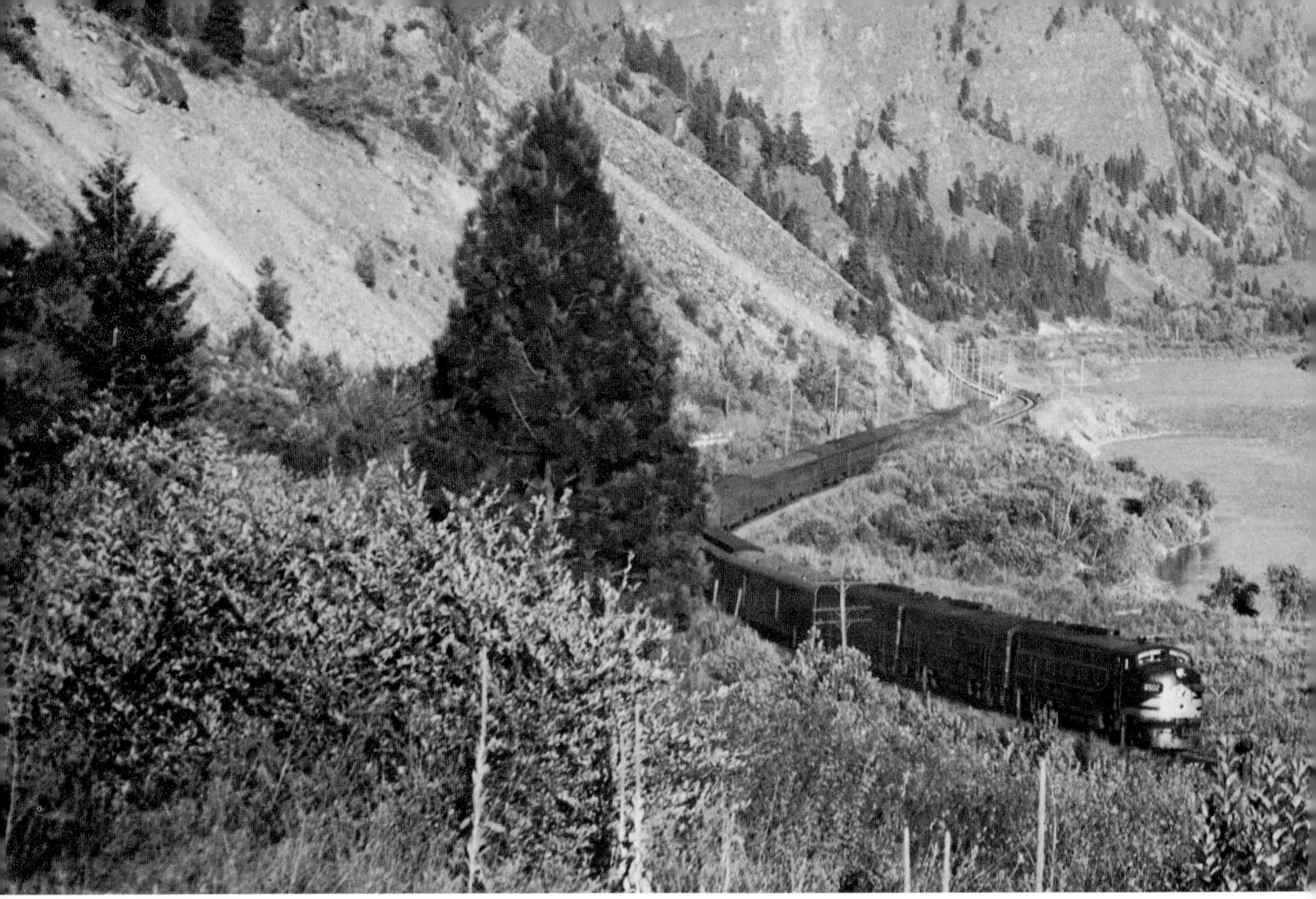

ROUTE OF THE NORTH COAST LIMITED
SEATTLE
SANDPOINT
SPOKANE
VANCOUVER
MISSOULA
PASCO
PORTLAND
BISMARK
FARGO
BUTTE
MINNEAPOLIS
S. P. & S.
LIVINGSTON
BILLINGS
ST. PAUL
LA CROSSE
CHICAGO
NORTHERN PACIFIC
Drawn By: Sy Dykhouse III

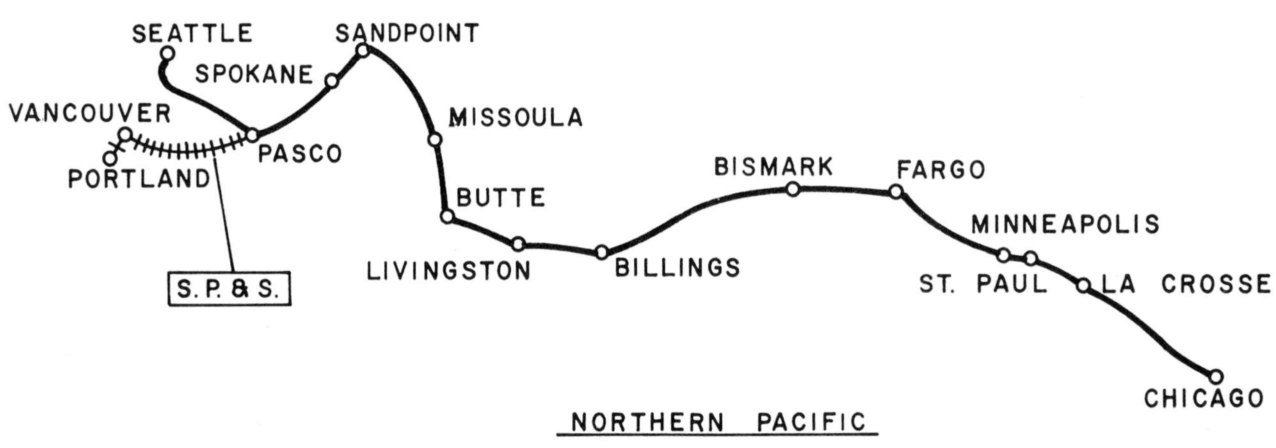

THE NORTHERN PACIFIC'S North Coast Limited began operation in 1900 between St. Paul and Seattle. Later service was extended to Chicago over the Chicago and North Western Railway. Can you imagine how different railroad history might have been had that operation continued?

The North Coast Limited was always a popular train and was streamlined in 1947. The dome cars came in 1954 along with a new two tone green color scheme. The newest cars in service on the North Coast Limited were the Slumber-coaches added in 1959. This photo shows the NP's streamlined North Coast Limited along the Clarks Fork River in Western Montana in pre-vista dome days. The scenery shown here typifies much of what can be seen along the route of the North Coast Limited, and was directly responsible for inspiring the NP management to operate domes on trains 25 and 26. (Burlington Northern)

FORMER NORTHERN PACIFIC dome coach No. 556 in the two tone green color scheme. The Northern Pacific owned eight such cars series 549 through 556. The CB&Q owned two additional cars, No. 557 and 558; and the SP&S one, No. 559. All were painted in the NP color scheme. (Patrick C. Dorin)

FORMER PULLMAN sleeping car No. 310 is a Budd Company constructed dome car with 4 roomettes, 4 duplex single rooms (under dome) and 4 double bedrooms. Several of these cars have been modified for lounge car service in the dome. The domes of these modified cars seat 24 passengers at small tables. The new service replaced the former observation lounge cars and was called "Lounge-in-the-Sky." (Budd Company)

THE VISTA DOME NORTH COAST LIMITED is shown here in the beautiful Jefferson Canyon about 30 miles west of Bozeman, Montana and near Three Forks, where the Madison, Jefferson and Gallatin Rivers meet to form the Missouri. (Burlington Northern)

CB&Q FIRST NO. 32, the North Coast Limited, roars through Alma, Wisconsin at nearly 80 miles per hour with two "E" units and 12 cars, including two dome coaches and two dome sleepers. The photo was taken during the summer of 1967. (Bob Lorenz)

FINAL RUN of the combined "Empire Builder/North Coast Limited" on BN rails between Chicago and Minneapolis. In the background is the Halstead Street commuter passenger station in Chicago, Illinois. (John H. Kuehl)

FORMER NP DOME "Lounge-in-the-Sky" sleeper No. 378 on the rear of train No. 25 departing the Chicago Union Station in March, 1971. (Patrick C. Dorin)

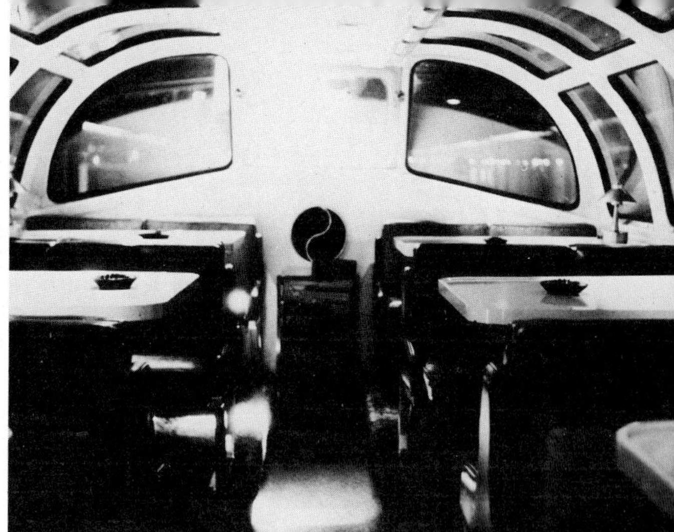

INTERIOR OF THE DOME "Lounge-in-the-Sky" showing table seating of car NP 378. (Patrick C. Dorin)

BURLINGTON NORTHERN TRAIN NO. 25, the combined North Coast Limited/Empire Builder departs Chicago Union Station with a consist of 14 cars, including 6 dome cars in March, 1971. The last five cars of the train made up the North Coast Limited section. (Patrick C. Dorin)

THE NORTHERN PACIFIC'S domeliner, the North Coast Limited, is shown here during a station stop at Butte, Montana. This photo shows the usual power assignment of three units for 25 and 26. The two-tone color scheme of light and dark green for the North Coast Limited was one of the most distinctive of all color schemes to be found on any transportation system equipment. The slogan, "Mainstreet of the Northwest," splashed across the sides of the passenger motive power would be especially true today of the Burlington Northern. (Harold K. Vollrath)

BURLINGTON NORTHERN NO. 25 during a station stop at Billings, Montana. (J. DeVries)

THE NORTH COAST LIMITED being backed into the Chicago Union Station on a sunny but smoggy day in the summer of 1964. (J. W. Swanberg)

The *Vista-Dome* NORTH COAST LIMITED—

SCHEDULE

No. 25—Daily—West Example of Daily Service		Miles	Completely Air-Conditioned, Wire-Recorded Music, Controlled Radio Reception, Stewardess-Nurse Service	No. 26—Daily—East Example of Daily Service	
			Central Time		
Sunday	12 10 pm	0	Lv..CHICAGO (C. B. & Q.)..Ar.	1 45 pm	Tuesday
"	6 55 pm	427	Ar.......ST. PAUL.......Lv.	7 00 am	"
"	7 15 pm	0	Lv. ST. PAUL, via N. P. Ry. Ar.	6 40 am	"
"	7 40 pm	11	Ar.....MINNEAPOLIS....Lv.	6 15 am	"
"	7 50 pm	11	Lv.....MINNEAPOLIS.....Ar.	6 10 am	"
"	6 00 pm	0	Lv........DULUTH.......Ar.	7 05 am	Tuesday
"	6 11 pm	4	Lv.......SUPERIOR.......Ar.	6 50 am	"
Sunday	11 54 pm	252	Ar........Fargo........Ar.	1 42 am	Tuesday
Monday	1 35 am	344	Ar......Jamestown......Lv.	12 10 am	"
"	3 20 am	446	Ar........Bismarck.......Lv.	10 20 pm	Monday
			Mountain Time		
"	2 41 am	451	Ar........Mandan.......Ar.	9 04 pm	"
"	4 29 am	552	Ar.......Dickinson......Lv.	7 19 pm	"
"	6 22 am	657	Ar........Glendive.......Lv.	5 19 pm	"
"	7 46 am	736	Ar.......Miles City......Lv.	3 48 pm	"
"	8 45 am	781	Ar........Forsyth.......Lv.	2 59 pm	"
"	10 31 am	883	Ar........Billings.......Lv.	1 13 pm	"
Monday	a10 35 am	......	Lv........Billings........Ar.	a10 15 pm	Monday
"	a12 55 pm	......	Ar..CODY (Yellowstone)..Lv.	a 7 45 pm	"
Monday	12 35 pm	999	Ar.......Livingston......Lv.	11 06 am	Monday
"	a12 40 pm	......	Lv.......Livingston......Ar.	a 9 00 pm	"
			Yellowstone Park		
"	a 2 30 pm	......	Ar.......Gardiner.......Lv.	a 7 30 pm	"
Monday	1 31 pm	1023	Ar.......Bozeman......Lv.	10 11 am	Monday
"	3 30 pm	1121	Ar.........Helena.........Lv.	7 40 am	"
"	3 56 pm	1118	Ar.........Butte........Lv.	7 45 am	"
"	6 14 pm	1238	Ar.......Missoula.......Lv.	5 18 am	"
			Pacific Time		
"	10 38 pm	1496	Ar........Spokane.......Lv.	10 45 pm	Sunday
Tuesday	1 27 am	1642	Ar...PASCO via N. P. Ry...Lv.	7 50 pm	"
"	3 31 am	1731	Ar........YAKIMA.......Lv	5 50 pm	"
"	4 29 am	1768	Ar......ELLENSBURG.....Lv.	4 45 pm	"
"	7 35 am	1892	Ar. SEATTLE (King St. Sta.) Lv.	1 30 pm	"
"	b 7 35 am	1889	Ar........TACOMA.......Lv.	b 1 00 pm	Sunday

Spokane-Portland

Monday	10 47 pm	0	Lv...Spokane (N. P. Ry.)..Ar.	10 38 pm	Sunday
Tuesday	2 40 am	146	Lv..Pasco (S. P. & S. Ry.).Ar.	7 05 pm	"
"	7 00 am	379	Ar.......Portland.......Lv. via S. P. & S. Ry.	3 00 pm	"

California Via Puget Sound

458 Daily		408 Daily		Pacific Time	459 Daily		457 Daily	
Tu.	5 00	Tu.	11 10	Lv.........Seattle.........Ar.	6 00	Su.	1 30	Su.
Tu.	6 02	Tu.	12 16	Lv.........Tacoma.........Ar.	4 15	Su.	12 31	Su.
Tu.	9 15	Tu.	3 20	Ar.........Portland.........Lv.	11 45	Sa.	9 30	Su.

19 Daily		11 Daily		9 Daily		Southern Pacific	20 Daily		10 Daily		12 Daily	
Tu.	11 00	Tu.	4 00	Tu.	7 35	Lv....Portland....Ar.	7 40	Sa.	11 25	Su.	8 45	Su.
We.	b 6 55	We.	b8 15	Tu.	b10 55	Ar.....Oakland...Lv.	b10 45	Fri.	b 8 00	Su.	b4 35	Sa.
We.	7 20	We.	8 50	Tu.	11 30	Ar..San Francisco.Lv.	10 20	Fri.	7 20	Su.	3 50	Sa.
Th.	10 00	We.	7 00	We.	10 00	Ar...Los Angeles..Lv.	5 40	Fri.	6 05	Sa.	5 40	Sa.

a—During Park Season Only. b—Connection is bus operated.

NOW . . .

Economy-minded travelers may purchase private room sleeping accommodations on COACH tickets in

SLUMBERCOACHES on the Vista-Dome

NORTH COAST LIMITED

EQUIPMENT

TRAIN No. 25 (Westbound) (Operates via Butte)

Observation Lounge Sleeping Car—
Chicago to Seattle, 4 Double Bedrooms, 1 Compartment, Lounge-Buffet, Radio. (Car 259.)

Pullman Standard Sleeping Cars—
Chicago to Portland, 8 Duplex Roomettes, 6 Roomettes, 4 Double Bedrooms. (Car 257.)
Chicago to Seattle, **Vista-Dome,** 4 Double Bedrooms, 4 Duplex Single Rooms, 4 Roomettes. (Cars 256 and 258.)
Chicago to Seattle, 8 Duplex Roomettes, 6 Roomettes, 3 Double Bedrooms, 1 Compartment. (Car 255.)

ALL-ROOM SLUMBERCOACH—Chicago to Seattle, 24 Single Rooms, 8 Double Rooms—may be purchased on **COACH** ticket. Car SC 25.

Dining Car—
Chicago to Seattle. Pasco to Portland, via S. P. & S.

Vista-Dome Reclining Chair Coaches (Leg rests).
Chicago to Portland. (Car C-252.)
(Via S. P. & S. Ry. Pasco to Portland.)
Chicago to Seattle. (Car C-250).
Seats in Dome sections are not reserved. All other coach seats are reserved, at no additional cost. Advance reservation necessary.

Reclining Chair Coaches—
Chicago to Seattle. (Cars C-251 and C-254.) **Leg rests.**
Chicago to Portland. (Car C-253.)
Pasco to Seattle. (Car C-270.)
Pasco to Portland, 60 Seat—Unreserved
(Via S. P. & S. train No. 1 Pasco to Portland).

Lewis & Clark Traveller's Rest Buffet-Lounge—
Chicago to Seattle. Featuring select and a la carte meals, snacks and beverages.

TRAIN No. 26 (Eastbound) (Operates via Butte)

Observation Lounge Sleeping Car—
Seattle to Chicago, 4 Double Bedrooms, 1 Compartment, Lounge-Buffet, Radio. (Car 269.)

Pullman Standard Sleeping Cars—
Seattle to Chicago, 8 Duplex Roomettes, 6 Roomettes, 3 Double Bedrooms, 1 Compartment. (Car 265.)
Portland to Chicago, 8 Duplex Roomettes, 6 Roomettes, 4 Double Bedrooms. (Car 267.)
Seattle to Chicago, **Vista-Dome,** 4 Double Bedrooms, 4 Duplex Single Rooms, 4 Roomettes. (Cars 266 and 268.)

ALL-ROOM SLUMBERCOACH—Seattle to Chicago—24 Single Rooms, 8 Double Rooms—may be purchased on **COACH** ticket. Car SC 26.

Dining Car—
Seattle to Chicago. Portland to Pasco, via S. P. & S.
(For meal prices and sample menus, see Page 4.)

Vista-Dome Reclining Chair Coaches (Leg rests).
Seattle to Chicago. (Car C-260.)
Portland to Chicago. (Car C-262.)
Seats in Dome sections are not reserved. All other coach seats are reserved at no additional cost. Advance reservation necessary.

Reclining Chair Coaches—
Seattle to Chicago. (Cars C-261 and C-264.) **Leg rests.**
Portland to Chicago. (Car C-263.)
Seattle to Pasco. (Car C-270.)
Portland to Pasco; 60 Seat—Unreserved
(Via S. P. & S. No. 2 Portland to Pasco).

Lewis & Clark Traveller's Rest Buffet-Lounge—
Seattle to Chicago. Featuring select and a la carte meals, snacks and beverages.

Time from 12:01 midnight to 12:00 noon shown in light face type; **time from 12:01 noon to 12:00 midnight shown in heavy face type.**

Source: NP Time Table
May 27, 1962

IT IS TRAIN TIME AT BILLINGS, Montana. CB&Q train No. 30 en route to Denver awaits its 1:30 PM departure time while Northern Pacific No. 26, the Vista Dome North Coast Limited loads passengers, mail and express for points east on the Northern Pacific and Burlington Railroads. (Louis A. Marre)

AS BUSINESS DECLINED on the sleeping car trade between Chicago and Portland on the North Coast Limited, and six of the NP and CB&Q sleeper domes were converted to sleeper dome lounges; the three companies no longer operated a dome sleeper between Chicago and Portland. With that development, the SP&S dome sleeper was repainted in the SP&S color scheme of olive green and tan. The car is shown here in AMTRAK service in Chicago on March 26, 1972. (John H. Kuehl)

THE CAPITOL LIMITED was placed in service in 1923 between New York City, Baltimore, Washington, D. C. and Chicago. The train was always equipped with the finest of passenger equipment. The train was All–Pullman from 1923 to 1958 when it was combined with the All–Coach Columbian, an equally fine train.

The Capitol Limited became a "Domeliner" in December, 1950 as part of an up grading program of B&O passenger services. About the same time the train received two-unit diners and stainless steel Pullmans with the most up to date accommodations. The train remained a fine way to travel between Chicago and Washington right up until the time of AMTRAK. However, the trains lost their domeliner status in 1968. This photo shows the Capitol Limited after receiving the new "Strata Dome" (from C&O's Chessie – see Chapter 19) and other stainless steel passenger equipment. Note the power combination of one E-7 and two F-3's heading up the 14 car All–Pullman Domeliner. (Baltimore and Ohio)

THE BALTIMORE AND OHIO Railroad operated three dome sleepers over its system. The cars, originally built for C&O's Chessie, were named as follows:
Starlight Dome
Moonlight Dome
Sunlight Dome
(Baltimore & Ohio)

AN INTERIOR VIEW of the former B&O sleeper Strata Dome. (Baltimore and Ohio)

THREE "E" UNITS BACK BALTIMORE & OHIO No. 7, the Shenandoah, into Chicago for an earlier than advertised arrival October 12, 1962. The night before, floodlights on the dome sleeper helped night owls view the Potomac Valley west of Washington, D. C. (Jim Scribbins)

THE DAY IS NOVEMBER 8, 1969 and rail fans are observing for the last time the departure of the domeliner Capitol Limited from Chicago's Grand Central Station. In addition to the dome coach (fourth car in the train), this historic train also included an SP baggage car, three flat top coaches, three sleepers, C&O diner-lounge-observation (originally built for a "Chessie" connection) and a B&O business car. From November 9, 1969 thru April 30, 1971, all C&O and B&O trains arrived and departed from the C&NW Madison Street Station. Grand Central, which also served the Wisconsin Central (now Soo Line) and Chicago Great Western has now been dismantled. (John H. Kuehl)

B&O'S EASTBOUND DOMELINER the Capitol Limited swings off the lift bridge over the South Branch of the Chicago River during August, 1967. The "St. Charles Airline" is on the right and IC's Central Station is clearly seen in the far background to the left of E-8A No. 1445. (John H. Kuehl)

A BALTIMORE & OHIO dining car cook leans out of the C&O observation dining car and catches a welcome breeze, as the eastbound Capitol Limited accelerates out of Grand Central Station in Chicago on a hot summer day in August, 1969. (John H. Kuehl)

A B&O DOME COACH WAS PAINTED light blue and silver for the American Railroad's Centennial train for 1969. In November of that year, the car wore B&O emblems at each end. The photo was taken on the occasion of the arrival of the first Capitol Limited at the C&NW depot in Chicago. (John H. Kuehl)

THE EASTBOUND DOMELINER, the Capitol Limited sprints across the bridge over the Calumet River at about 95th Street in Chicago. Bringing up the rear in splendid fashion is the beautiful "Metcalf," one of a number of identical cars originally built for the C&O. (John H. Kuehl)

ROUTE OF THE B. & O. STRATA DOMES
DETROIT
CHICAGO
TOLEDO
GARY
DESHLER
FOSTORIA
YOUNGSTOWN
AKRON
LIMA
PITTSBURGH
CUMBERLAND
HARPERS FERRY
DAYTON
CINCINNATI
WASHINGTON D. C.
Drawn By: Sy Dykhouse III

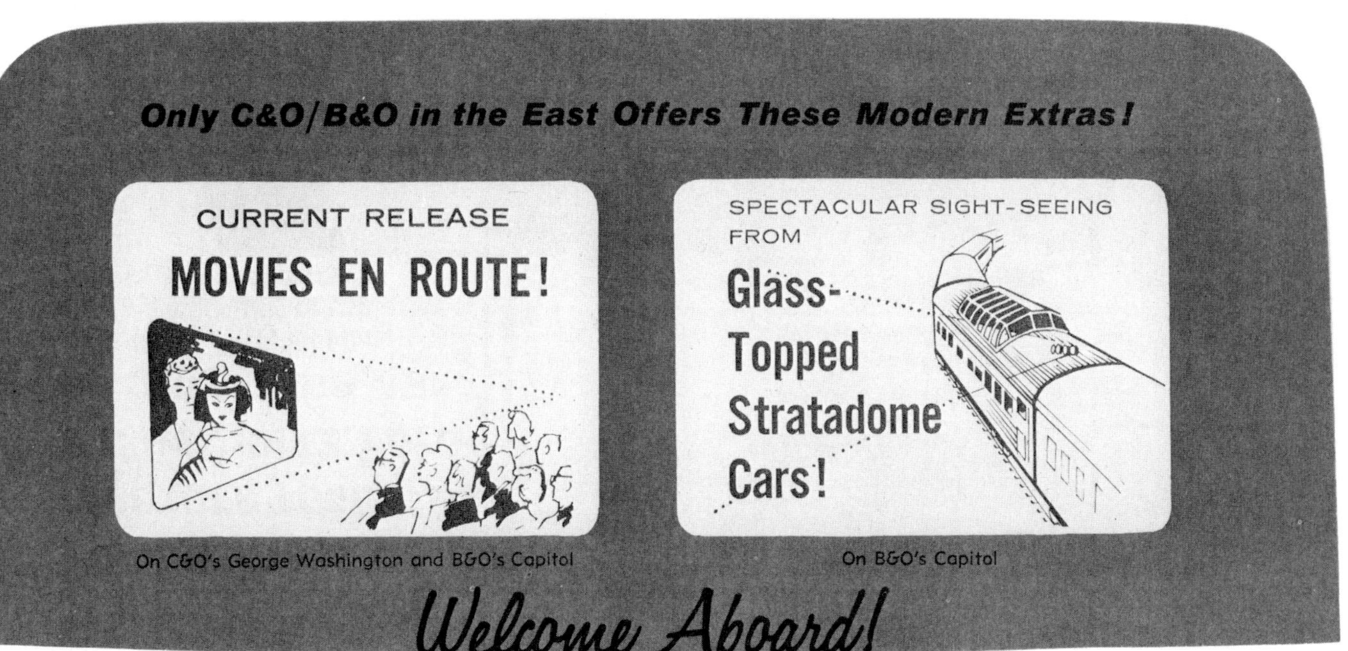
Only C&O/B&O in the East Offers These Modern Extras!
CURRENT RELEASE
MOVIES EN ROUTE!
On C&O's George Washington and B&O's Capitol
SPECTACULAR SIGHT-SEEING FROM
Glass-Topped Stratadome Cars!
On B&O's Capitol
Welcome Aboard!

Table 1 — Baltimore and Washington to Pittsburgh, Cleveland, Toledo, Detroit, Chicago

Miles	Westward Baltimore to Chicago	Dav'l't Speed-liner 21 Daily	Chicago Express 153 9 Daily	Ambassador 19 Daily	Columbian 25 Daily	Capitol Limited 5 Daily	Clevo. Night Express 17 Daily	Shenandoah 7 Daily
	(EASTERN STANDARD TIME) Lv BALTIMORE—	AM	PM	PM	PM	PM	PM	PM
0.0	Mt. Royal Station	9.30	12.30	4.00	4.00	4.00		9.55
1.5	Camden Station	9.35	12.35	4.05	4.05	4.05	8.25	10.00
38.3	Ar WASHINGTON	10.15	1.25	4.50	4.50	4.50	9.10	10.45
38.3	Lv WASHINGTON	10.30	2.45	5.15	5.15	5.30	9.30	11.15
45.2	Silver Spring	10.41	2.59	5.29	h5.29	5.44	9.43	11.23
93.4	Harpers Ferry	11.29	3.52	6.23			10f40	
100.7	Shenandoah Junction		4.02				10.51	12.30
111.6	Martinsburg	11.51	4.21	6.50	‡6.50	‡7.04	11.17	12.50
184.2	Ar Cumberland	1.20	6.02	8.22			12.50	2.17
184.2	Lv Cumberland	1.23	6.12	8.30	‡8.30	‡8.45	1.05	2.22
221.3	Meyersdale		7.12					
233.1	Rockwood		7.30					
276.4	Ar Connellsville	3.23	8.33	10.42			3.15	4.35
276.4	Lv Connellsville	3.25	8.38	10.45	10‡45	10‡57	3.23	4.41
319.4	McKeesport	4.16	9.31	11.37	11‡37	11‡49	4.13	5.30
324.6	Braddock (P. & L. E. Sta.)		c9.41					c5.46
334.4	Ar Pittsburgh (P. & L. E. Sta.)	4.40	10.00	12.04	12.04	12.15	4.40	6.05
334.4	Lv Pittsburgh (P. & L. E. Sta.)	*6.00*	10.20	12.08	12.08	12.25	5.05	6.25
381.6	New Castle	▼*7.04*	11.28		u1.09		6.10	7.26
399.9	Youngstown	▼*7.35*	11.53	1.32	r1.32		6.37	7.50
453.7	Ar Akron (Union Station)		1.08	2.30	2.30			8.55
	Ar Akron (Howard Street)						7.42	
	Ar Cleveland (Lee Rd., Shaker Hts.)	*8.51*						
	Ar Cleveland (Union Terminal)	*9.05*					8.50	
453.7	Lv Akron (Union Station)	Connecting service to Youngstown and Cleveland via P. & L. E.—Erie R. R.	1.08	2.30	2.30			8.55
527.6	Ar Willard		2.28	3.45	3.45	4.07		10.15
527.6	Lv Willard		2.55	4.00	4.27	4.27		10.20
551.8	Tiffin		3.23		r4.50			10.45
564.3	Fostoria		3.41	x4.51	r5.02			11.03
590.0	Ar Deshler		4.16		5.28			11.33
	Lv Deshler		*4.48					*1.40*
	Ar Toledo (Union Station)		a*5.60*	a6.25				a*2.30*
	Ar Detroit (Michigan Cent. Sta.)		*7.35*	7.50				*4.00*
590.0	Lv Deshler		4.16		5.28			11.33
615.0	Defiance		4.45		r5.52			11.58
655.5	Ar Garrett (E. S. T.)		5.39		6.32	6.32		12.39
655.5	Lv Garrett (C. S. T.)		4.44		5.37	5.37		11.44
717.3	La Paz		■5.52		g6.33	g6.33		12y43
772.5	Gary		6.55		a7.26	a7.26		1.38
786.6	Ar South Chicago		7.15		7.46	7.46		2.01
796.3	Ar 63rd Street, Chicago		7.31		8.02	8.02		2.18
805.8	Ar CHICAGO		8.00		8.30	8.30		2.45
	(Grand Central Station) (CENTRAL STANDARD TIME)	PM	AM	AM	AM	AM	AM	PM

No. 5—DAILY
THE CAPITOL LIMITED

Club Car—
Baltimore to Chicago. (Buffet.) (Radio.)
Observation Lounge Car—
Washington to Chicago—5 Double B. R. (Buffet.) (Radio.)
Strata Dome Car—
Washington to Chicago—5 Roomettes, 1 Single Bedroom, 3 D. R. (Each D. R. accommodates 2 persons.)
Sleeping Cars—
Baltimore to Chicago—16 Duplex Roomettes, 4 Double B. R.
Washington to Chicago—16 Duplex Roomettes, 4 Double B. R.
Washington to Chicago—10 Roomettes, 6 Double B.R. (2 cars.)
Dining Car..........Washington to Chicago.
Stewardess-Nurse—Baltimore to Chicago.

No. 7—DAILY
THE SHENANDOAH

Lounge Car—
Washington to Chicago—8 Sec. (Buffet.) (Radio.)
Strata Dome Car—
Washington to Chicago (on odd dates except the 31st) —5 Roomettes, 1 Single Bedroom, 3 D. R. (Each D. R. accommodates 2 persons.)
Sleeping Cars—
Baltimore to Chicago—16 Duplex Roomettes. 4 Double B. R.
Washington to Chicago—10 Roomettes, 5 Double B.R. (on even dates).
Washington to Pittsburgh—10 Roomettes, 6 Double B. R. (May be occupied in Pittsburgh until 8.00 a. m.)
(Sleepers open at Washington **10.00 p. m.**)
Dining-Lounge Car.Pittsburgh to Chicago.
Coach Lounge Car..Baltimore to Chicago.
Recl. Seat Coach....Baltimore to Chicago.
Stewardess-Nurse—Washington to Chicago.

No. 25—DAILY
THE COLUMBIAN

Dining Car..........Baltimore to Chicago.
Slumbercoach—
Baltimore to Chicago—24 Single Rooms, 8 Double Rooms.
Recl. Seat Coaches—
(Coach seats reserved in advance without charge.)
Baltimore to Chicago. (Lounge Rooms.)
Washington to Chicago. (Lounge Rooms.)
Strata Dome Lounge Car..Washington to Chicago.
Observation Coach-Lounge Car—
Washington to Willard. (Buffet.) (Radio.)
Stewardess-Nurse—Washington to Chicago.

Source: B&O Time Table Oct. 26, 1958

CHAPTER 8

The Santa Fe Chiefs

The first Chief was born in 1926 and the Super Chief came along in 1936. These trains were equipped with standard cars until the late 1930's. The first dome lounge cars did not arrive until late 1950. After placing the cars on display for a short while, the new Pleasure Dome Lounge Cars went into service on the Super Chief on January 28, 1951. On the same day, the Super Chief received a new dining car that runs as a companion car to the Dome Lounge. These cars have operated on the Super Chief from 1951 through 1972, over 20 years of continuous service.

The Company owned six of these beautiful cars. Five were in regular operation, with one as a spare so that continuous service may be offered while one of the regulars is in the shops.

The dome car has three levels, the first of which is the lower level lounge under the dome that seats 10. The main level of the car includes the main lounge and the Turquoise Room. The main lounge in the forward section has individual lounge chairs and sofas seating fourteen and also a table arrangement seating four for a total of eighteen. Private parties of up to ten persons can be served dinner or refreshments in the Turquoise Room. When not reserved for private use, all passengers may enjoy this beautiful room for refreshments which are served from the lower lounge. The Pleasure Dome is reached by a stairway from the main level and has glare proof windows. The seating arrangement includes in addition to four double seats, eight individual deep-cushion swivel chairs.

The second train to receive domes on the Santa Fe was the El Capitan. Five Dome-Lounge Cars, series 506 to 513 (called Big Domes as they were full-length domes) were originally operated on former trains 21 and 22 from delivery in 1954 to July, 1956 when the El Capitan was equipped with Hi-Level equipment. At the same time (1954), three Dome Lounge Cars (series 506 to 513) were used in trains 11 and 12 between Chicago and Oklahoma City. Trains 11 and 12 were the Kansas Cityan and the Chicagoan. When Train 11 was combined with train 19 between Chicago and Kansas City the dome lounge operated on train 9 to Kansas City, thence train 11 to Oklahoma City and train 12 Oklahoma City to Chicago. Later the dome lounge operated on train 11 Kansas City to Wichita and train 12 Wichita to Chicago.

As stated previously, the El Capitan received its Hi-Level equipment from the Budd Company in the summer of 1956. These cars are 15½ feet in height and provide passengers with a panoramic view of the countryside from a vantage point a full four feet higher than in a standard or regular chair car. The train consist also includes a high level dining car and a hi-level lounge car.

The dome type lounge (actually it is not a dome car in the strict definition of the word, but does have roof skylights. The only thing lacking is the "see-ahead" view.) cars seat a total of 86 passengers on the two levels. The upper level has table and lounge seats for sixty passengers and this area is used for serving refreshments. The lower level, the Kachina Room, has

THE SANTA FE CHIEF was placed in service in the 1920's and the Super Chief came in 1936. The Santa Fe always operated the finest of passenger trains, and continued that tradition with the addition of dome cars in the 1950's. The first train to receive domes was the Super Chief. The All–Pullman extra fare train was equipped with a "Pleasure Dome Lounge" car on January 28, 1951. This photo shows train No. 17, the Super Chief powered by four "F" units and a consist of 12 cars, gliding through Cajon Pass, California. The sixth car is the Pleasure Dome Lounge of this All–Pullman domeliner. (Sante Fe)

table arrangement seating for 26 and snack type meal service is provided all day. The Hi-level equipment including the lounge has operated on the El Capitan from 1956 through 1972, a total of 16 continuous years.

When the El Capitan went Hi-level in 1956, the Dome Lounges were reassigned to the Chief between Chicago and Los Angeles. The Dome cars remained in service on 19 and 20 until the train was discontinued on May 13, 1968.

In 1954, the Santa Fe also took delivery of 6 Dome Lounge Dormitory cars. These cars were assigned to the new San Francisco Chief operating between Chicago and Richmond, California through the famous San Joaquin Valley. This equipment operated on trains 1 and 2 until October 18, 1968. At that time, the Dome Lounge Dorms were taken out of service on 1 and 2 and placed in service on the Texas Chief, trains 15 and 16. The Dome Lounges that were formerly operated on the Chief, and were in Texas service from May 1968 until October were then placed in service on the San Francisco train. An operation that continued until AMTRAK took over.

The Santa Fe owned two types of Big Dome Lounge Cars. The first eight (series 506 to 513) contained on the lower level a bar, a 28 seat lounge section, a private desk for writing letters and a Nurse's room. The second group's (series 550 to 555) lower level contained a small cocktail lounge and a dormitory section for the crew. The Domes of both groups were identical. The total seating capacity of the dome sections was 75 passengers with angled sofas (for two people) that permitted a passenger to enjoy the American panorama without craning his neck. The sofas provided seating for 57 passengers, while at the rear of the dome there were 18 seats at tables that made up a refreshment lounge. The two groups of dome cars were purchased at the same time.

The Santa Fe has provided the public with some of the finest domeliners to be operated anywhere in the world. Even in the face of rising costs, Santa Fe passenger trains were in 1971 still providing excellent service between Chicago and the Great Southwest. (See Chapter 21, AMTRAK, for present Santa Fe service.)

PLEASURE DOME LOUNGE CAR No. 502 is one of six short domes operated by the Sante Fe. The six cars (500 to 505) were built by Pullman in 1950 and have operated exclusively on the Super Chief. (Santa Fe)

THE LOWER LEVEL of the Pleasure Dome car is a gathering place for refreshments and hors d'oeuveres before dinner. (Santa Fe)

THE SANTA FE owned and operated eight Chair–Lounge–Dome cars (as they were called on the Santa Fe) series 506 to 513. The equipment was built by the Budd Company in 1954 and is similar to the former Great Northern Great Dome lounge cars, also built by the Budd Company. Note the steel bars at each end of the dome placed there to prevent icicles at tunnel portals from breaking dome windows and causing injury to passengers. (Santa Fe)

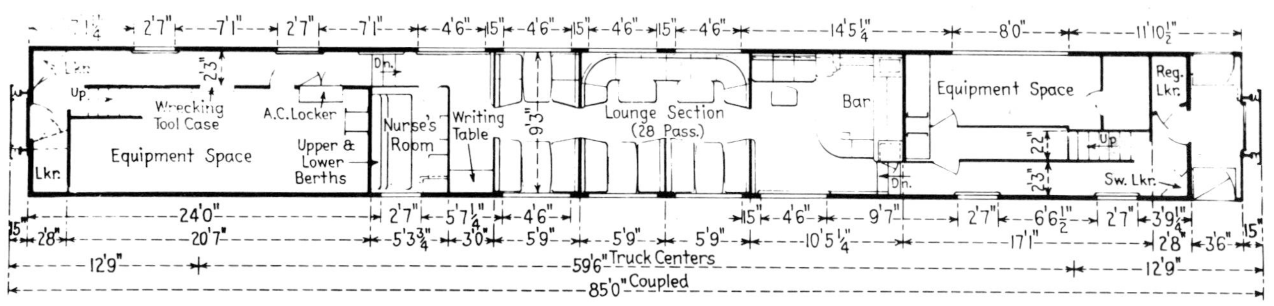

FLOOR PLAN FOR THE Santa Fe Chair–Lounge–Dome cars showing both levels. (Budd Company)

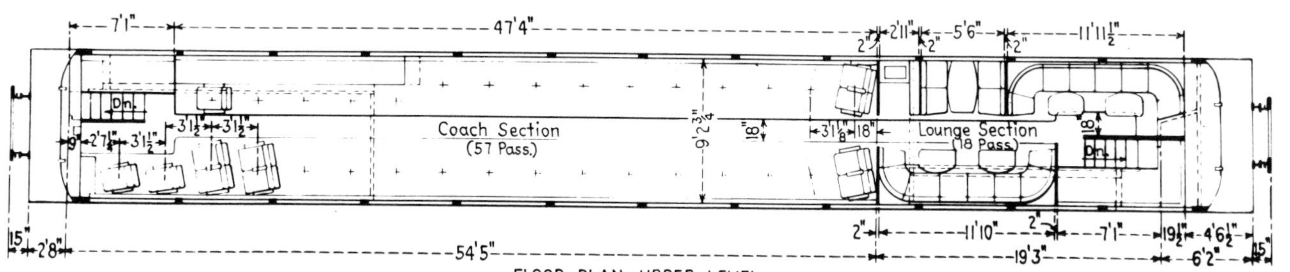

ROUNDING ONE OF THE CURVES of the double horseshoe curve near Ribera, New Mexico is the Santa Fe's pre Hi-level All–Coach domeliner, the El Capitan. Trains 21 and 22 carried a full length dome lounge until the new equipment arrived in 1956. (Santa Fe)

THE SANTA FE PURCHASED six Chair–Lounge–Dome–Dormitory cars for use on the San Francisco Chief, series 550 to 555. These cars were identical to the 506 to 513 series, except the lower level contained a crew dormitory section instead of a full lounge. (Santa Fe)

INTERIOR OF SANTA FE Big Dome Lounge showing both chair and table seating. The arrangement of the domes for both sets of equipment (506 to 513 and 550 to 555) was virtually identical. (Santa Fe)

A 12 CAR SAN FRANCISCO CHIEF crosses the Muir trestle near Glen Frazer, California with the dome lounge dormitory car cut in behind the coaches and ahead of the dining car. (Santa Fe)

SANTA FE NO. 1, the San Francisco Chief, rolls through Abo Canyon, New Mexico with Hi-level chair cars in the 21 car consist including one dome lounge dormitory, which is located behing the hi-level cars. (Santa Fe)

SANTA FE NO. 16, the domeliner Texas Chief pauses at Joliet, Illinois before completing the last leg of its Texas–Chicago run. The consist on this April 11, 1970, is two baggage cars, three hi-level chair cars, one dome lounge, one dining car and three Pullmans, (John H. Kuehl)

THE TIME IS JULY, 1956 and the Hi-level El Capitan has just gone into service. Originally the train consisted of a baggage car, a dormitory-baggage car with a modified roof to match the Hi-level equipment, three Hi-level Chair Cars, Hi-level dining car, Hi-level lounge and four more Hi-level Chair Cars. A truly beautiful train that provided the ultimate in Chair Car comfort. (Santa Fe)

THE SANTA FE purchased 6 Hi-level lounge cars with roof sky lights. The six cars, series 575 to 580, can operate only with other Hi-level equipment and have served on the El Capitan exclusively since their purchase. (Santa Fe)

INTERIOR OF HI-LEVEL lounge showing the two seat table arrangements. (Santa Fe)

INTERIOR OF THE HI-LEVEL lounge showing the full length of the car. Note the service elevator near the attendant, and also the stairway leading to the lower level Kachina Coffee Shop. (Santa Fe)

SANTA FE FIRST NO. 17, the Super Chief, departs Chicago during the summer of 1969. The photo was taken from the 18th Street Bridge in Chicago. (John H. Kuehl)

THE FINAL RUN OF Santa Fe No. 1, the domeliner San Francisco Chief departing Chicago on April 30, 1971. The train always ran with "F" units until very close to the end when a combination of one passenger FP-45 and one freight F-45 were occasionally operated along with one of the steam generators converted from former baggage cars. (John H. Kuehl)

FROM LEFT TO RIGHT we see Sante Fe first No. 17, the Super Chief behind two FP-45's; and second No. 17, the El Capitan behind five "F" units on August 4, 1969. (John H. Kuehl)

Westbound Condensed Transcontinental Schedules

Miles	Table A	No. 19 The Chief Sleeping Cars and Chair Cars Daily Example		No. 123 The Grand Canyon Via La Junta Daily Example		No. 1 San Francisco Chief Sleeping Cars and Chair Cars Daily Example		No. 17 The Super Chief Extra Fare Standard Sleeping Cars Daily Example		No. 17 El Capitan Extra Fare Coach Passengers Daily Example	
.0	Lv Chicago (C.S.T.)	9.10 AM	Sun	11.00AM	Sun	3.15PM	Sun	6.30 PM	Sun	6.30 PM	Sun
37.5	" Joliet	9.55 AM	"	11.55AM	"	4.05PM	"	7.20 PM	"	7.20 PM	"
89.6	" Streator	10.40 AM	"	12.50PM	"	C4.50PM	"	⊠ 8.05 PM	"	⊠ 8.05 PM	"
130.1	" Chillicothe	11.15 AM	"	1.30PM	"	w5.25PM	"	⊠ 8.40 PM	"	⊠ 8.40 PM	"
177.5	" Galesburg, Ill.	11.59 AM	"	2.20PM	"	C6.10PM	"	⑰ 9.25 PM	"	⑰ 9.25 PM	"
232.9	" Ft. Madison, Ia.	12.50 PM	"	3.30PM	"	7.00PM	"	10.20 PM	"	10.20 PM	"
451.1	Ar Kansas City, Mo.	4.35 PM	"	8.50PM	"	10.30PM	"	1.55 AM	Mon	1.55 AM	Mon
451.1	Lv Kansas City, Mo.	4.55 PM	"	9.30PM	"	10.50PM	"	2.05 AM	"	2.05 AM	"
490.8	" Lawrence, Kan.			10.10PM	"	f11.30PM	"				
516.9	" Topeka			10.50PM	"	11.55PM	"				
578.2	" Emporia	g 6.40 PM	"	12.30AM	Mon	1.10AM	Mon				
636.2	" Newton	7.50 PM	"	2.10AM	"	2.25AM	"	5.05 AM	"	5.05 AM	"
669.1	" Hutchinson	8.20 PM	"	2.55AM	"			ZZ5.35 AM	"	ZZ5.35 AM	"
789.3	Ar Dodge City (C.S.T.)	10.07 PM	"	5.15AM	"			7.15 AM	"	7.15 AM	"
789.3	Lv Dodge City, Kan. (M.S.T.)	9.10 PM	"	4.25AM	"			6.18 AM	"	6.18 AM	"
991.7	Ar La Junta, Colo.	11.59 PM	"	8.00AM	"			8.55 AM	"	8.55 AM	"
.0	Lv Denver	7.50 PM	Sun								
74.8	" Colorado Springs	9.38 PM	"								
119.3	" Pueblo	10.45 PM	"								
183.2	Ar La Junta	11.50 PM	"								
991.7	Lv La Junta	12.15 AM	Mon	8.25AM	Mon	Via Amarillo — For schedule Newton to Belen see table 7, page 23		9.00 AM	Mon	9.00 AM	Mon
1098.3	" Raton, N. M.	2.33 AM	"	11.00AM	"			11.18 AM	"	11.18 AM	"
1206.3	" Las Vegas	4.33 AM	"	1.10PM	"			1.15 PM	"	1.15 PM	"
1270.5	Ar Lamy	6.05 AM	"	3.14PM	"			2.50 PM	"	2.50 PM	"
1288.6	Ar Santa Fe (Motor Coach)	6.45 AM	Mon	3.55PM	Mon			3.30 PM	Mon	3.30 PM	Mon
.0	Lv Santa Fe (Motor Coach)	5.20 AM	Mon	2.30PM	Mon			2.05 PM	Mon	2.05 PM	Mon
1338.1	Ar Albuquerque	7.30 AM	Mon	4.35PM	Mon			4.15 PM	Mon	4.15 PM	Mon
636.2	Lv Newton (C.S.T.)					2.25AM	Mon				
663.4	" Wichita					3.10AM	"				
697.5	" Wellington, Kan.					4.00AM	"				
1010.4	Ar Amarillo, Tex.					10.00AM	"				
.0	Lv Amarillo, Tex.					10.35AM	Mon				
121.6	Ar Lubbock, Tex.					1.00PM	"				
1010.4	Lv Amarillo, Tex.					10.10AM	Mon				
1114.1	Ar Clovis, N. M. (C.S.T.)					12.15PM	"				
1114.1	Lv Clovis (M.S.T.)					11.50AM	"				
1244.9	" Vaughn					1.50PM	"				
1353.9	Ar Belen					3.50PM	"				
1338.1	Lv Albuquerque	7.40 AM	Mon	5.00PM	Mon			4.25 PM	Mon	4.25 PM	Mon
1499.2	" Gallup, N. M.	10.00 AM	"	7.28PM	"	6.12PM	Mon	6.45 PM	"	6.45 PM	"
1627.1	" Winslow, Ariz.	11.47 AM	"	9.50PM	"	8.00PM	"	8.32 PM	"	8.32 PM	"
1685.5	" Flagstaff	‡12.51 PM	"	11.05PM	"	nn 9.05PM	"	tt 9.37 PM	"	tt 9.37 PM	"
1719.4	Ar Williams	‡ 1.33 PM	"	12.05AM	Tues.	9.44PM	"	‡ 10.17 PM	"	‡10.17 PM	"
1719.4	Lv Williams	▣ 1.45 PM	Mon	14 ‡ 4.15AM	Tues.						
1783.7	Ar Grand Canyon	▣ 3.30 PM	"	‡ 7.00AM	"						
.0	Lv Grand Canyon	▣11.30 AM	Mon	15 ‡ 8.00PM	Mon	▣ 7.40PM	Mon	▣ 7.46 PM	Mon	▣ 7.40 PM	Mon
64.3	Ar Williams	▣ 1.15 PM	"	‡10.20PM	"	▣ 9.25PM	"	▣ 9.25 PM	"	▣ 9.25 PM	"
1719.4	Lv Williams	‡ 1.33 PM	Mon	12.05AM	Tues.	9.44PM	Mon	‡ 10.17PM	Mon	‡10.17 PM	Mon
1742.4	Ar Ash Fork			1.07AM	"	10.40PM	"	J 11.02PM	"	J11.02 PM	"
1742.4	Lv Ash Fork			2.10AM	Tues.	2.10AM	Tues	2.10AM	Tues	2.10 AM	Tues
1799.5	Ar Prescott			3.45AM	"	3.45AM	"	3.45AM	"	3.45 AM	"
1936.8	Ar Phoenix			8.30AM	"	8.30AM	"	8.30AM	"	8.30 AM	"
1742.4	Lv Ash Fork			1.07AM	Tues	10.40PM	Mon	J 11.02 PM	Mon	J11.02 PM	Mon
1769.8	" Seligman, Ariz. (M.S.T.)	3.02 PM	Mon	1.53AM	"	11.22PM	"	11.43 PM	Tues.	11.43 PM	Tues
1918.8	Ar Needles, Calif. (P.S.T.)	4.30 PM	"	3.50AM	"	12.45AM	Tues	12.56 AM	"	12.56 AM	"
1918.8	Lv Needles	4.40 PM	"	4.00AM	"	12.55AM	"	1.06 AM	"	1.06 AM	"
2086.4	Ar Barstow	7.30 PM	"	7.30AM	"	3.45AM	"	3.52 AM	"	3.52 AM	"
2086.4	Lv Barstow	7.35 PM	"	7.45AM	"	↓		3.57 AM	"	3.57 AM	"
2167.5	Ar San Bernardino	9.28 PM	"	9.55AM	"			5.52 AM	"	5.52 AM	"
2177.9	Ar Riverside	RR	"	10.25AM	"			RR	"	RR	"
2192.9	Ar Pomona	S10.01 PM	"					S6.31 AM	"	S6.31 AM	"
2217.8	Ar Pasadena	10.39 PM	"					7.20 AM	"	7.20 AM	"
.0	Lv Pasadena (Motor Coach)	⑧10.45 PM	Mon					⑧ 7.40 AM	Tues	⑧7.40 AM	Tues
26.5	Ar Long Beach " "	⑧11.50 PM	"					⑧ 8.55 AM	"	⑧8.55 AM	"
2223.7	Ar Los Angeles (P.S.T.)	11.15 PM	Mon	12.10PM	Tues			8.00 AM	Tues	8.00 AM	Tues
		No. 80		No. 74				No. 72		No. 72	
.0	Lv Los Angeles (P.S.T.)	11.45 PM	Mon	1.30PM	Tues			9.30 AM	Tues	9.30AM	Tues
127.9	Ar San Diego (P.S.T.)	3.00 AM	Tues	4.15PM	"	↓		12.15 PM	"	12.15PM	"
				Motor Coach		No. 1					
2086.4	Lv Barstow (P.S.T.)			⑲ 7.45AM	Tues.	3.55AM	Tues				
2227.4	Ar Bakersfield			⑲10.45AM	"	7.20AM	"				
				No. 63							
2227.4	Lv Bakersfield			2.30PM	"	7.45AM	"				
2337.8	Ar Fresno			4.25PM	"	9.40AM	"				
2395.8	" Merced			5.25PM	"	10.40AM	"				
2461.1	" Stockton			6.31PM	"	11.50AM	"				
2495.5	" Pittsburg			7.08PM	"	f 12.31PM	"				
2529.3	Ar Richmond			7.55PM	"	1.30PM	"				
				MotorCoach		MotorCoach					
2529.3	Lv Richmond			8.00PM	Tues.	1.35PM	Tues.				
2537.3	Ar Berkeley			8.25PM	"	2.00PM	"				
2540.2	" Oakland			8.35PM	"	2.10PM	"				
2547.2	Ar San Francisco (P.S.T.)			8.40PM	Tues.	2.15PM	Tues				

Source: Santa Fe Time Table Spring-Summer 1960

Chicago, Kansas, Oklahoma and Texas

Read down | Read up

No. 23 See Note A Daily	No. 15 Texas Chief Daily	Miles	Table 3	No. 24 See Note A Daily	No. 16 Texas Chief Daily
AM	PM			PM	AM
B 9.00	**5.00**	0	Lv..Chicago, Ill. (C.S.T.)..Ar	G **9.00**	10.00
9.55	**5.50**	38	Lv..........Joliet..........Lv	**8.04**	8.48
......	(4) **6.08**	58	Lv.......Coal City........Lv	**7.40**	8.24
10.45	**6.35**	90	Lv........Streator........Lv	**7.08**	7.55
11.25	**7.10**	130	Lv.......Chillicothe.......Lv	**6.20**	7.15
12.15	**7.55**	177	Lv......Galesburg, Ill.......Lv	**5.25**	6.30
1.25	**9.05**	232	Lv...Ft. Madison, Iowa....Lv	**4.25**	5.35
E **2.58**	**10.15**	311	Lv.....La Plata, Mo......Lv	**2.55**	4.20
3.35	(23) **10.48**	346	Lv.......Marceline.......Lv	**2.20**	(26) 3.45
4.17	....	385	Lv.......Carrollton.......Lv	**1.44**	....
5.40	12.40	449	Ar....Kansas City, Mo.....Lv	**12.30**	2.05
No. 211	↓			**No. 212**	↑
6.05		449	Lv....Kansas City, Mo.....Ar	**12.10**	
6.32		475	Lv......Olathe, Kan.......Lv	11.30	
7.00		506	Lv........Ottawa.........Lv	11.00	
7.28		532	Lv........Garnett.........Lv	10.28	
7.55		558	Lv..........Iola..........Lv	10.02	
8.05		566	Lv.......Humboldt.......Lv	9.54	
8.20		575	Lv........Chanute........Lv	9.45	
8.48		605	Lv.......Cherryvale.......Lv	9.12	
9.10		614	Lv......Independence......Lv	9.00	
9.31		637	Lv......Caney, Kan.......Lv	8.31	
9.55		655	Lv....Bartlesville, Okla.....Lv	8.10	
f**10.30**		686	Lv.......Collinsville.......Lv	7.35	
11.00		705	Ar......Tulsa, Okla.......Lv	7.15	
No. 23				**No. 24**	
A **6.00**	1.00	449	Lv....Kansas City, Mo.....Ar	A**12.15**	1.40
6.40	1.48	489	Lv.....Lawrence, Kan......Lv	11.15	12.45
7.15	2.25	515	Lv........Topeka........Lv	10.40	12.15
(5) **7.50**	....	550	Lv.......Osage City.......Lv	(40) 9.55	....
C **8.30**	3.30	577	Lv.......Emporia.......Lv	J 9.25	**11.00**
9.40	4.35	650	Ar........Newton........Lv	8.15	**9.55**
A **9.45**	4.45	650	Lv........Newton........Ar	A 8.05	**9.45**
PM	5.25	677	Lv........Wichita........Lv	AM	**9.05**
	6.10	715	Lv........Winfield........Lv		**8.15**
See	6.30	728	Lv...Arkansas City, Kan....Lv	See	**8.00**
Table	f 6.43	740	Lv.....Newkirk, Okla......Lv	Table	f **7.38**
No. 1	7.10	753	Lv.......Ponca City.......Lv	No. 2	**7.25**
for	7.45	786	Lv.........Perry.........Lv	for	**6.45**
Schedule	8.15	817	Lv........Guthrie........Lv	Schedule	**6.10**
West of	9.10	848	Lv.....Oklahoma City.....Lv	West of	**5.40**
Newton	9.40	865	Lv.........Norman.........Lv	Newton	**5.00**
....	10.12	881	Lv.........Purcell.........Lv	....	**4.40**
....	10.38	903	Lv......Pauls Valley......Lv	....	**4.06**
....	11.34	948	Lv........Ardmore........Lv	....	**3.15**
....	(14)11.52	965	Lv......Marietta, Okla.....Lv	....	(18) **2.55**
....	**12.22**	988	Ar....Gainesville, Texas....Lv	....	**2.30**
....	▣ **2.25**	988	Lv....Gainesville, Texas....Ar	....	▣ **2.05**
....	▣ **3.05**	1018	Ar........Denton........Lv	....	▣ **1.30**
....	**12.22**	988	Lv....Gainesville, Texas....Ar	....	**2.30**
....	**1.40**	1052	Ar.......Fort Worth.......Lv	....	**1.08**
....	† **2.10**	1052	Lv.......Fort Worth.......Ar	....	† **12.25**
....	▣ **3.25**	1083	Ar.........Dallas.........Lv	....	▣11.10
....	▣11.10	0	Lv.........Dallas.........Ar	....	▣ **2.25**
....	† **12.25**	31	Ar.......Fort Worth.......Lv	....	† **1.10**
....	**2.00**	1052	Lv.......Fort Worth.......Ar	....	**12.53**
....	**2.42**	1081	Lv........Cleburne........Lv	....	**12.23**
....	(28) **3.53**	1155	Lv.......McGregor.......Lv	....	(29)11.07
....	**4.20**	1180	Ar........Temple........Lv	....	10.45
....	▣ **7.00**	0	Lv........Temple.........Ar	▣ **8.55**	▣ 8.45
....	▣ **8.50**	69	Lv.........Austin.........Lv	▣ **7.15**	▣ 7.10
....	▣**10.45**	148	Ar......San Antonio......Lv	▣ **5.30**	▣ 5.00
....	**4.30**	1180	Lv........Temple.........Ar	....	10.40
....	**6.31**	1291	Ar.....Belleville Yard.....Lv	....	8.51
....	(47) **7.14**	1332	Lv.......Rosenberg.......Lv	....	(48) 8.13
....	**8.30**	1368	Ar.Houston, Texas (C.S.T.).Lv	....	7.20
	PM				AM

TEXAS CHIEF—Trains 15 and 16—Daily

Chicago—Kansas City—Oklahoma City—Ft. Worth—Houston

Big Dome Lounge Car . . . Chicago and Houston.
Chair Cars . . . Chicago—Houston.
Dining Car . . . Chicago—Houston.
Sleeping Cars . . . Chicago—Ft. Worth.
Chicago—Houston.
Chicago—Topeka—May be occupied at Topeka (westbound) until 7:30 a.m. Ready (eastbound) at 9:30 p.m.
Roomettes, Bedrooms, and Suites.

Source: Santa Fe Time Table
July 1, 1970

Transcontinental Train Equipment

SUPER CHIEF

Trains 17 and 18

Chicago, Kansas City and Los Angeles

Extra-fare, private room and suites streamliner service. Radio and recorded musical programs in every room.

Dormitory Baggage Car.......Chicago and Los Angeles.

Sleeping Car.......Chicago and Los Angeles—2 D.R., 4 Comps., 4 Double Bedrooms: Car 174 (westbound); Car 184 (eastbound).

Chicago and Los Angeles—2 D. R., 4 Comps., 4 Double Bedrooms. Car 172 (westbound); Car 182 (eastbound).

Chicago and Los Angeles—10 Roomettes, 6 Double Bedrooms: Car 171 (westbound); Car 181 (eastbound).

Turquoise Room-Pleasure Dome Lounge Car.......Chicago and Los Angeles.

Dining Car.......Chicago and Los Angeles. Serves all meals. (Fred Harvey Service):

Sleeping Car.......Chicago and Los Angeles—10 Roomettes, 6 Double Bedrooms: Car 176 (westbound); Car 186 (eastbound).

Kansas City and Los Angeles—10 Roomettes, 6 Double Bedrooms. Car 170 (westbound); Car 180 (eastbound).

Ready for occupancy (Westbound) 9:30 pm. May be occupied at Kansas City (Eastbound) until 8:00 am.

June 9 through September 12, 1960 reclining seat leg rest chair cars, also separate car and lounge car will be operated for chair car passengers. All chair car seats reserved. See page 45 for special service charge.

THE CHIEF

Trains 19 and 20

Chicago, Kansas City, Denver, Albuquerque, Los Angeles and San Diego

Pullman and Chair Car streamliner service.

All chair car seats reserved. $2.00 service charge between Chicago and Los Angeles, with similar charge between intermediate points

Reserved seat reservation required.

Dormitory Baggage Car.....Chicago and Los Angeles.

Sleeping Car.......Chicago and Los Angeles—10 Roomettes, 3 Double Bedrooms, 2 Compartments. Car 196 (westbound); Car 206 (eastbound).

Chicago and Los Angeles—10 Roomettes, 6 D. B. R. Car 198 (westbound). Car 208 (eastbound).

Phoenix to Ash Fork—6 Sec., D. R., 4 D. B. R. (On connecting train) Car 420 (eastbound only).

Tulsa to Chicago—10 Roomette, 3 D. B. R., 2 Comps. (On No. 48 to Kansas City). Car 481.

Topeka to Chicago—6 Sec,, 6 Roomette, 4 double bedroom. (On No. 6 to Kansas City).

Kansas City to Chicago—10 Roomettes, 6 D. B. R. Car 201.

Kansas City to Chicago—10 Roomettes, 5 D. B. R. Car 203.

Kansas City to Chicago—6 Section, 6 Roomette, 4 Double Bedroom. Car 66.

Big Dome Lounge Car......Chicago and Los Angeles.

Dining Car.......Chicago and Los Angeles. (Fred Harvey Service).

Snack Car.......Phoenix to Ash Fork. (On connecting train).

Sleeping Car.......Denver and Los Angeles—6 Section, 6 Roomettes, 4 D. B. R. (On No. 27 Denver to Pueblo: No. 200 Pueblo to La Junta; on No. 191 La Junta to Pueblo; on No. 28 Pueblo to Denver.) Car 190 (westbound); Car 204 (eastbound).

Reserved Seat Chair Cars ..Chicago and Los Angeles (reclining seats). Car 500-501 and 507 (westbound); Car 600-601 and 607 (eastbound). Denver and Los Angeles. Car 508 (westbound); Car 608 (eastbound).

EL CAPITAN

Trains 17 and 18

Hi-Level Streamlined El Capitan Equipment

Chicago, Kansas City, Albuquerque and Los Angeles

Chair-car streamliner service. Extra Fare.

Courier-Nurse Service. Radio and recorded musical programs.

(All seats Reserved. Reservation required.)

Baggage Dormitory Car....Chicago and Los Angeles.

Hi-Level Chair Car........Chicago and Los Angeles (68 seats) Car 900 and 906 (westbound); Car 800 and 807 (eastbound).

Chicago and Los Angeles (72 seats) Car 903 and 904 (westbound); Car 803 and 804 (eastbound).

Hi-Level Dining Car.......Chicago and Los Angeles. Serving all meals. Fred Harvey Service.

Hi-Level Lounge Car.......Chicago and Los Angeles.

SAN FRANCISCO CHIEF

Trains 1 and 2

Chicago, Kansas City, Topeka, Amarillo, Richmond and San Francisco

Pullman and Chair Car Streamliner Service.

Courier-Nurse Service.

All chair car seats reserved. $2.00 service charge between Chicago an Richmond-San Francisco with similar charge between intermediate points

Reserved seat reservation required.

Baggage Car..............Chicago and Richmond.

Sleeping Car..............Chicago and Richmond—10 Roomettes, 3 D. B. R., 2 Comp Car 18 (westbound); Car 28 (eastbound).

Chicago and Richmond—4 D. R., 1 Double Bedroom Pullma Lounge. Car 19 (westbound); Car 29 (eastbound).

Ash Fork to Phoenix—6 Sec., D. R., 4 D. B. R. (On connecti train) Car 419 (westbound only.) Ready to occupy 10.45 p. at Ash Fork.

Chicago to Tulsa-10 Roomette, 3 D. B. R., 2 Compartments (No. 47 from Kansas City) Car 471.

Chicago and Lubbock—6 Section, 6 Roomette, 4 D. B. R. (C No. 93 Amarillo to Lubbock; on No. 94 Lubbock to Amarillo Car 15 (westbound); Car 20 (eastbound).

Kansas City and Richmond—10 Roomettes, 6 D. B. R. (Ready f occupancy at Kansas City 9:30 pm. May be occupied eastbou until 7:30 am. at Kansas City.) Car 14 (westbound); Car (eastbound).

Houston and Richmond—8 Section, 2 Comps., 2 D. B. R. (On N 66-75 to Clovis: on No. 76-65 from Clovis.) Car 10 (westbound Car 22 (eastbound).

Big Dome Lounge Car......Chicago and Richmond

Dining Car..............Chicago and Richmond. Serving all meals. (Fred Harvey Service

Snack Car..............Ash Fork to Phoenix (On connecting train).

Reserved Seat Chair Cars Chicago and Richmond Car 300, 301 and 307 (westbound); Car 40 401 and 407 (eastbound). Houston and Richmond. Car 3 (westbound; Car 408 eastbound.) Chicago and Clovis. Car 3 (westbound; Car 409 (eastbound).

THE GRAND CANYON

Trains 123 and 124 Via La Junta and Albuquerque

Chicago, Kansas City, Topeka, and Los Angeles

Pullman and Chair Car Service.

Dormitory Lounge Car......Chicago and Los Angeles.

Sleeping Car..............Chicago and Los Angeles—8 Section, 2 Compartment, 2 Doub Bedroom Car 237 (westbound); Car 247 (eastbound).

Chicago and Los Angeles via Grand Canyon—2 D. R., 4 Com partment, 4 D. B. R. Car 236 (westbound). Car 246 (eastbound Daily until September 15, 1960.

Kansas City and Los Angeles—24 Duplex Roomette. Car 23 (westbound); Car 245 (eastbound).

Dallas to Los Angeles—6 Sec., 6 Roomette, 4 D. B. R. (On N 112-77-75-1 Dallas to Barstow) Car 231 (westbound).

Los Angeles to Dallas—6 Sec., 6 Roomette, 4 D. B. R. (On N 2-76-78-111 from Winslow.) Car 241 (eastbound).

Dining Car:..............Chicago and Los Angeles. (Fred Harvey Service).

Chair Cars..............Chicago and Los Angeles. Dallas and Los Angeles Car 770 (wes bound); Car 780 (eastbound).

Club Lounge-Car..........Los Angeles and San Diego. (On connecting train).

EXPLANATORY NOTES: Sec.—Section; D. R.—Drawing-room; Comp.—Compartment; Obs. | Observation; D. B. R.—Double Bedroom.

Source: Santa Fe Time Table Spring-Summer 1960

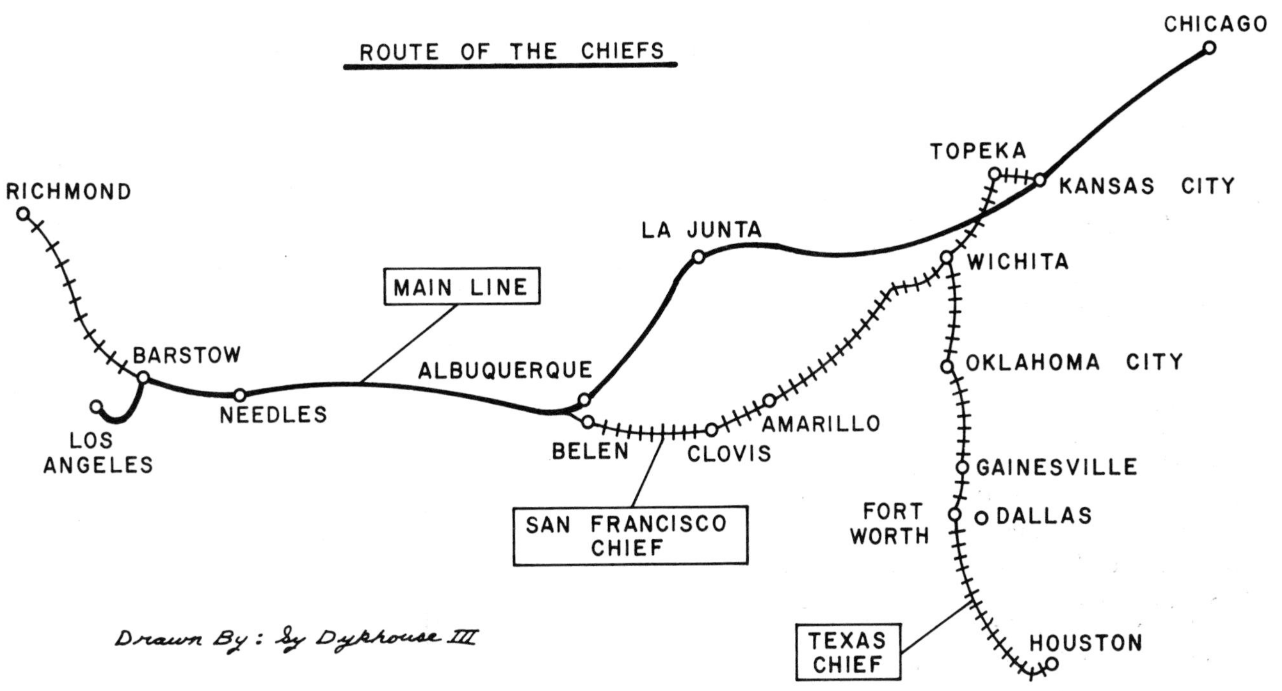
ROUTE OF THE CHIEFS
CHICAGO
TOPEKA
KANSAS CITY
RICHMOND
LA JUNTA
WICHITA
MAIN LINE
BARSTOW
ALBUQUERQUE
OKLAHOMA CITY
NEEDLES
AMARILLO
LOS ANGELES
BELEN
CLOVIS
GAINESVILLE
FORT WORTH
DALLAS
SAN FRANCISCO CHIEF
TEXAS CHIEF
HOUSTON
Drawn By: Sy Dykhouse III

CHAPTER 9

The Union Pacific "Cities" and the Challenger

The Union Pacific Railroad has operated Dome Cars on its Western "Cities" fleet since 1955. Initially, the Railroad equipped its Challenger and City of Portland with a Dome Coach and a Dome Observation Lounge Car. The City of Los Angeles received a Dome Observation Lounge the same year and was the only Dome Car on the train.

About the time the UP trains began operating over the Milwaukee Road instead of the Chicago and North Western between Chicago and Omaha, the Dome Dining Cars arrived. This equipment was assigned to the City of Los Angeles and the City of Portland. Shuffeling of this equipment and the addition of Milwaukee Road Super Domes began in 1957.

First of all in 1957, the spare Super Dome from the combined Olympian and Twin Cities Hiawatha (See Chapter 13, second paragraph) were assigned to trains 111 and 112, the City of Denver, replacing the Pub Cars on that run. (The Pub club lounge cars were then assigned to the Streamliner City of Las Vegas.) This arrangement continued until the City of Portland and the City of Denver were combined between Chicago and Denver. The Union Pacific then advertised the City of Denver as having three Dome Cars. The City of Portland and City of Denver operated in this manner until 1967. In that year, the UP began cutting the Denver Cars out of the Portland train at North Platte or vice versa. From then on, Number 105 and 111, and 106 and 112 operated separately west of North Platte. However, Dome Cars were discontinued on the Denver run.

The Challenger carried a single Dome Coach until it was combined with the City of Los Angeles on April 28, 1956. The Dome Lounge, which had operated for a short time on 107 and 108, was placed in operation on the City of St. Louis between Kansas City and Los Angeles. The Challenger, from 1956 through 1967, operated separately only during the Summer and Holiday Seasons of the year. When it did, it carried a single Dome Coach plus a Milwaukee Road Super Dome during the Summer Seasons of 1962 through 1964. The addition of Super Domes, however, was not always a regular operation between Chicago and Los Angeles.

With the consolidation of the City of Los Angeles and the Challenger between Chicago and the West Coast during the off seasons, Number 103 and 104 carried three Dome Cars. This method of operation continued until the Summer of 1970, when the City of Los Angeles lost its Dome Diner. The City of Portland had lost its Dome Diner in 1968. However both the Portland and Los Angeles trains continued to carry Dome Coaches and Dome Lounges prior to AMTRAK in 1971.

As stated previously, the City of St. Louis received a Dome Lounge in 1955 from the former Challenger. Later in 1958, the Union Pacific and Wabash Railroads ordered 6 Dome Coaches for operation between St. Louis and Los Angeles. This operation continued until 1968 when through operation between St. Louis and Los Angeles was terminated. In that year, the UP renamed Numbers 9 and 10, the City of Kansas City and the Norfolk and Western con-

UNION PACIFIC 2ND NO. 103, at Cheyenne, Wyoming with four "E" units and 18 cars. Although not visible in the photo, the All-Coach Challenger consist includes two dome cars, a dome coach and a full length Milwaukee Road Super Dome Lounge car. The photo was taken in July, 1963. (Louis A. Marre and Gordon B. Mott)

MILWAUKEE ROAD TRAIN NO. 104 at Savanna, Illinois in August, 1968. (William S. Kuba)

SOUTHERN PACIFIC TRAIN NO. 102, the City of San Francisco, sprints across the Nevada desert as it heads for the Utah border and the Great Salt Lake. The huge consist of the train has a rainbow of colors including grey SP diesels (Alco PA's), SP grey baggage cars, SP silver and red equipment and the ever popular Union Pacific yellow. The Southern Pacific dome lounge, auto-mat car and diner will be replaced at Ogden with Union Pacific food and beverage cars. (Dick Steinheimer)

THE FP-45 NO. 1 dwarfs the "F" unit as the pair lead Milwaukee Road domeliner No. 112 eastbound at Marion, Iowa in June, 1969. (William S. Kuba)

THE FINAL RUN of the Milwaukee Road–Union Pacific train No. 103, the combined "Cities" departs from Chicago behind an A–B–A set of Union Pacific E-9's. (John H. Kuehl)

Condensed Schedules between Chicago and Portland, Seattle

WESTBOUND—READ DOWN / EASTBOUND—READ UP

105● Domeliner City of Portland Daily one day for example		Elevation	Mls.	Table D THE MILWAUKEE ROAD UNION PACIFIC Central Time	106● Domeliner City of Portland Daily one day for example	
PM				Union Station	AM	
3.00	Sun.	595	0	Lv CHICAGO (CMStP&PRR) Ar	10.15	Tue.
① 3.45	"	560	37	Lv Elgin Ar	③ 9.21	"
4.25	"	570	80	Lv Davis Jct Ar	8.43	"
5.28	"	599	138	Lv Savanna Ar	7.41	"
6.59	"	848	227	Lv Marion (Cedar Rapids) Ar	6.04	"
8.58	"	967	362	Lv Perry Ar	3.58	"
11.25	"	1033	488	Ar OMAHA (CMStP&PRR) Lv	1.50	"
11.50	"	1033	488	Lv OMAHA (U.P.R.R.) Ar	1.30	"
1.24	Mon.	1447	570	Ar Columbus Lv	12.01	"
2.35	"	1864	632	Ar Grand Island Lv	11.05	Mon.
3.32	"	2149	674	Ar Kearney Lv	10.19	"
5.35	"	2802	769	Ar North Platte (C.T.) Lv	8.55	"
				Mountain Time		
4.55	"	2802	769	Lv North Platte Ar	7.30	"
6.20	"	3467	851	Ar Julesburg Lv	6.02	"
9.15	"	6060	995	Ar Cheyenne Lv	3.30	"
10.30	"			Lv Cheyenne Ar	3.00	"
11.52	"	7151	1051	Ar Laramie Lv	1.30	"
1.39	"	6747	1168	Ar Rawlins Lv	11.40	"
3.27	"	6263	1287	Ar Rock Springs Lv	f 9.45	"
4.00	"	6083	1302	Ar Green River Lv	9.25	"
4.10	"	6083	1302	Lv Green River Ar	9.15	"
5.18	"	6913	1372	Lv Kemmerer Lv	f 7.55	"
8.05	"	4463	1546	Ar Pocatello Lv	4.45	"
12.25	Tue.	4463	0	Lv Pocatello Ar	C 2.05	Mon.
1.30	"	4708	51	Ar Idaho Falls Lv	C 12.55	"
8.15	Mon.	4463	1546	Lv Pocatello Ar	4.30	Mon.
......	......	4337	1571	Ar American Falls Lv	......	......
..B...	"	4282	1605	Ar Minidoka Lv	..B..	"
9.46	"	3970	1654	Ar Shoshone Lv	2.40	"
9.55	Mon.	3970	1654	Lv Shoshone Ar	K 2.30	Mon.
11.25	"	5816	1723	Ar Sun Valley Lv	K 12.35	Mon.
6.15	Mon.	5816		Lv Sun Valley Ar	K 4.40	Mon.
7.30	"	3970		Ar Shoshone Lv	K 2.50	"
9.46	Mon.	3970	1654	Lv Shoshone Ar	2.40	Mon.
10.40	"	2562	1706	Ar Glenns Ferry Lv	1.45	"
11.55	"	2692	1781	Ar Boise Lv	12.20	Mon.
12.18	Tue.	2489	1800	Ar Nampa Lv	11.55	Sun.
1.50	"	2116	1882	Ar Huntington (M.T.) Lv	10.36	"
				Pacific Time		
12.51	"	2116	1882	Lv Huntington Ar	9.35	"
2.05	"	3438	1930	Ar Baker Lv	8.15	"
5.20	"	1069	2056	Ar Pendleton Lv	5.01	"
7.40	"	98	2188	Ar The Dalles Lv	2.45	"
9.30	"	29	2272	Ar Portland (U.P.R.R.) Lv	1.00	"
9.45	Tue.	29	2272	Lv Portland Ar	No. 460 12.05	Sun.
12.34	"	13	2417	Ar Tacoma Lv	9.01	"
1.30	"	15	2455	Ar SEATTLE (P.T.) Lv	8.05	"
PM					AM	

Reference Notes

① Stops to take revenue passengers for Marion or beyond. Does not carry passengers locally from Chicago to Elgin. Consult suburban timetable for service between these stations.

③ Stops to leave revenue passengers from Marion or beyond. Does not carry passengers locally from Elgin to Chicago. Consult suburban timetable for service between these stations.

B Stops to leave revenue passengers from Omaha, Denver and East and take revenue passengers for Portland, Spokane or beyond.

C Idaho Falls, Idaho is rail gateway to Yellowstone and Grand Teton National Parks. During summer season (June 10 thru August 26) coaches (from Salt Lake City and through Pocatello) set out for occupancy at Idaho Falls (6:30 A.M. inbound; 9:30 P.M. outbound). Motor buses then transport passengers to and from Yellowstone and Grand Teton National Parks.

f Stops to take or leave revenue passengers.

K Motor Bus. This service is provided passengers arriving or departing Shoshone and holding proper tickets to and from Sun Valley, Idaho. No bus service during period Sun Valley is closed Oct. 20 to Dec. 16 and Apr. 1 to May 1.

● Limited handling of baggage on these trains; consult Agent.

C.T. Central Time.

M.T. Mountain Time.

P.T. Pacific Time.

Condensed Schedules between Chicago and Denver

WESTBOUND—READ DOWN / EASTBOUND—READ UP

111● City of Denver Daily one day for example		Mls.	Table E THE MILWAUKEE ROAD UNION PACIFIC Central Time	112● City of Denver Daily one day for example	
PM			Union Station	AM	
3.00	Sun.	0	Lv CHICAGO (CMStP&PRR) Ar	10.15	Mon.
① 3.45	"	37	Lv Elgin Ar	③ 9.21	"
4.25	"	80	Lv Davis Jct Ar	8.43	"
5.28	"	138	Lv Savanna Ar	7.41	"
6.59	"	227	Lv Marion (Cedar Rapids) Ar	6.04	"
8.58	"	362	Lv Perry Ar	3.58	"
11.25	"	488	Ar OMAHA (CMStP&PRR) Lv	1.50	"
11.50	"	488	Lv OMAHA (U.P.R.R.) Ar	1.30	"
1.24	Mon.	570	Ar Columbus Lv	12.01	"
2.35	"	632	Ar Grand Island Lv	11.05	Sun.
3.32	"	674	Ar Kearney Lv	10.19	"
5.35	"	769	Ar North Platte (C.T.) Lv	8.55	"
			Mountain Time		
4.50	"	769	Lv North Platte Ar	7.15	"
6.00	"	851	Ar Julesburg Lv	5.55	"
6.49	"	908	Ar Sterling Lv	4.58	"
8.15	"	1001	Ar La Salle Lv	3.33	"
9.15	"	1048	Ar DENVER (U.P.R.R.) Lv	2.45	"
AM			*Mountain Time*	PM	

EQUIPMENT

DOMELINER "CITY OF PORTLAND"

Nos. 105 and 106—Daily.

Between Chicago and Portland

Pullman Sleeping Cars
  Roomettes and Double Bedrooms
Dome Lounge Car for Sleeping Car passengers
Dining Car (Club and a la carte service)
Dome Coach (Seats reserved; dome seats not reserved)
Reclining Seat-Leg Rest Coaches—all seats reserved

Between Portland and Seattle

Reclining Seat Coaches—(Not Reserved)

All tickets honored except: Banana Messengers, Caretakers, Commutation, Drover, Circus or Show Scrip.

"CITY OF DENVER"

No. 111 and 112—Daily.

Between Chicago and Denver

Pullman Sleeping Cars
  Roomettes and Double Bedrooms
  Reclining Seat-Leg Rest Coaches—all seats reserved.
Dome Lounge Car for Sleeping Car Passengers. Chicago-North Platte
Dining Car (Club and a la carte service). Chicago-North Platte
Cafe Lounge Car—North Platte-Denver, Meal Service and Beverages

Source: Milwaukee Road Time Table
April 28, 1968

Table C Condensed Schedules between CHICAGO and LOS ANGELES

WESTBOUND—READ DOWN | EASTBOUND—READ UP

27-9 National Parks Special Saturdays only. See Note ▣		13-27-9 Daily Example		103 Domeliner City of Los Angeles Daily Example		107 Challenger Domeliner Daily Example		Elevation	Mls.	CHICAGO AND NORTH WESTERN UNION PACIFIC	108 Challenger Domeliner Daily Example		104 Domeliner City of Los Angeles Daily Example		10-28-14 Daily Example	
PM		AM		PM		AM				*Central Standard Time*	AM		AM		PM	
1.30	Sat.	10.45	Sun	7.15	Sun	9.00	Sun	614	0	Lv..CHICAGO (C. & N.W. Ry.)..Ar	7.45	Tue	10.30	Tue	6.15	Tue
......	"	11.01	"	......	"	......	"	630	9	" ....Oak Park.......... "	......	"	......	"	K6.01	"
..O...	"	11.33	"	......	"	......	"	720	36	" ....Geneva.......... "	..C..	"	......	"	5.28	"
......	"	12.05	"	......	"	..O..	"	884	58	" ....De Kalb.......... "	6.32	"	......	"	5.04	"
......	"	12.25	"	......	"	......	"	795	75	" ....Rochelle.......... "		"	......	"	4.45	"
3.11	"	12.55	"		"	......	"	772	98	" ....Dixon.......... "	......	"	......	"	4.20	"
3.29	"	1.17	"	...B...	"	10.45	"	649	110	" ....Sterling.......... "	5.45	"	8.33	"	4.07	"
4.10	"	2.15	"	9.36	"	11.20	"	598	138	" ....Clinton.......... "	5.12	"	8.00	"	3.33	"
5.32	"	3.54	"	10.53	"	12.36	"	731	219	" ....Cedar Rapids........ "	3.53	"	6.41	"	2.10	"
6.48	"	5.30	"	......	"	1.44	"	884	289	" ....Marshalltown........ "	..E..	"	......	"	12.45	"
7.28	"	6.30	"	12.28	Mon	2.17	"	917	327	" ....Ames.......... "	2.19	"	..E..	"	12.03	"
7.58	"	7.02	"	12.53	"	2.41	"	1138	340	" ....Boone.......... "	1.57	"	4.45	"	11.34	"
10.35	"	10.30	"	3.10	"	5.00	"	1033	488	Ar...OMAHA (C. & N.W. Ry.)...Lv	11.45	Mon	2.35	"	8.00	"
AM		AM		AM		PM					PM		PM		PM	
11.40	Sat.	11.40	Sun	11.40	Sun	9.00	Sat	918	0	Lv MINNEAPOLIS (C. & N.W. Ry.) Ar	6.50	Tue	6.50	Tue	6.50	Tue
12.10	"	12.10	"	12.10	"	9.45	"	703	11	" ....ST. PAUL.......... "	6.15	"	6.15	"	6.15	"
8.00	"	8.00	"	8.00	"	5.30	"	991	......	" ....ROCHESTER.......... "	7.57	"	7.57	"	7.57	"
6.25	"	6.25	"	6.25	"	6.45	Sun	1100	277	" ....SIOUX CITY.......... "	11.50	"	11.50	"	11.50	"
8.40	"	8.40	"	8.40	"	9.05	"	1033	377	Ar...OMAHA (C. & N.W. Ry.)...Lv	9.25	"	9.25	"	9.25	"
11.00	Sat.	11.00	Sun	3.25	Mon	5.10	Sun	1033	488	Lv....OMAHA (U. P. R. R.)....Ar	11.35	Mon	2.20	Tue	7.00	Tue
2.00	Sun.	2.00	Mon	5.24	"	7.07	"	1864	632	Ar..........Grand Island..........Lv	9.26	"	12.11	"	3.50	"
5.20	"	5.20	"	7.10	"	8.51	"	2802	769	Ar..........North Platte..........Lv	7.33	"	10.18	Mon	12.45	"
	"									*Mountain Standard Time*						
4.55	"	4.55	"	6.15	"	7.56	"	2802	769	Lv..........North Platte..........Ar	6.28	"	9.13	"	11.00	Mon
10.00	"	10.00	"	9.35	"	11.17	"	6060	995	Ar..........CHEYENNE..........Lv	3.25	"	6.15	"	7.00	"
11.35	"	11.35	"	11.04	"	12.44	Mon	7151	1051	" ....Laramie.......... "	2.05	"	4.50	"	4.20	"
1.50	"	1.50	"	12.59	"	2.30	"	6747	1168	" ....Rawlins.......... "	12.15	"	3.00	"	2.00	"
4.25	"	4.25	"	3.15	"	4.36	"	6083	1302	" ....Green River.......... "	10.00	"	12.40	"	11.10	"
6.50	"	6.50	"	5.05	"	6.25	"	6745	1402	" ....Evanston.......... "	8.09	"	10.49	"	8.50	"
8.45	"	8.45	"	6.45	"	8.00	"	4298	1478	Ar..........Ogden..........Lv	6.40	"	9.15	"	7.00	"
9.05	"	9.05	"	6.55	"	8.10	"	4298	1478	Lv..........Ogden..........Ar	6.30	"	9.05	"	6.05	"
10.00	"	10.00	"	7.40	"	8.55	"	4251	1515	Ar......SALT LAKE CITY......Lv	5.45	"	8.20	"	5.05	"
10.30	"	10.30	"	7.50	"	9.05	"	4251	1515	Lv......SALT LAKE CITY......Ar	5.35	"	8.10	"	4.45	"
3.00	Mon	3.00	Tue	......	"	......	"	5091	1757	Ar..........Lund..........Lv	......		......	"	12.05	Mon
A 4.15	Mon	A 4.15	Tue	......	......	......	......	5805	1790	Ar.....CEDAR CITY (Bus).....Lv	......	......	......	......	A10.45	Sun
										Zion-Bryce-Grand Canyon Nat'l Parks						
A 1045	Sun.	A 1045	Mon	......	......	......	......	5805	......	Lv.....CEDAR CITY (Bus).....Ar	......	......	......	......	A 4.15	Mon
3.00	Mon	3.00	Tue	......	"	......	Mon	5091	1757	Lv..........Lund..........Ar	......	Sun	......	"	12.05	Mon
4.08	"	5.08	"	......	Tue	......	"	4396	1839	Ar..........Caliente..........Lv	......	"	......	"	10.15	Sun
	"									*Pacific Standard Time*						
7.05	"	7.05	"	2.45	"	3.50	"	2034	1965	" ....Las Vegas.......... "	8.50	"	11.25	Sun	6.30	"
1.00	"	1.00	"	7.50	"	8.50	"	1076	2231	" ....San Bernardino........ "	3.30	"	6.08	"	12.20	"
1.30	"	1.30	"	f 8.15	"	f 9.15	"	866	2261	" ....Riverside.......... "	f 3.07	"	f 5.43	"	11.55	"
2.50	"	2.50	"	9.10	"	10.10	"	205	2293	" ....East Los Angeles........ "	2.20	"	4.50	"	10.50	"
3.15	"	3.15	"	9.30	"	10.30	"	270	2299	Ar..LOS ANGELES (U. P. R. R.)..Lv	2.00	"	4.30	"	10.30	"
PM		PM		AM		PM					PM		PM		AM	

EQUIPMENT—Regularly assigned through cars are air-conditioned

DOMELINER "CITY OF LOS ANGELES"—Nos. 103 and 104 Daily. Some of these cars do not operate every trip. Consult ticket agent for particulars.

Between Chicago and Los Angeles.
- 10 Roomette, 6 Double Bedroom Sleeping Car.
- 4 Double Bedroom-4 Compt.-2 D.R. Sleeping Cars.
- 5 Double Bedroom-2 Compt.-2 D. R. Sleeping Cars.
- Cafe-Lounge Car. (for Coach passengers.)
- Dining Car. Astra Dome Observation Lounge Car.
- Leg Rest Coaches. (seats reserved.)

Between Minneapolis-St. Paul and Los Angeles.
- 6 Section-6 Roomette-4 Double Bedroom Sleeping Car (In C. & N. W. Nos. 203 and 204 between Minneapolis and Omaha.)

Between New York and Los Angeles.
- 10 Roomette, 6 Double Bedroom Sleeping Car (In N. Y. C. System No. 59 westbound and No. 68 eastbound between New York and Chicago).
- 10 Roomette, 6 Double Bedroom Sleeping Car. (In Penn. R. R. No. 1 westbound and No. 48 eastbound between New York and Chicago.)

"CHALLENGER" DOMELINER—Nos 107 and 108.

Between Chicago and Los Angeles. **Daily.**
- Leg Rest Coaches (Seats reserved). Dining Car.
- Astra-Dome Coach (Seats reserved.)
- 14 Section Sleeping Car.
- 10 Roomette, 6 Double Bedroom Sleeping Car.
- Astra Dome Observation Lounge Car.

Between Omaha and Los Angeles.
- Leg Rest Coach .(Seats reserved.)

No. 10-28-14 Daily.

Los Angeles to Chicago:
- Sleeping Car Service. **Sections, Roomettes and** Bedrooms. (Change at Ogden)
- Dining Car Service.
- Lounge Car Service.
- Coaches. (Seats reserved. Change at Ogden.)

NATIONAL PARK SPECIAL—No. 27-9. Saturdays only.

Chicago to Los Angeles.
- Bedrooms, Roomettes and Sections (Change at Ogden).
- Reclining Seat Coach Service. (Seats reserved. Change at Ogden.)
- Cafe Lounge Car and Dining Car Service

No. 13-27-9. Daily.

Between Chicago and Los Angeles:
- Sleeping Car Service. Sections, Roomettes and Bedrooms. (Change at Ogden.)
- Lounge Car Service.
- Dining Car Service.
- Coaches (Seats reserved Ogden to Los Angeles (Change at Ogden.)

No Extra Fares On Any Trains

Reference Notes for pages 10 and 11.

▣ The National Park Special, Train No. 2 will be operated fro Chicago Saturday only June 18 throu August 27, connectin with Union Pacif Train No. 27 a Omaha.

A Bus connection.

B Stops to receive reve nue passengers for Og den, Utah and beyon

C Stops to dischar revenue passenge from Council Bluf and beyond.

E Stops to dischar revenue passenge from Ogden, Uta and beyond.

f Stops to receive discharge revenue pas sengers.

H Operates from Ne York EVEN date during Apr., May Aug. ODD dates dur ing June, July, Sep Operates from Sa Francisco ODD date during Apr., May Aug. EVEN dates dur ing June, July, Sept

J Note—Operates fro New York ODD date during Apr., May Aug. EVEN dates dur ing June, July, Sep Operates from Sa Francisco EVEN date during Apr., May Aug. ODD dates dur ing June, July, Sept

K Stops only to dis charge revenue pas sengers.

L On Saturdays Sleep ing Car leaves New York 10.10 p.m. o No. 29, arrives Chica go on Sundays 2.35 pm

O Stops to receive reve nue passengers fo Council Bluffs an beyond.

P Stops to discharge revenue passengers from east of Cheyenne

Source: C&NW Time Table April 24, 1955

ST. LOUIS, KANSAS CITY, DENVER AND PACIFIC COAST POINTS

Read Down | **Read Up**

209-9-103 Daily (Domeliner "City of St. Louis")	203 Daily ("City of Kansas City")	Mls.	TABLE 6		104-10-210 Daily (Domeliner "City of St. Louis")	212 Daily ("City of Kansas City")
PM	AM		CENTRAL STD. TIME		PM	PM
3 40	9 15	.0	Lv St. Louis, Mo. (Union Station)	Ar	**2 55**	**9 40**
4 00	9 30	5.6	Lv Delmar Blvd.	Ar	**2 20**	**9 15**
....	9 50	22.8	Lv St. Charles	Lv	**g 1 49**	**b 8 44**
....	....	59.0	Lv Truesdale—Warrenton	Lv	......	**8 07**
....	c10 42	83.3	Lv Montgomery	Lv	......	**7 41**
....	....	90.9	Lv Wellsville▲	Lv	......	**7 31**
5 39	11 06	109.1	Lv Mexico	Lv	**12 32**	**7 07**
5 56	11 26	123.2	Ar Centralia	Lv	**12 19**	**6 49**
6 55	**12 25**	123.2	Lv Centralia	Ar	11 20	**5 50**
7 40	**1 10**	144.9	Ar Columbia	Lv	10 35	**4 45**
4 45	10 35	144.9	Lv Columbia	Ar	**1 10**	**7 40**
5 50	11 20	123.2	Ar Centralia	Lv	**12 25**	**6 55**
5 56	11 26	123.2	Lv Centralia	Ar	**12 19**	**6 49**
6 20	11 52	147.1	Ar Moberly	Lv	11 52	**6 20**
6 23	11 59	147.1	Lv Moberly	Ar	11 47	**6 15**
....	**12 20**	168.1	Lv Salisbury	Lv	......	**5 53**
....	**12 38**	186.1	Lv Brunswick	Lv	......	**5 33**
....	**1 05**	209.8	Lv Carrollton	Lv	......	**5 07**
....	**1 40**	234.5	Lv Henrietta●	Lv	......	**4 43**
8 45	**2 55**	278.1	Ar Kansas City (C. S. T.)	Lv	9 40	**3 55**
9 20	PM	278.	Lv Kansas City, Mo. (C. S. T.) (Un. Pac.)	Ar	9 05	PM
7 50	....	918.	Ar Denver, Colo. (M. S. T.) (Un. Pac.)	Lv	**8 20**	....
7 00	....	1496.	Ar Ogden, Utah (M. S. T.)	Lv	9 10	....
8 20	....	1532.	Ar Salt Lake City, Utah (M. S. T.)	Lv	7 35	....
12 30	....	2316.	Ar Los Angeles, Calif. (P. S. T.)	Lv	**1 30**	....
7 50	....	1496.	Lv Ogden (M. S. T.) (S. P.)	Ar	8 40	....
12 50	....	2281.	Ar San Francisco (P. S. T.)	Lv	**2 15**	....
8 55	....	1496.	Lv Ogden (M. S. T.) (Un. Pac.)	Ar	5 35	....
11 55	....	1564.	Ar Pocatello, Idaho (M. S. T.)	Lv	2 45	....
12 25	....	1564.	Lv Pocatello (M. S. T.)	Ar	2 05	....
1 30	....	1615.	Ar Idaho Falls, Idaho (M. S. T.) ⊙	Lv	12 55	....
8 05	....	918.	Lv Denver (M. S. T.) (Un. Pac.)	Ar	**3 30**	....
9 00	....	2278.	Ar Portland, Ore. (P. S. T.) (U. P.)	Lv	**12 30**	....
12 27	....	2423.	Ar Tacoma, Wash. (P. S. T.) (Un. Pac.)	Lv	9 01	....
1 30	....	2461.	Ar Seattle (P. S. T.) (Un. Pac.)	Lv	8 05	....
PM					AM	

Coach Seat Reservations are Required for Domeliner **"City of St. Louis",** between St. Louis, Kansas City and Western Points.

RESERVED COACH SEAT CHARGES DOMELINER "CITY OF ST. LOUIS"

BETWEEN ST. LOUIS, MO.

AND		AND	
Kansas City, Mo.	None	Milford, Utah	$2.50
Manhattan, Kans.	$1.50	Caliente, Nev.	2.75
Oakley, Kans.	1.75	Las Vegas, Nev.	3.00
Denver, Colo.	2.00	Los Angeles, Calif.	3.00
Cheyenne, Wyo.	2.00	Elko, Nev.	3.50
Ogden, Utah	2.00	Reno, Nev.	4.00
Salt Lake City, Utah	2.00	San Francisco, Calif.	4.00

To intermediate points not shown, charges will be the same as shown to the next points beyond.

CITY OF SAN FRANCISCO

DAILY SERVICE BETWEEN

CHICAGO, OMAHA and SAN FRANCISCO

ST. LOUIS—KANSAS CITY—DENVER AND PACIFIC COAST

TRAINS 203 AND 212 "CITY OF KANSAS CITY"

Chair Car (Buffet Service)
St. Louis—Kansas City

TRAINS 209-9-103 AND 104-10-210 Domeliner "CITY OF ST. LOUIS"

Dome Coach, St. Louis-Los Angeles

Dome Lounge Car, Ogden-Los Angeles

Club-Lounge Car, St. Louis—Los Angeles

Dining Car Service, St. Louis—Los Angeles—San Francisco

Reserved Seat Coaches (Reclining Seats—Leg Rests)
St. Louis—Los Angeles (No. 95 WB, No. 105 EB)
St. Louis—Los Angeles (No. 96 WB, No. 106 EB)
St. Louis—San Francisco (No. 98 WB, No. 1035 EB)

Standard Sleeping Cars
St. Louis—Los Angeles (No. 94 WB, No. 104 EB)
6-Rmtte, 4-DBR, 6 Sec.

ST. LOUIS—COUNCIL BLUFFS, IA.

TRAINS 211 AND 214

Reclining Chair Cars
St. Louis—Council Bluffs

Source: N&W Time Table
Oct. 30, 1966

OVERLAND ROUTE

CHICAGO - OGDEN - RENO - SACRAMENTO - OAKLAND - SAN FRANCISCO
ST. LOUIS - KANSAS CITY - DENVER - SALT LAKE CITY - SAN FRANCISCO

WESTBOUND—Read Down				EAST-BOUND Read Up
Elev.	City of San Francisco No. 101 Daily	Mls.		City of San Francisco No. 102 Daily
595	6 00	0	Lv CHICAGO (C.T.) CMStP&P..Ar	11 59
1033	2 55	488	Lv Omaha (C.T.) U.P...........Lv	3 30
6060	10 45	995	Lv Cheyenne (M.T.)............Lv	5 40
6083	4 25	1302	Lv Green River................Lv	11 50
4298	8 00	1478	Ar Ogden (M.T.) U.P...........Lv	8 35
480	9 30	0	Lv St. Louis (C.T.) (M.P.).....Ar	5 10
748	3 00	279	Ar Kansas City (C.T.) (M.P.)..Lv	11 30
748	8 00	279	Lv Kansas City (C.T.) (U.P.)..Ar	9 15
5188	7 15	919	Lv Denver (M.T.) (U.P.)......Lv	8 45
6060	9 30	1025	Ar Cheyenne (M.T.) (U.P.)....Lv	6 00
6060	10 45	1025	Lv Cheyenne (M.T.) (U.P.)....Ar	5 10
4298	7 00	1508	Ar Ogden (M.T.) (U.P.)......Lv.	8 35
5490	#7 30	0	Lv Butte (M.T.) U.P ....Ar	7 30
4708	12 55	212	Lv Idaho Falls..............Lv	1 40
4463	2 45	263	Lv Pocatello................Lv	12 25
4298	5 35	397	Ar Ogden (M.T.) U.P........Lv	†8 55
4251	6 30	0	Lv Salt Lake City...........Ar	●10 50
4298	7 20	36	Ar Ogden...................Lv	●10 05
			Westbound—set watch back one hour. Eastbound—set watch ahead one hour.	
4298	8 30	0	Lv OGDEN, UTAH (M.T.) ......Ar	8 05
5629	10 40	176	Lv Wells (P.T.)................Lv	3 50
5062	11 30	227	Lv Elko........................Lv	w2 55
4896	12 11	249	Lv Carlin......................Lv	w2 25
4495	f1 06	307	Lv Battle Mountain (a)..........Lv	fw1 17
4332	2 01	366	Lv Winnemucca...............Lv	12 23
4195	f2 31	399	Lv Imlay.......................Lv	f11 51
3978	3 11	439	Lv Lovelock...................Lv	11 09
4010	f4 01	495	Lv Hazen......................Lv	f10 20
4423	5 15	537	Lv Sparks.....................Lv	9 35
4496	5 30	540	Lv RENO.......................Lv	9 07
5825	6 25	575	Lv Truckee (To Lake Tahoe).....Lv	8 05
2424	8 38	640	Lv Colfax.....................Lv	5 45
1273	f9 17	658	Lv Auburn (R.R. St.)............Lv	f5 22
168	9 50	676	Lv Roseville..................Lv	4 58
42	10 30	693	Ar SACRAMENTO.............Lv	4 25
42	10 45	693	Lv SACRAMENTO.............Ar	4 15
51	....	707	Lv Davis......................Lv	f3 50
7	11 39	733	Lv Suisun-Fairfield............Lv	3 23
7	12 05	751	Lv Martinez...................Lv	3 02
10	12 15	756	Lv Crockett (To Vallejo).........Lv	2 48
38	12 40	770	Ar Richmond..................Lv	2 27
16	12 57	776	Ar Berkeley...................Lv	2 15
9	1 15	780	Ar OAKLAND (16th St.) ⊕.....Lv	2 05
13	1 45	786	Ar SAN FRANCISCO (3rd St.) ⊕Lv	1 30

BOISE, WINNEMUCCA STAGES (Daily)

10 40	1 30	Lv Winnemucca(P.T.).............Ar	6 10	12 50
4 15	6 45	Lv Caldwell (M.T.)................Lv	2 25	9 15
4 30	7 00	Lv Nampa.........................Lv	2 00	8 45
5 00	7 30	Ar Boise (M.T.)...................Lv	1 30	8 15

KLAMATH FALLS VIA ALTURAS
WESTERN GREYHOUND LINES (Daily)

7 00	7 30	Lv Reno..........................Ar	9 20	6 35
8 50	9 21	Lv Susanville.....................Ar	7 01	4 50
11 05	12 01	Lv Alturas........................Ar	4 45	2 35
1 15	2 08	Ar Klamath Falls.................Lv	2 45	12 35

RENO-FALLON
NEVADA CENTRAL MOTOR LINES INC.

d9 00	c4 30	*8 00	Lv Reno...........Ar	c9 20	* 4 00	d8 20
d10 20	c5 50	*9 20	Ar Fallon..........Lv	c8 00	* 2 40	d7 00

TRAINS 101-102
STREAMLINER CITY OF SAN FRANCISCO

(SUBJECT TO SPECIAL CITY OF SAN FRANCISCO CHARGE ALSO RESERVED SEAT CHARGE)

Meal and Lounge Service: Chicago–San Francisco.

Sleeping Car: Chicago–San Francisco. (Roomettes, Bedrooms.)

Chair Cars: Chicago–San Francisco. Reclining leg rest seats.

Kansas City-San Francisco. Westbound on U.P. No. 9-103 to Ogden. Eastbound on U.P. No. 104-10 to Kansas City. Reclining leg rest seats.

Reserve seats in advance.

Pillow service available at nominal charge.

Porter Service.

Checked Baggage Handled: San Francisco–Reno, Nev. and intermediate (except Roseville, Auburn, Colfax, Truckee via PMT truck and subject to delay—no pets).

Reno–Ogden (all intermediate service via PMT truck and subject to delay—no pets or remains).

Service to and from scheduled stops Ogden–Chicago, except no service at intermediate points between Omaha–Chicago.

No checked baggage between Kansas City–St. Louis.

FOR FOOTNOTES COMMON TO ALL SCHEDULES SEE SUNSET ROUTE PAGE.

●—Bus operates from Greyhound Station. Union Pacific Interstate tickets honored.

#—Tuesday, Friday and Sunday only.

†—Monday, Thursday and Saturday only.

a—North Battle Mountain station on the Western Pacific.

c—Daily except Sunday.

d—Sunday only

w—W.P. Station.

Source: Southern Pacific Time Table
June 22, 1969

CHAPTER 10

The Missouri Pacific Eagles

The first diesel powered streamlined passenger train on the Missouri Pacific was the Missouri River Eagle placed in service between St. Louis and Omaha on March 10, 1940. This train started a chain of events that led to the inauguration of the Colorado Eagle on June 21, 1942. This new train replaced the Scenic Limited operating between St. Louis and Denver. On August 15, 1948, the famed Sunshine Special was replaced by the Texas Eagle streamliners operating between St. Louis and Fort Worth, El Paso, Galveston, Houston and San Antonio. During the life span of the Eagles from 1940 to 1971, Dome cars were to operate on three of the trains during most or part of their careers.

The first three Dome Coaches (called Planetarium Coaches by the MoPac) arrived on the property in June, 1948. These were initially assigned to the Colorado Eagle. The Dome Cars (one for each set of equipment for the overnight St. Louis – Denver train) shared the train consist with three sleepers (one a Denver - Wichita Car), a flat top coach, a Grill-coach and Diner Lounge Car. This equipment remained much the same until Feb. 1, 1964 when the name Colorado Eagle was dropped along with the sleepers and dining and lounge facilities between St. Louis and Denver. For a short while, a Diner-Parlor Car was placed in operation between St. Louis and Kansas City. The entire train was discontinued on April 2, 1966.

1952 brought more Dome Coaches to the MoPac. Four of the cars went into operation on the Texas Eagles. Trains No. 1 and 2 carried a Dome between St. Louis and Fort Worth. Trains 21 and 22 handled their Dome Coach between St. Louis and San Antonio. On September 18, 1961, the two sections of the Texas Eagles were combined into one train out of St. Louis. The Dome cars continued to operate between the same cities as they had since their purchase.

By 1964 however, business was declining, and changes were made in the operation of the Dome Cars. First of all, the pair of Domes off the Colorado Eagle were shifted to the Missouri River Eagle where they remained in operation until 1967. On the Texas service, only one Dome Coach operated in each set of equipment out of St. Louis instead of the previous two. In this case, the St. Louis – San Antonio car remained. However, the Road then placed the surplus Domes on trains 21 and 22 between New Orleans and Fort Worth. This operation also continued until 1967. At that time, all Domes were withdrawn from service and six were subsequently sold to the Illinois Central Railroad.

All told, the MoPac owned a total of eight Dome Coaches. Seven were normally assigned to the Eagles at all times, with the eighth providing extra service or use as a spare when the regular equipment was in the shops. The Domes operated for 20 of the 31 years of the Missouri Pacific Eagle Passenger Service.

THE FIRST EAGLE was placed in service in 1940, and it started a chain reaction that led to a whole fleet of Eagle Streamliners on the Missouri Pacific. Domes from the Budd Company were added to the Colorado Eagle in 1948. This photo shows Missouri Pacific No. 12, the Colorado Eagle, en route to St. Louis from Denver with a 10 car consist including two Budd built dome coaches. (Missouri Pacific)

THE BUDD COMPANY built three dome coaches for the MoPac in 1948. The original series of this equipment was 890, 891 and 892. The three cars, all owned by the Missouri Pacific, were later numbered 590 thru 592 and were eventually sold to the Illinois Central Railroad after many years of service on the Colorado Eagle. (Missouri Pacific)

ROUTE OF THE EAGLES

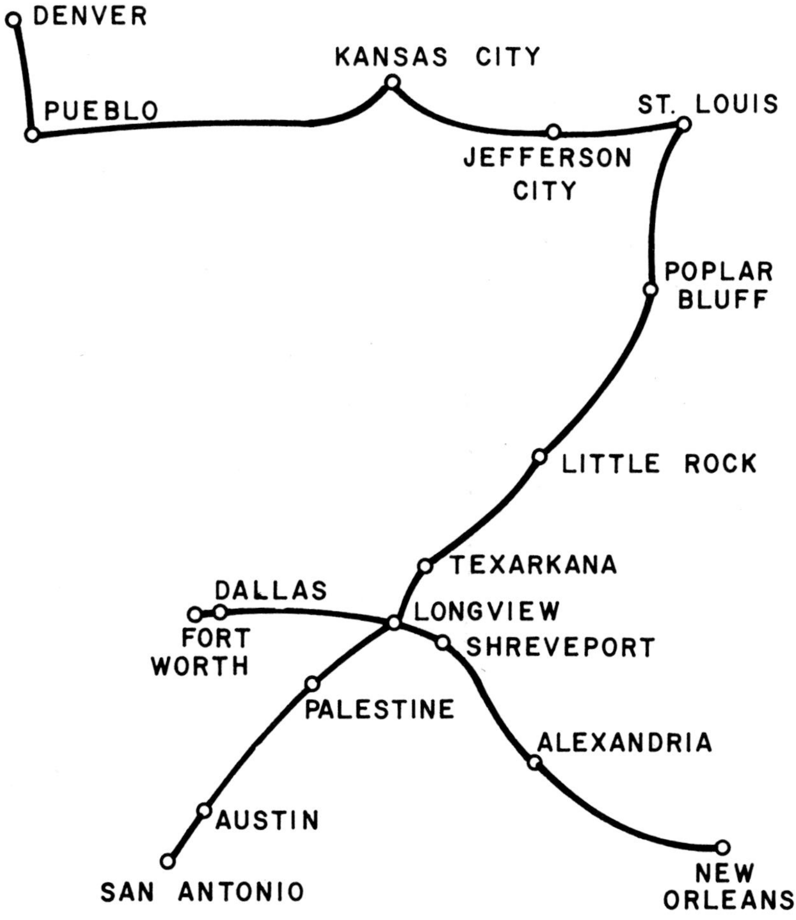

MISSOURI PACIFIC LINES

Drawn By: Sy Dykhouse III

THE NEXT TRAINS TO RECEIVE domes were the Texas Eagles. This photo shows the domeliner Texas Eagle at San Antonio, Texas with Electro–Motive Division passenger diesel No. 7003. The unusual thing about this unit is that it was originally assigned to the Colorado Eagle. Note the two road names – Missouri Pacific and Rio Grande – and the train name Colorado Eagle on the nose. (Harold K. Vollrath)

PULLMAN STANDARD BUILT FOUR DOME COACHES for the Missouri Pacific and one for the Texas & Pacific in 1952. The equipment was originally numbered 893 to 896 and T&P 200, but later renumbered 593 to 597. These five dome cars were purchased for service on the Texas Eagles and remained in that service until 1967. All carried 42 revenue seats, except No. 593 which carried 52 seats. All of the cars were sold to the Illinois Central in 1967 except for No. 595, which was retired the same year. (Missouri Pacific)

INTERIOR VIEW of lower level of dome coach constructed by Pullman Standard looking forward toward the stairs leading to the dome. The interiors were equipped with over the seat lighting and drapes. (Missouri Pacific)

INTERIOR VIEW of the dome section of coaches built by Pullman Standard looking toward rear and down stairs to lower level. (Missouri Pacific)

ST. LOUIS — KANSAS CITY — OMAHA

	17	Miles		TABLE 9 9-27-64			16	
...	8.50	0	Lv	ST. LOUIS, MO. (CST)	Ar	....	5.10	....
...	2.20	279	Ar	KANSAS CITY, MO.	Lv	....	11.30	....
...	2.40	279	Lv	KANSAS CITY, MO.	Ar	....	11.10	....
...	3.15	307	Lv	Leavenworth, Kan.	Lv	....	10.20	....
...	3.20	309	Lv	Fort Leavenworth	Lv	....	10.15	....
...	3.42	328	Lv	Atchison	Lv	....	9.55	....
...	★ 4.05	349	Lv	Everest	Lv	....	....	....
...	4.24	367	Lv	Hiawatha, Kan.	Lv	....	9.09	....
...	4.42	382	Lv	Falls City, Neb.	Lv	....	8.53	....
...	5.11	411	Lv	Auburn	Lv	....	8.23	....
...	5.35	433	Lv	Nebraska City	Lv	....	7.59	....
...	5.50	444	Lv	Union	Lv	....	7.45	....
...	★ 6.06	459	Lv	Plattsmouth	Lv	....	★ 7.28	....
...	6.55	478	Ar	OMAHA, NEB. (Un. Sta.)	Lv	....	7.00	....

THE DOMELINER TEXAS EAGLE powered by 3 "E" units at St. Louis Union Station on August 20, 1966. By this date, Numbers 1 and 2 were assigned but one dome coach between St. Louis and San Antonio, instead of the original two. The spare domes from the Colorado Eagle and from the Texas Eagle were reassigned to the Missouri River Eagle and trains 21 and 22 between New Orleans and Fort Worth. (J. W. Swanberg)

ST. LOUIS — LITTLE ROCK — TEXARKANA
NEW ORLEANS — ALEXANDRIA — SHREVEPORT
DALLAS — FORT WORTH — EL PASO — LOS ANGELES

7	3	1	Miles	TABLE 1 3-21-65		2	4	8
12.45	1.00	5.30	0	Lv ST. LOUIS, MO. (CST)	Ar	8.30	5.45	11.00
★ 1.55	★ 2.09	★ 6.35	45	Lv De Soto	Lv		4.04	
			54	Lv Blackwell	Lv		f 3.50	
			60	Lv Cadet	Lv		f 3.42	
	★ 2.31		64	Lv Mineral Point	Lv		f 3.36	
	★ 2.40		73	Lv Irondale	Lv		f 3.25	
2.45	2.50		79	Lv Bismarck	Lv		3.17	8.49
			86	Lv Middlebrook	Lv		f 3.04	
3.03	3.07		92	Lv Arcadia-Ironton	Lv		2.54	8.27
			102	Lv Glover	Lv		f 2.38	
			111	Lv Annapolis	Lv		f 2.26	
			115	Lv North Des Arc	Lv		f 2.20	
3.50	★ 3.53		130	Lv Piedmont	Lv		2.01	7.42
			138	Lv Mill Spring	Lv		f 1.49	
	★ 4.15		149	Lv Williamsville	Lv		1.36	
4.55	♧ 4.50	9.00	169	Ar POPLAR BLUFF	Lv	4.55	1.10	6.55
5.05	5.00	9.10	169	Lv POPLAR BLUFF	Ar	4.45	♧12.50	6.45
★ 5.20	★ 5.15		184	Lv Neelyville, Mo	Lv		f 12.25	
5.33	§ 5.27		195	Lv Corning, Ark	Lv		12.10	ϕ 6.13
			202	Lv Knobel	Lv		12.01	
			206	Lv Peach Orchard	Lv		★11.50	
			218	Lv O'Kean	Lv		★11.30	
6.38	6.05	★10.01	229	Lv Hoxie	Lv		11.15	★ 5.40
★ 7.03			255	Lv Tuckerman	Lv		★10.40	
7.25	6.45	10.30	264	Lv Newport	Lv		10.25	5.05
			281	Bradford	Lv		f 10.03	
★ 7.53	7.20		291	Lv Bald Knob	Lv		9.50	
			296	Judsonia	Lv		9.42	
8.05	★ 7.30		300	Lv Kensett-Searcy	Lv		9.35	
★ 8.20			316	Lv Beebe	Lv		9.10	
♧ 9.30	8.30	11.55	349	Ar LITTLE ROCK	Lv	2.05	8.25	3.45
11.25	8.50	12.20	349	Lv LITTLE ROCK	Ar	1.50	7.40	3.30
11.49			372	Lv Benton	Lv		★ 7.00	
12.10	9.40		392	Lv Malvern	Lv		6.40	2.30
12.35	10.05		414	Lv Arkadelphia	Lv		6.10	2.03
12.55	10.30		429	Lv Gurdon	Lv		5.55	1.46
1.15	10.48		446	Lv Prescott	Lv		5.35	
1.40	11.07		461	Lv Hope	Lv		5.20	1.12
2.30	12.10	3.15	493	Ar TEXARKANA, ARK.-TEX.	Lv	11.25	4.45	♧12.35
27	↓	↓		(For Austin-San Antonio-Mexico—See Table 4.) (For Houston— See Tables 4-5.)		↑	↑	28
3.00	12.55	3.40	493	Lv TEXARKANA, ARK.-TEX.	Ar	11.15	4.15	12.15
3.27	1.22	★ 4.05	517	Lv Atlanta	Lv	★10.40	2.55	• 11.22
4.00	■ 1.51	★ 4.30	544	Lv Jefferson	Lv	★10.15	2.25	• 10.56
4.52	2.25	4.50	560	Lv Marshall	Lv	10.00	2.10	10.40
5.27	3.10	5.30	583	Ar LONGVIEW, TEX.	Lv	9.30	1.30	10.10
		21				22		
5.27	3.10	6.06	583	Lv LONGVIEW, TEX.	Ar	8.15	1.30	10.10
5.40	3.24	6.20	596	Lv Gladewater	Lv	7.08	12.33	9.40
★ 5.50			606	Lv Big Sandy	Lv	■ 7.00	12.25	
6.25	4.07	6.55	629	Lv Mineola	Lv	6.40	12.05	9.15
★ 6.39		★ 7.09	642	Lv Grand Saline	Lv	★ 6.25	11.46	
★ 6.56		7.30	660	Lv Wills Point	Lv	6.09	11.25	★ 8.44
★ 7.10		7.45	676	Lv Terrell	Lv	5.55	11.05	★ 8.30
★ 7.34	5.16	8.10	695	Lv Mesquite	Lv	5.35	★10.40	8.10
8.00	5.45	9.00	710	Ar DALLAS	Lv	5.05	10.15	7.40
8.40	6.10	9.25	710	Lv DALLAS	Ar	4.40	9.20	7.20
	6.26	9.41	722	Lv Grand Prairie	Lv	4.18	★ 8.56	6.54
★ 9.00	6.35	9.50	728	Lv Arlington	Lv	4.09	★ 8.48	6.47
9.20	7.00	10.20	742	Ar FT. WORTH (CST)	Lv	3.50	8.30	6.30

(For El Paso-California — See Table 3)

23		21	Miles	TABLE 2 3-14-65		22		24
7.25		8.30	0	Lv NEW ORLEANS (CST)	Ar	5.35		8.10
7.34		8.39	2	Lv Carrollton Ave	Ar	5.10		7.55
★ 8.05		9.10	17	Lv Avondale	Lv	4.40		7.27
8.57		10.13	70	Lv Donaldsonville	Lv	3.10		6.20
f 9.10		10.28	81	Lv White Castle	Lv	★ 2.51	(Box Dinner)	6.03
9.23		10.45	91	Lv Plaquemine	Lv	2.40		5.50
9.37		11.10	96	Lv Addis (For Baton Rouge)	Lv	2.24		5.28
f 9.51			111	Lv Rosedale	Lv			f5.11
f 9.56			115	Lv Mariongouin	Lv			f5.05
f 10.20		★11.49	135	Lv Melville	Lv	★ 1.45		4.39
10.55		12.24	169	Lv Bunkie	Lv	1.13		4.05
ⓐ11.30		1.15	200	Ar ALEXANDRIA	Lv	12.25		3.15
11.55		1.35	200	Lv ALEXANDRIA	Ar	12.03		2.55
1.05		2.34	253	Lv Natchitoches	Lv	11.10		1.50
3.10		4.15	327	Lv SHREVEPORT, LA.	Lv	10.01		12.30
f 3.28			343	Lv Waskom, Tex.	Lv			f 11.44
3.50		5.05	370	Ar MARSHALL	Lv	8.55		11.20
27		↓				↑		28
4.52		5.15	370	Lv MARSHALL	Ar	8.45		ⓐ10.40
5.27		6.06	393	Lv LONGVIEW	Lv	8.15		10.10
5.40		6.20	406	Ar Gladewater	Lv	7.08		9.40
6.25		6.55	439	Ar Mineola	Lv	6.40		9.15
8.00		9.00	520	Ar DALLAS	Lv	5.05		7.40
8.40		9.25	520	Lv DALLAS	Ar	4.40		7.20
9.20		10.20	552	Ar FORT WORTH (CST)	Lv	3.50		6.30

(For El Paso-California—See Table 3)

23			Miles	TABLE 3 3-14-65		26		
↓								
10.05			742	Lv FT. WORTH (CST)	Ar	⊕ 1.00	⊕Connecting Service to Dallas (Via Texas Motor Coaches — Rail tickets honored)	
			773	Lv Weatherford	Lv	12.13		
			787	Lv Millsap	Lv	★11.53		
			814	Lv Gordon	Lv	★11.26		
			822	Lv Strawn	Lv	★11.19		
			837	Lv Ranger	Lv	11.01		
			847	Lv Eastland	Lv	10.46		
			856	Lv Cisco	Lv	10.35		
12.45			882	Lv Baird	Lv	10.02		
1.35			903	Lv Abilene	Lv	9.28		
			920	Lv Merkel	Lv	★ 8.54		
2.17			944	Lv Sweetwater	Lv	8.30		
f 3.11			972	Lv Colorado City	Lv	♧ 7.44		
3.55			1009	Ar BIG SPRING	Lv	6.45		
4.20			1009	Lv BIG SPRING	Ar	6.25		
f 4.41			1030	Lv Stanton	Lv	f 6.05		
5.20			1049	Lv Midland	Lv	5.45		
♧ 6.15			1069	Lv Odessa	Lv	4.56		
7.00			1105	Lv Monahans	Lv	4.01		
			1119	Lv Pyote	Lv	★ 3.43		
7.54			1143	Lv Pecos	Lv	3.22		
8.19			1162	Lv Toyah	Lv	2.58		
			1194	Lv Kent	Lv	★ 2.20		
9.52			1231	Lv Van Horn	Lv	1.45		
10.40			1264	Lv Sierra Blanca (CST)	Lv	★ 1.10		
11.45			1357	Ar EL PASO, TEX. (MST)	Lv	10.25		
				Southern Pacific Lines				
2.50			1357	Lv EL PASO, TEX. (MST)	Ar	5.00		
8.45			1668	Ar TUCSON, ARIZ.	Lv	10.00		
11.35			1790	Ar PHOENIX, ARIZ.	Lv	7.15		
8.15			2169	Ar LOS ANGELES (PST)	Lv	8.30		

Source: Missouri Pacific Railroad Time table April 1, 1965

EQUIPMENT

The Texas Eagle

Trains No. 1-21-41 42-22-2

All Coach Seats Reserved.

Sleepers—

St. Louis — Ft. Worth
(10 Rmte. 6 DBR) [19-28]
(14 Rmte. 4 DBR) [17-29]

St. Louis — Alexandria
(14 Rmte. 4 DBR) [312-1321]

St. Louis — Houston
(14 Rmte. 4 DBR) [211-1220]

St. Louis — Mexico City
(10 Rmte. 6 DBR) [102-101]

St. Louis — San Antonio
(14 Rmte. 4 DBR) [215-228]

New Orleans — Ft. Worth
(10 Rmte. 6 DBR) [213-222]
(May be occupied until 7:00 AM)

Diner—

St. Louis — San Antonio
Longview — Ft. Worth

Diner-Coach—

St. Louis — Houston [HU-16]

Dome Coaches—

St. Louis — San Antonio [SA-25]
New Orleans — Ft. Worth [NO-21]

Coaches—

St. Louis — Ft. Worth [FW-1]
St. Louis — Houston [HU-11]
St. Louis — San Antonio [SA-26]

No checked baggage or remains handled between St. Louis, Mo. and Palestine, Tex.

Trains 1-2 Connection for National Railways of Mexico

Aztec Eagle

Sleeper—

St. Louis — Mexico City
(10 Rmte. 6 DBR) [102-101]

Diner—

Nuevo Laredo — Mexico City

Coaches—

San Antonio — Laredo-Nuevo Laredo
Nuevo Laredo — Mexico City

Trains No. 31-32

Sleeper—

St. Louis — Alexandria
(14 Rmte. 4 DBR) [312-1321]

Coaches—

Little Rock — Alexandria

Trains No. 7-27 - 28-8 - 23-24

Grill Coach—

St. Louis — Ft. Worth
(Grill Service St. Louis—Little Rock; Marshall — Ft. Worth)

Coaches—

St. Louis — San Antonio
New Orleans — Ft. Worth

Trains No. 27-26

Coaches—

Ft. Worth — El Paso

Trains No. 3-4

Coaches—

St. Louis — Ft. Worth

Trains No. 37-38

Coaches—

Memphis — Little Rock

The Missouri River Eagle

Trains No. 17-16

Diner- Parlor Car—

St. Louis — Kansas City [51-61]

Dome Coach—

St. Louis — Omaha

Coach—

St. Louis — Omaha

Trains No. 11-12

Diner- Parlor Car—

St. Louis — Kansas City [111-121]

Coaches—

St. Louis — Denver

Trains No. 15-14

Coaches—

St. Louis — Kansas City

Grill Coach—

St. Louis — Kansas City

Trains No. 19-18

Sleeper—

St. Louis — Kansas City
(14 Rmte — 4 DBR.) [91-106]
(May be occupied at 10:00 PM and until 7:30 AM)

Coaches—

St. Louis — Kansas City

Trains No. 53-52

Coaches—

New Orleans — Houston

Trains No. 55-54

Coaches—

Houston — Brownsville (May be occupied at Houston until 6:00 AM)

RESERVED COACH SEAT CHARGES

Texas Eagles

TRAINS 1-21-41—42-22-2

Between ☞ And ☞	St. Louis, Mo.	Poplar Bluff, Mo.	Little Rock, Ark.
Poplar Bluff........Mo.	$0.50	....	....
Little Rock........Ark.	0.50	$0.50	....
Texarkana........Ark.	1.00	1.00	$0.50
Longview........Tex.	1.50	1.50	1.00
Palestine........Tex.	1.50	1.50	1.00
Houston........Tex.	1.50	1.50	1.50
Austin........Tex.	1.50	1.50	1.50
San Antonio........Tex.	1.50	1.50	1.50
Dallas........Tex.	1.50	1.50	1.00
Ft. Worth........Tex.	1.50	1.50	1.00

Between ☞ And ☞	Marshall, Tex.	Longview, Tex.	Dallas, Tex.	Ft. Worth, Tex.
New Orleans........La.	$1.00	$1.00	$1.00	$1.00
Addis........La.	.50	.50	1.00	1.00
Alexandria........La.	.50	.50	1.00	1.00
Natchitoches........La.	.50	.50	.50	.50
Shreveport........La.	.25	.50	.50	.50

Minimum Reserved Coach Seat Charge 25c (50 Miles or Less).

Capacity of sleepers shown in parenthesis—
(14 Rmte. 4 DBR) 14 Roomettes 4 Double Bedrooms.
(10 Rmte. 6 DBR) 10 Roomettes 6 Double Bedrooms.
Designating numbers of Sleepers and Coaches shown in brackets—[ ]
Note: Sleeper and parlor car numbers shown in dark face type Southbound and Westbound; Northbound and Eastbound in light face type.

April 1, 1965 All editions printed in U.S.A.

Source: Missouri Pacific Railroad Time Table April 1, 1965

TEXARKANA — SAN ANTONIO — MEXICO CITY

7	1	Miles	TABLE 4 3-14-65		2	8
3.35	3.40	493	Lv TEXARKANA, ARK.-TEX. (CST)	Ar	**11.15**	11.30
4.03	★ 4.05	517	Lv Atlanta	Lv	**★10.40**	9.45
4.36	★ 4.30	544	Lv Jefferson	Lv	**★10.15**	9.17
5.10	4.50	560	Lv Marshall	Lv	**10.00**	9.00
5.45	5.30	583	Ar LONGVIEW	Lv	**9.30**	8.30
6.05	5.50	583	Lv LONGVIEW	Ar	**9.10**	8.10
6.20	6.04	595	Lv Kilgore	Lv	**8.49**	7.22
6.50	....	605	Lv Overton	Lv	....	7.01
7.01	....	612	Lv Arp	Lv	....	6.46
7.15	6.36	619	Lv Troup	Lv	**8.19**	6.36
7.39	6.55	637	Lv Jacksonville	Lv	**7.58**	6.10
8.05	....	652	Lv Neches	Lv	....	f 5.42
8.45	7.40	664	Ar PALESTINE	Lv	**7.25**	5.30
↓	↓		(For Houston — See Table 5)		↑	↑
9.20	8.05	664	Lv PALESTINE	Ar	**7.01**	4.40
★ 9.32	....	674	Lv Tucker	Lv	....	★ 4.18
9.44	....	682	Lv Oakwood	Lv	....	4.02
10.10	....	701	Lv Buffalo	Lv	....	3.32
10.25	★ 8.48	708	Lv Jewett	Lv	**★ 6.06**	3.15
10.40	....	719	Lv Marquez	Lv	....	2.55
f10.58	....	733	Lv Easterly	Lv	....	2.30
f11.05	....	737	Lv New Baden	Lv	....	2.20
11.13	★ 9.26	741	Lv Franklin	Lv	**★ 5.34**	2.12
11.35	9.40	754	Lv Hearne	Lv	**5.21**	1.52
11.46	....	765	Lv Gause	Lv	....	1.09
12.06	10.05	775	Lv Milano	Lv	**★ 4.59**	12.47
12.36	10.18	784	Lv Rockdale	Lv	**4.50**	12.36
1.59	10.52	810	Lv Taylor	Lv	**4.25**	**11.45**
2.12	....	819	Lv Hutto	Lv	....	**11.20**
2.20	....	827	Lv Round Rock	Lv	....	**11.07**
3.27	11.32	845	Lv AUSTIN	Lv	**3.44**	**10.35**
3.45	....	855	Lv Manchaca	Lv	....	**9.43**
3.53	....	860	Lv Buda	Lv	....	**9.38**
4.03	....	866	Lv Kyle	Lv	....	**9.29**
4.23	**12.10**	875	Lv San Marcos	Lv	**★ 3.09**	**9.19**
★ 4.32	....	882	Lv Hunter	Lv	....	**★ 9.09**
4.46	**12.29**	893	Lv New Braunfels	Lv	**★ 2.52**	**8.59**
f 5.05	....	907	Lv Bracken	Lv	....	**f 8.40**
5.14	....	914	Lv Wetmore	Lv	....	**f 8.33**
5.45	**1.20**	924	Ar SAN ANTONIO	Lv	**2.15**	**8.15**
....	**1.45**	924	Lv SAN ANTONIO	Ar	**1.35**	....
....	**f 2.15**	947	Lv Lytle	Lv	**f12.35**	....
....	**f 2.21**	952	Lv Natalia	Lv	**f12.24**	....
....	**f 2.26**	957	Lv Devine	Lv	**f12.13**	....
....	**f 2.52**	978	Lv Pearsall	Lv	f11.34	....
....	**3.12**	994	Lv Dilley	Lv	11.09	....
....	**3.32**	1011	Lv Cotulla	Lv	10.34	....
....	**f 4.06**	1039	Lv Encinal	Lv	f 9.56	....
....	**f 4.20**	1050	Lv Callaghan	Lv	f 9.41	....
....	**5.20**	1078	Ar LAREDO, TEX. (CST)	Lv	9.05	....
			National Railways of Mexico			
....	**6.15**	1080	Lv NUEVO LAREDO, MEXICO	Ar	8.00	....
....	**10.23**	1236	Ar MONTERREY, MEXICO	Lv	3.50	....
....	9.07	1557	Ar SAN LUIS POTOSI, MEXICO	Lv	**6.31**	....
....	**8.10**	1881	Ar MEXICO CITY, MEXICO (CST)	Lv	8.10	....

Light figures indicate A. M.

For equipment, see page 3

Source: Missouri Pacific Railroad
Time Table
April 1, 1965

CHAPTER 11

The Blue Fleet of the Wabash

The Domeliners on the former Wabash Railroad include three different trains, not including the City of St. Louis which is covered in another chapter. The most famous of the three was the fleet leader, the Blue Bird, which operated between Chicago and St. Louis, Missouri. The other two trains were the Banner Blue and the City of Kansas City.

The Domeliner Blue Bird was formally christened on February 26, 1950 at the St. Louis Union Station. The Domeliner operated from that date until February 25, 1970 when it was discontinued on the Chicago – St. Louis run and replaced by a long distance Commuter Streamliner, The City of Decatur operating between Chicago and Decatur, Illinois.

The Domeliner, as it was originally built by the Budd Company, was a masterpiece of a passenger train. The original train was made up of six cars and powered by one E-7 or E-8 unit. The first car of the train was a Baggage – Coffee Shop Club Car. The baggage section included provision for the crew. These included lockers, water cooler and washroom facilities. The center of the car contained a lunch counter with nine leather upholstered stools. Beyond the partition toward the rear of the car was (and is) a twenty three passenger lounge section, with washrooms for ladies and gentlemen at the end of the car.

The next three cars were Dome Coaches. The cars carried a variety of color schemes which prevented unpleasant monotony. Each car was (and is) divided into two passenger sections. The forward section seats twenty and the rear thirty-four passengers. The seats on the main floor are individually reclining and rotating reversible of the sleepy hollow type. The Dome seats do not recline but are reversible. The train also carried a Dining Cocktail Lounge Car and a Dome Observation Parlor Car. Radio and recorded musical programs were provided throughout the entire train.

The popularity of the train brought about the addition of a Pullman built Dome Parlor Car. This car also included the famous Blue Bird Room, which was actually an enlarged Drawing Room that served from six to nine passengers.

During the mid-1950's, the Blue Bird also carried a 14 Roomette 4 Double Bedroom sleeper from San Antonio to Chicago on its north bound run. The car was part of the MKT's and Frisco's Texas Special and was routed via the Wabash to Chicago. The Blue Bird provided morning service to Chicago and afternoon service to St. Louis.

The companion train to the Blue Bird was the Banner Blue. The Banner Blue had been in operation since the 1920's and provided morning service to St. Louis and afternoon service to Chicago through 1967. The train became a Domeliner in the early 1960's when the Wabash added a dome coach from the original Blue Bird equipment. The train, in addition to the Dome Coach, consisted of an Observation Drawing Room Parlor Car, a Dining Lounge Car and one or two flat top coaches. The train also handled some head-end business.

The third train in the Blue Fleet of the Wabash, the City of Kansas City, operated between St. Louis and Kansas City and was a companion train to the City of St. Louis. In 1952, the Wabash transferred a Dome Coach to

THE WABASH RAILROAD BLUE BIRD and Banner Blue were trains of distinction since the 1920's, and the railroad was very proud of them. They were fabulous and fast. Prior to dieselization and dome cars, the trains were powered by Hudsons and usually ran with a six or seven car consist including a dining car, parlor car and a parlor observation. The standard trains were kept in prime condition right up until the days of dieselization and streamlining, or shall we say, domelining.

The first domeliner arrived in 1950, the Blue Bird. The original domeliner (as shown here) was powered by a single Electro Motive Division "E" unit which was the customary power prior to the N&W lease of the Wabash. The consist of this sharp little train was later expanded with a second dome parlor car and also a Pullman sleeper on its northbound run. (A Roomette–Bedroom sleeper off the MKT–Frisco's Texas Special from San Antonio, Texas.) The normal or usual consist in the 1950's was 7 or 8 cars southbound and 8 or 9 cars northbound, the Pullman being the extra car northward. Prior to its discontinuance in 1970, the train was powered by one GP-9 and consisted of one coffee shop baggage car and two coaches. The dome cars were gone. (Louis A. Marre)

THE ORIGINAL DOMELINER "Blue Bird" was built by the Budd Company. The color scheme of "Wabash Blue" and silver made the six car train very attractive to the eye. The Wabash Railroad was the only railroad to operate dome cars between Chicago and St. Louis before AMTRAK. This photo shows the original six car consist of one coffee shop baggage, three dome coaches, one dining-cocktail lounge car and one dome parlor observation car. (Norfolk & Western Railway)

LOOKING TOWARD THE rear of the car, this is the interior of the dome parlor observation originally built for the Blue Bird. The car is divided into four sections: The observation lounge (note the smaller movable chairs in the observation end), the dome and two parlor sections. The observation area has six lounge chairs plus two tables recessed on both sides of the rear door. The next section (shown in photo) contains 14 sleepy hollow parlor chairs that are fully adjustable and rotating. The central area under the dome contains lounges or rest rooms for the ladies and gentlemen and a drawing room with accommodations for five people. This room featured a private fully enclosed lavatory, a three seat sofa, two movable chairs and an illuminated closet with double doors. The front parlor section contains nine chairs. Lighting is flourescent and there are individual reading lamps above each chair in the baggage racks. The car was fully carpeted – and was a great way to travel between Chicago and St. Louis. (Norfolk & Western Railway)

the City of Kansas City, which provided morning service to Kansas City and afternoon service to St. Louis. This car was later transferred to operation on the Banner Blue. The train also carried an Observation Parlor Car with a Drawing Room, a Dining Car and a Coffee Shop Club for coach passengers. The train, usually powered by a single E unit, also handled Baggage Cars and a Rail Post Office Car.

By 1964, the City of Kansas City was minus its Dome Coach, Diner and Observation Parlor Car. The first Norfolk and Western timetable in 1964 listed the train as being equipped with a Chair Car and Buffet service. This equipment remained in operation until its discontinuance by early 1968. By the end of 1969, there were no dome cars operated on any train over the former Wabash lines of the Norfolk and Western Railway.

Altogether the former Wabash Railroad operated a total of six dome cars including the Dome Coach provided for the Union Pacific's City of St. Louis, four of the cars were built by Budd, the others by Pullman. The cars, although no longer on the former Wabash lines, were still in operation as of early 1971. However, that is another chapter.

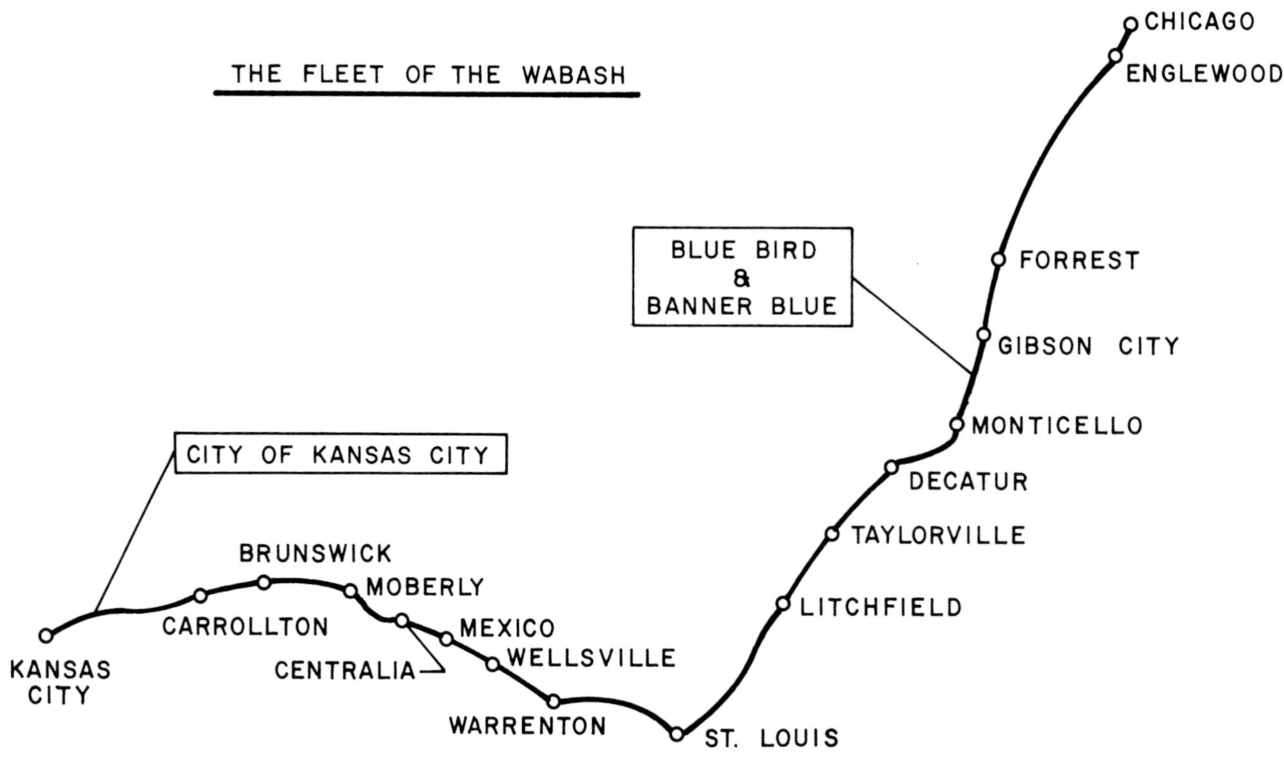

Drawn By: Sy Dykhouse III

THE BUDD COMPANY built three dome coaches for the Wabash in 1950 for the Blue Bird. The cars were originally numbered 200 to 202, but later were renumbered 1610 to 1612. The equipment contains 56 coach seats plus 24 more seats in the dome. The cars still wear their original color scheme (since the N&W adopted the Wabash colors for their passenger equipment) but are now lettered Norfolk and Western. (The Budd Company)

AFTER THE BLUE BIRD went into service in 1950, parlor car business increased at such a rate that the Wabash placed an order for a second dome parlor car for the train. The 1602 was a smooth side car but was painted to match the Budd built equipment. The beautiful car was built by Pullman Standard in 1952 and contained the famous "Blue Bird" room, a drawing room that accommodated up to nine passengers. To this writer's knowledge, this is the largest drawing room to be operated on any railroad. (Norfolk and Western Railway)

Hostess Service
Fashion Shows
Free Champagne
with Dinner
Recreation Car
Movies / Games
Song Fests
Television / Telephone
Strata Dome Pullman
on the FLORIDA SPECIAL

FLORIDA SPECIAL

First trip from New York December 16; first trip from Miami December 17.

Coach-Pullman Train—All seats reserved
Daily Between
New York-Washington and Miami
Extra Fare

Read Down — Read Up

NYNH&H 3 / PRR 107 / RF&P 87 / ACL 87	TABLE A — EASTERN STANDARD TIME	NYNH&H 28 / PRR 106 / RF&P 88 / ACL 88
2 00 AM	Lv **Boston** .... NYNH&H Ar	**11 55 PM**
2 26 AM	Lv Route 128 .... " Ar	**11 33 PM**
3 20 AM	Lv Providence .... " Ar	**10 50 PM**
5 52 AM	Lv New Haven .... " Ar	**8 31 PM**
7 30 AM	Ar **New York** (Grand Central Ter.)." Lv	**7 00 PM**
10 45 AM	Lv **New York** (Penn. Station)..... PRR Ar	**6 15 PM**
10 59 AM	Lv Newark .... " Ar	**5 59 PM**
12 14 PM	Lv Philadelphia (30th St.) .... " Ar	**4 37 PM**
12 42 PM	Lv Wilmington .... " Ar	**4 09 PM**
1 45 PM	Lv Baltimore .... " Ar	**3 10 PM**
2 25 PM	Ar **Washington** .... " Lv	**2 30 PM**
2 55 PM	Lv **Washington** .... RF&P Ar	**1 55 PM**
[19]**3 12 PM**	Lv Alexandria .... " Ar	**1 30 PM**[19]
5 05 PM	Ar **Richmond** .... " Lv	11 45 AM
5 15 PM	Lv **Richmond** .... ACL Ar	11 35 AM
[2]**5 45 PM**	Lv Petersburg .... " Ar	10 58 AM[2]
7 10 PM	Lv Rocky Mount .... " Ar	9 25 AM
8 30 PM	Lv Fayetteville .... " Ar	7 55 AM
10 00 PM	Ar Florence .... " Lv	6 40 AM
10 10 PM	Lv Florence .... " Ar	6 30 AM
11 30 PM	Ar Charleston .... " Lv	....
1 10 AM	Ar Savannah .... " Lv	3 35 AM
3 35 AM	Ar **Jacksonville** .... " Lv	1 15 AM
3 45 AM	Lv **Jacksonville** .... " Ar	1 05 AM
6 20 AM	Ar Orlando .... " Lv	**10 10 PM**
9 35 AM	Ar West Palm Beach Lv	**6 43 PM**
9 56 AM	Ar Delray Beach Lv	**6 20 PM**
10 06 AM	Ar Deerfield Beach (Boca Raton) .. Lv	**6 09 PM**
10 25 AM	Ar Fort Lauderdale Lv	**5 55 PM**
10 35 AM	Ar Hollywood Lv	**5 40 PM**
11 25 AM	Ar **Miami** Lv	**5 15 PM**

(For Special Service Charge in Reserved Seat Coaches, see Page 5.)

see Page 5

Hostess and Passenger Representative between New York and Miami

Coach Attendant Service

EXTRA FARE

In Coach—$2.50 **In Pullman—$5.00**

MODERN STREAMLINED EQUIPMENT

Type Car	Car No.	Between	Accommodations
Coaches	FS-4	New York-Miami	54 Reclining, reserved seats
	FS-3	New York-Miami	54 Reclining, reserved seats
	FS-2	New York-Miami	54 Reclining, reserved seats
	FS-1	Washington-Miami	54 Reclining, reserved seats
Diner		Washington-Miami	
Recreation Car		New York-Miami	
Sleepers	FS-20	New York-Miami	10 Roomettes, 6 Double Bedrooms
	FS-21	New York-Miami	6 Double Bedrooms, Bar-Lounge
Diner		New York-Miami	
Sleepers	FS-22	New York-Miami	11 Double Bedrooms
	FS-23	New York-Miami	7 Double Bedrooms, 2 Drawing Rooms
	FS-24	New York-Miami	7 Double Bedrooms, 2 Drawing Rooms
	FS-25	New York-Miami	4 Double Bedrooms, 4 Compartments, 2 Drawing Rooms
Strata Dome Sleeper	FS-26	Richmond-Miami	5 Roomettes, 1 Single Bedroom, 3 Compartments

Source: ACL Time Table
Oct. 31, 1965

ROUTE OF THE SOUTHERN CRESCENT

NEW YORK — WASHINGTON — CHARLOTTE — ATLANTA — BIRMINGHAM — NEW ORLEANS

READ DOWN				READ UP	
1	5	Miles	(ET) Eastern Time (CT) Central Time	6	2
9 55	*12 55*	......	Lv *Boston*.................(PC) *Mass.* Ar	*1 55*	*6 55*
2 40	*5 25*	......	Ar *New York (Penn. Sta.)*..........*N. Y.* Lv	*9 30*	*2 10*
6 50	*9 35*	......	Ar *Washington*..................*D. C.* Lv	....	*10 00*
3 00 PM	7 30 PM	......	Lv **New York Penna Sta.(PC)..(ET)N. Y.** Ar	7 00 AM	12 38 PM
3 16	7 46	......	Newark.....................N. J.	6 39	12 22
4 00	8 29	......	Trenton....................."	5 50	11 35
4 29	8 57	......	**North Philadelphia** ....Pa.	5 23	11 07
4 39	9 06	......	Philadelphia (30th St. Station)....."	4 50	10 58
5 08	9 39	......	Wilmington..................Del.	4 14	10 29
6 09	10 40	......	**Baltimore Penna Sta.**..........Md.	3 05	9 25
6 50	11 20	......	Ar Washington...............D. C. Lv	2 25	8 40
7 25	12 25	.0	Lv **Washington**......(SOU)..(ET). D. C. Ar	1 55	7 50
7 43	12 50	8.2	**Alexandria**...................Va.	1 31	7 10
a 8 16	a 1 22	32.6	**Manassas**....................."	....	......
8 47	1 57	67.4	**Culpeper**....................."	12 10	......
9 08	b 2 17	84.7	**Orange**......................."	....	......
9 40	2 45	112.2	Ar **Charlottesville (Union Sta.)**..... " Lv	11 20	5 20
9 40	2 56	112.2	Lv **Charlottesville (Union Sta.)**..... " Ar	11 20	5 20
h	......	160.0	Sweet Briar ...."	....	......
10 50	3 50	165.1	Ar **Monroe** ...." Lv	10 10	4 20
10 55	4 20	165.1	Lv **Monroe** ...." Ar	9 50	4 15
11 04	4 30	172.5	Ar **Lynchburg** ...." Lv	9 40	4 05
11 11	4 42	172.5	Lv **Lynchburg** ...." Ar	9 37	4 05
r 11 37	f 5 08	195.8	**Altavista** ...."	r 9 05	......
......	f 5 31	218.2	Chatham ...."	....	......
12 21	5 57	235.8	Ar **Danville**..................." Lv	8 27	2 50
12 31	6 08	235.8	Lv **Danville**..................." Ar	8 15	2 41
j 1 00	6 40	259.9	Reidsville...................**N. C.**	c 7 46	......
1 25	7 15	283.9	Ar **Greensboro**................." Lv	7 18	1 50
1 35	7 40	283.9	Lv Greensboro ...." Ar	7 03	1 50
1 53	7 59	299.2	**High Point**. ...."	6 42	1 20
......	8 09	306.0	Thomasville ...."	c 6 31	......
......	8 21	316.8	Lexington ...."	c 6 19	......
2 35	8 45	333.7	Ar **Salisbury**..................." Lv	5 58	12 46
......	z 8 55	.0	Lv Salisbury...................." Ar	z 5 45	......
......	z 12 55	138.9	Ar Asheville...................." Lv	z 1 45	......
2 40	8 55	333.7	Lv **Salisbury**..................." Ar	5 53	12 40
......	9 15	348.9	**Kannapolis** ...."	....	......
3 03	9 29	356.4	Concord......................."	5 24	......
3 25	9 50	375.2	Ar **Charlotte**..................." Lv	5 02	11 45
3 40	10 15	375.2	Lv **Charlotte**..................." Ar	4 45	11 37
......	p10 34	389.1	Belmont ...."	....	......
4 11	10 52	399.3	**Gastonia** ...."	4 16	11 12
......	p11 06	410.6	Kings Mountain ...."	....	......
......	p11 21	423.9	**Blacksburg** ....**S. C.**	....	......
......	11 32	432.3	Gaffney......................."	....	......
5 13	11 52	452.6	Ar Spartanburg ...." Lv	3 21	10 15
5 13	12 05	452.6	Lv Spartanburg ...." Ar	3 15	10 15
......	p12 28	471.0	Greer ...."	....	......
5 55	12 50	484.1	Ar **Greenville**..................." Lv	2 40	9 35
6 05	1 10	484.1	Lv **Greenville**..................." Ar	2 25	9 30
......	1 23	495.8	Easley........................."	....	......
......	1 30	502.7	Liberty........................"	....	......
......	f	510.2	Central........................"	....	......
f 6 39	1 44	514.2	Clemson......................."	f 1 34	f 8 47
......	2 01	522.7	**Seneca**........................"	....	......
......	2 13	531.6	Westminster...................."	....	......
n 7 15	2 29	547.3	**Toccoa**......................Ga.	q 1 00	f 8 15
......	2 49	559.9	**Cornelia**......................."	....	......
......	f 3 01	572.2	**Lula**.........................."	....	......
8 00	3 18	584.6	**Gainesville**...................."	12 20	7 35
....	f	594.1	Flowery Branch................"	....	......
....	3 38	600.9	Buford........................"	....	......
....	f 3 48	612.7	Duluth........................"	....	......
8 55	4 20	633.3	Ar **Atlanta Peachtree Sta.**..........." Lv	11 25	6 40
9 10	....	633.3	Lv **Atlanta Peachtree Sta**.......(ET) Ga. Ar	....	6 25
10 48	....	735.0	**Anniston**...............(CT) Ala.	....	3 16
12 30	....	798.9	Ar Birmingham..................." Lv	....	1 55

Trains 1 and 2 (vertical labels): PC 173 / PC 126; The Southern Crescent—Private Room Pullman Cars—Reserved Seat Coaches
Trains 5 and 6 (vertical labels): PC 155 / PC 140; The Piedmont—Private Room Pullman Car—Reserved Seat Coaches

1 Operates Tuesdays Thursdays Sundays		TRI-WEEKLY BETWEEN BIRMINGHAM-NEW ORLEANS	2 Operates Mondays Wednesdays Fridays
Read Down			Read Up
12 45	798.9	Lv Birmingham ....(CT) Ala. Ar	1 40
1 56	854.3	Tuscaloosa......................"	12 27
r 2 21	879.7	Akron............................"	r12 01
e 2 30	888.9	Eutaw............................"	e11 53
e 2 55	914.9	Livingston........................"	e11 28
r 3 04	924.2	York............................."	r11 20
3 50	951.3	Ar Meridian ....Miss. Lv	10 55
3 55	951.3	Lv Meridian ...." Ar	10 50
5 03	1007.7	Laurel..........................."	9 40
5 40	1036.6	Hattiesburg......................"	9 05
5 57	1052.9	Purvis............................"	8 46
6 24	1076.4	Poplarville ...."	8 22
g 6 50	1100.3	Picayune........................."	g 7 57
7 09	1118.6	Slidell..........................La.	7 38
8 07	1151.5	New Orleans (Carrollton Ave.)..........."	6 52
8 25	1153.8	Ar New Orleans (Un. Pass. Term.)......" Lv	6 45

SOUTHERN PACIFIC'S "SUNSET," TRAINS 1 AND 2, OPERATING BETWEEN NEW ORLEANS — LOS ANGELES.

Read Down			Read Up
Departs New Orleans Wednesdays Fridays Mondays	Miles	OPERATES TRI-WEEKLY SLEEPING CAR, DINER-LOUNGE, CHAIR CARS, AUTOMATIC BUFFET CAR.	Departs Los Angeles Fridays Sundays Tuesdays
12:01 PM	.0	Lv New Orleans, La...................(CT).... Ar	(3) 8:10 PM
8:25 PM (1)	363.0	Ar Houston, Texas................................ Lv	(3) 12:15 PM
1:15 AM (2)	569.0	Ar San Antonio, Texas........................... Lv	(3) 7:50 AM
1:05 PM (2)	1177.0	Ar El Paso, Texas....................(MT).... Lv	(2) 6:20 PM
7:00 PM (2)	1488.0	Ar Tucson, Arizona Lv	(2) 11:10 AM
9:50 PM (2)	1608.0	Ar Phoenix, Arizona Lv	(2) 8:15 AM
6:30 AM (3)	2033.0	Ar Los Angeles, Cal.................(PT).... Lv	10:00 PM

SP 1 (read down) — SP 2 (read up)

(1) First Day. (2) Second Day. (3) Third Day.

The Southern Crescent — No. 1-2 — All-Reserved

DINING CAR—
Washington-Atlanta (Daily)
Atlanta-New Orleans (Note 1)

TAVERN-LOUNGE CAR—
Washington-Atlanta (Daily)

PARLOR-DOME CAR—(Note 1)

West	East	Between	Type
100	200	Atlanta-New Orleans	21 Parlor Seats

RECLINING SEAT COACHES—Reservation Charge Applying.

South	North	Between (Note 2)	Type
3	3	Washington-Birmingham or New Orleans	52-Seat
5	5	Washington-Atlanta	52-Seat
10	10	New York-Birmingham or New Orleans	52-Seat
12	12	New York-Birmingham or New Orleans	52-Seat

SLEEPING CARS—

South	North	Between	Type
22	22	Washington-Atlanta	DR,MR,Bft.-Lge. (Daily)
28	52	Washington-Atlanta	10-Rmtte 6-DBR (Daily)
SR-41	S-41	New York-Birmingham	10-Rmtte 6-DBR (Note 3)
West	East	Between	Type
SW-1	SE-1	New York-Los Angeles	10-Rmtte 6-DBR (Note 4)

Note 1. Tri-Weekly, Atlanta to New Orleans Tues., Thurs., Sun.; New Orleans to Atlanta Mon., Wed., Fri.

Note 2. Cars 3, 10, and 12 operate to and from New Orleans Tri-Weekly, prefixed "N", and operate to and from Birmingham four days a week, prefixed "B." See Schedules.

Note 3. Cars SR-41/S-41 operate four days each week, departing New York on Tues., Thurs., Fri., Sun.; and departing Birmingham on Tues., Thurs., Sat., Sun.

Note 4. Cars SW-1/SE-1 operate Tri-Weekly, departing New York on Mon., Wed., Sat.; and departing Los Angeles on Tues., Fri., Sun.

NEW YORK-LOS ANGELES VIA SLEEPER, WITH AN OVERNIGHT STOP IN EXOTIC NEW ORLEANS

The good old days are here again—only they're better! Southern has teamed up with two other railroads to bring you the Transcontinental Rail Cruise: luxurious sleeping car service from coast to coast.

Between Atlanta and New Orleans, you can ride Southern's beautiful dome car for an unbeatable view of the countryside. In New Orleans, you may wish to enjoy an evening on the town, with your sleeping car room as your hotel.

Sleepers leave New York and Washington on Monday, Wednesday, and Saturday. They leave Los Angeles on Tuesday, Friday, and Sunday.

The Nancy Hanks No. 8-7 — Daily — ATLANTA — MACON — SAVANNAH

Read Down 8	Miles	(Eastern Time)	Read Up 7
6 00	.0	Lv Atlanta (Spring St. Sta.) (ET) (CofGa) Ga. Ar	1 00
6 52	42.3	Griffin .... " "	11 58
7 12	60.5	Barnesville................ " "	11 37
r 7 28	76.5	Forsyth .... " "	r11 18
8 05	102.8	Ar Macon.................... " " Lv	10 50
8 15	102.8	Lv Macon.................... " " Ar	10 45
8 39	123.1	Gordon .... " "	10 10
9 21	158.5	Tennille................... " "	9 30
u 9 35	171.5	Davisboro.................. " "	u 9 15
9 54	186.8	Wadley .... " "	8 58
u10 05	197.4	Midville................... " "	u 8 46
10 25	214.9	Millen..................... " "	8 23
10 49	236.4	Dover .... " "	8 02
v11 21	265.9	Springfield................ " "	v 7 29
11 59	290.5	Ar Savannah................ " " Lv	7 00

EQUIPMENT: Reclining Seat Coaches (All seats reserved-no reservation charge.) Grill Car. DOME Coach. No checked baggage handled on this train.

CHAPTER 13

The Milwaukee Road Super Domes

The Milwaukee Road purchased 10 Full length Dome Lounge Cars from Pullman Standard in 1952 for operation on three of the Hiawathas. The cars were equipped with 68 Dome Seats and 28 seats in the lower level room. The lower level room is designated a Cafe Lounge on the Milwaukee Road. They entered service in January, 1953.

Four of the cars were assigned to the Morning and Afternoon Twin Cities Hiawathas, and the remaining six to the Olympian Hiawatha. The 10 cars remained in the Twin Cities and Pacific North West service until 1957 when the Olympian Hi was combined with the eastbound Morning Hi and the westbound Afternoon Hi between Chicago and Minneapolis. At first the combined trains carried two Super Domes (and two Dining Cars) between Chicago and Minneapolis. Gradually this operation ceased, and the two spare Domes (as the result of the consolidation) were temporarily assigned to the Milwaukee Road – Union Pacific City of Denver. This operation continued until the City of Denver and City of Portland were combined between Chicago and Denver. The remaining eight continued their Chicago – Minneapolis – Seattle runs until the Olympian Hiawatha was discontinued on May 22, 1961. This meant that the Milwaukee Road has six spare Domes. From 1961 until their sale to the Canadian National in 1964, the Super Domes received various assignments that included Summer operation on the Challenger between Chicago and Los Angeles, service between Chicago and Madison, and also on trains 23, 27, 12 and 58 between Chicago and Milwaukee. At the end of 1964, six of the cars were sold to the Canadian National.

Since 1964, the four remaining Super Domes remained in a stable operation on the pair of Twin Cities Hiawathas until January 23, 1970, when the Afternoon Hi was discontinued. The Milwaukee Road then operated two Super Domes for the Morning Hi with the remaining two in storage until the inauguration of AMTRAK.

Although the Super Domes lacked see ahead visability, they were swell cars from which to view the Wisconsin Dells, the Wisconsin Driftless area, the Mississippi River Country, and the Rocky Mountains. They were purchased at a cost of $320,000 a piece and despite cut backs in Hiawatha service, the equipment had operated for 18 continuous years; a tribute to Pullman Standard's craftsmanship.

MILWAUKEE ROAD NO. 3, the Afternoon Twin Cities Hiawatha departs Chicago on its run to Minneapolis and St. Paul. The Super Dome, in nearly all instances, ran ahead of the dining car as is shown here. (J. W. Swanberg)

THE FIRST MILWAUKEE ROAD HIAWATHA was born in 1935. The train set passenger record after record and in 1939 became a double daily service between Chicago and the Twin Cities. Meanwhile, the Olympian achieved Hiawatha status in 1947. Five years later, three of the six Hi's received Super Dome lounge cars for service between Chicago, Milwaukee, St. Paul, Minneapolis, Seattle and Tacoma. The three Hiawathas, the Morning and Afternoon Twin Cities and the Olympian, traveled through some of America's finest scenery, such as the Wisconsin Dells shown here. (The Milwaukee Road)

MILWAUKEE ROAD NO. 5 departs from the new Milwaukee Road depot beneath Milwaukee's high-level bridge. There are but two more trips and then the fleet Indian will be temporarily discontinued for this is April 28, 1971, and AMTRAK is just around the bend. From the rear are parlor car "Wisconsin Valley," diner No. 125 and Super Dome No. 59. (Jim Scribbins)

TOP PHOTO – The Milwaukee Road purchased 10 Super Dome Lounge cars in 1952 from Pullman Standard. They were originally operated on the Olympian and Twin Cities Hiawathas. Two of the ten cars remained in the Twin Cities service until May 1, 1971.

LOWER LEFT – Interior of the Cafe Lounge section of the Super Dome Lounge car.

LOWER RIGHT – Interior of the dome section of the Milwaukee Road lounge cars. (All photos – The Milwaukee Road)

THE SUPER DOMELINER, the Olympian Hiawatha (train No. 16), swings around a curve as it picks up speed behind Little Joe electric No. E20. The train, with its mixed consist of maroon and orange and UP yellow color scheme passenger equipment, will soon by pulling into Three Forks, Montana. The Olympian Hiawatha was nearly always assigned just one Super Dome lounge car, which was coupled ahead of the diner for the use of both coach and Pullman passengers. (Dick Steinheimer)

A LONE PASSENGER WAITS on the platform of the Ringling, Montana depot as train No. 15, the Olympian Hiawatha, rolls in behind rebuilt General Electric power, the E-22 A and B. The time is 1956. (Dick Steinheimer)

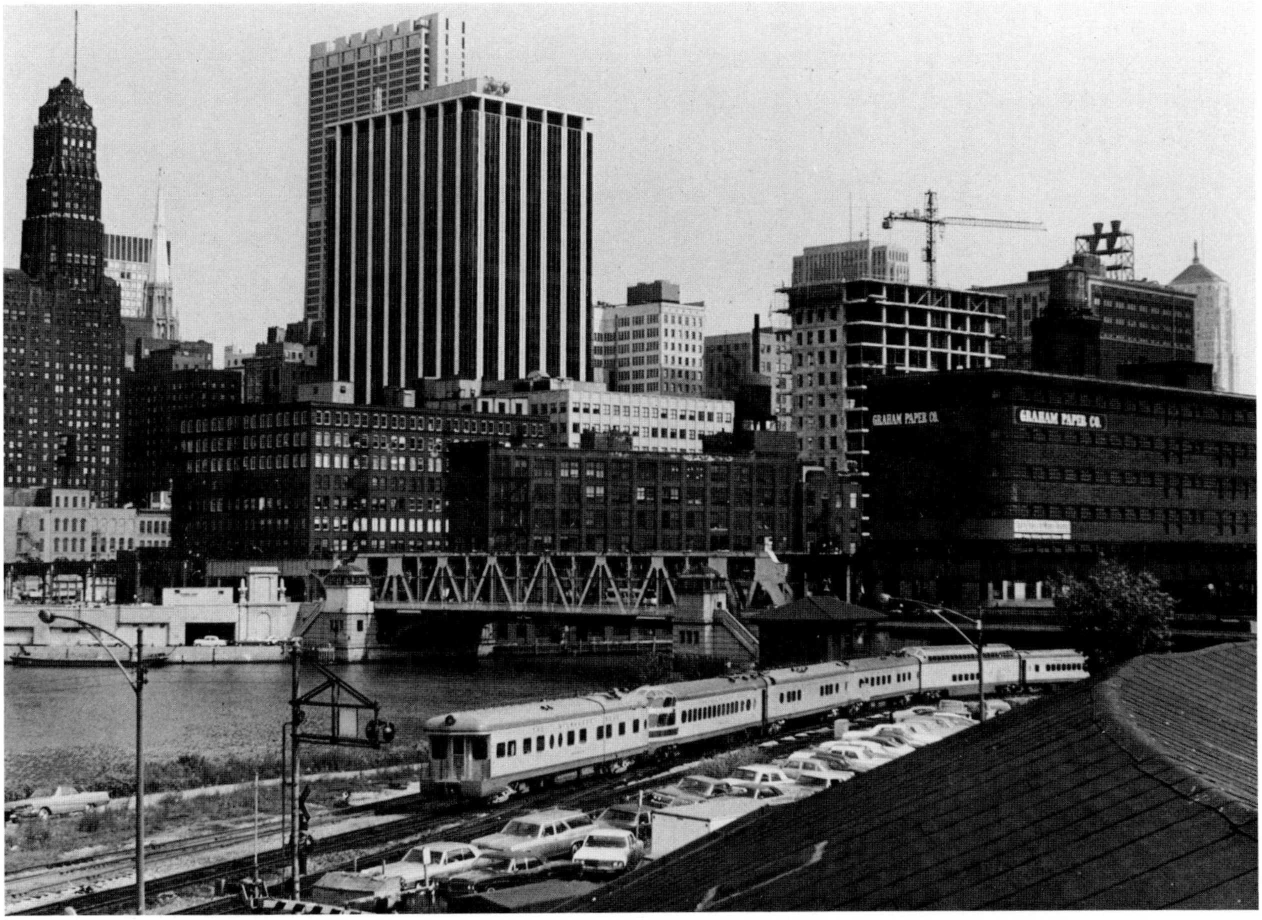

MILWAUKEE ROAD NO. 6, the Morning Twin Cities Hiawatha, arrives Chicago with a Super Dome, a dining car, a tap lounge car, parlor observation and a business car on the rear of the Super Domeliner. (John H. Kuehl)

THE FINAL WESTBOUND run of the Milwaukee Road's No. 5 departs Chicago on that "enigmatic" April 30, 1971. The next day, the Empire Builder began running on virtually the Hiawatha's old time schedule to Minneapolis. (John H. Kuehl)

SUPER DOME NO. 59 did the honors on April 30, 1971 for domeliner service on the last Hiawatha to depart Chicago prior to AMTRAK. (John H. Kuehl)

ROUTE'S OF THE SUPER DOMES

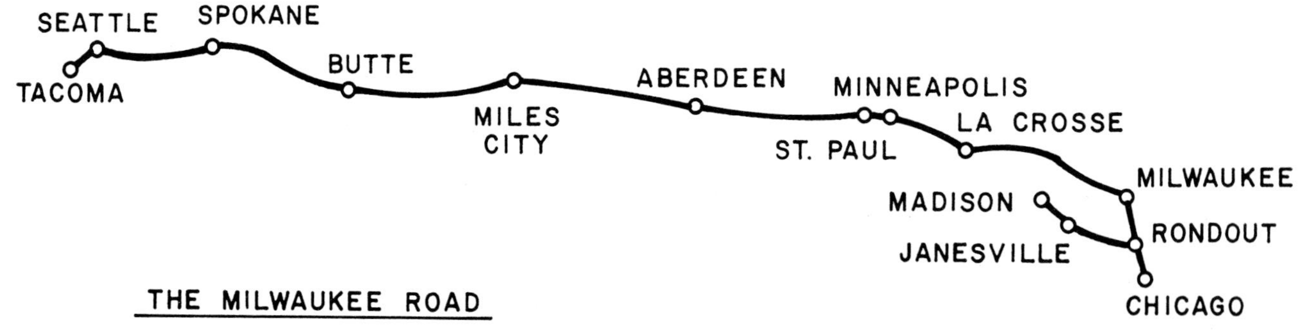

Drawn By: Sy Dykhouse III

Condensed Schedules between Chicago and Seattle-Tacoma
Super Dome Olympian HIAWATHA

No Extra Fare

A new TRAVEL DINE SLEEP *package* on the Olympian HIAWATHA between Chicago and the Pacific Northwest.

TRAVEL This Travel-Dine-Sleep package applies to all accommodations including berths, roomettes and bedrooms.

DINE The advance purchase of meal coupons permits a selection from the REGULAR menu at ONE-THIRD savings.

SLEEP A coach ticket entitles you to a soft reclining seat with adjustable leg-rests. It will also be honored in Lower and Upper berths which have been reduced 15% in price.

ASK YOUR TRAVEL AGENT for DETAILS

READ DOWN — READ UP

Olympian Hiawatha 15 Daily one day for example		Table A	Olympian Hiawatha 16 Daily one day for example	
		Union Station		
1.00 PM	Sun.	Lv Chicago . . . . *Central Standard Time* Ar	2.55 PM	Tue.
2.23 PM	"	Lv Milwaukee . . . . Ar	1.25 PM	"
5.22 PM	"	Lv LaCrosse . . . . Ar	10.10 AM	"
7.47 PM	"	Lv St. Paul Lv	8.05 AM	"
8.15 PM	"	Ar Minneapolis Lv	7.30 AM	"
8.40 PM	"	Lv Minneapolis . . . . Ar	6.35 AM	"
2.00 AM	Mon.	Lv Aberdeen . . . . Ar	1.05 AM	"
2.35 AM	"	Lv Mobridge . . *Mountain Standard Time* Ar	10.35 PM	Mon.
8.05 AM	"	Lv Miles City Lv	5.20 PM	"
11.30 AM	"	Lv Harlowton Lv	1.50 PM	"
1.57 PM	"	Ar Three Forks Lv	10.48 AM	"
①	"	Ar / Lv Gallatin Gateway▲ . . . . Entrance Yellowstone Park Lv / Ar	①	"
1.57 PM	"	Lv Three Forks . . . . Ar	10.48 AM	"
3.50 PM	"	Ar Butte Lv	9.05 AM	"
4.55 PM	"	Ar Deer Lodge Lv	8.15 AM	"
6.20 PM	"	Ar Missoula Lv	6.33 AM	"
8.45 PM	"	Lv Avery . . . . *Pacific Standard Time* Ar	2.15 AM	"
11.59 PM	"	Ar Spokane Lv	11.05 PM	Sun.
7.55 AM	Tue.	Ar Seattle Lv	3.30 PM	"
9.00 AM	"	Ar Tacoma Lv	2.15 PM	"

① During Yellowstone Park Season only. See table 15

EQUIPMENT

All Cars are air-conditioned

Olympian HIAWATHA—Nos. 15 and 16

Between Chicago and Seattle-Tacoma

Pullman Sleeping Cars
10 Roomettes—6 Double Bedrooms (151) (161)

Pullman Touralux Sleeping Cars
14 Sections (A-15) (A-16)

Dining Car

Super Dome Car with Cafe Lounge
Beverage Service

Reclining Seat Lounge Coaches
with leg rests (154-155) (164-165)

Between Minneapolis and Seattle-Tacoma

Pullman Sleeping Cars
8 Double Bedroom Skytop Lounge (150) (160)

All Coach seats reserved

Super Dome Cars open to all passengers, no additional charge.

Source: Milw. Rd. Time Table
Sept. 25, 1960

Condensed Schedules between Chicago—Milwaukee—St. Paul—Minneapolis

READ DOWN — READ UP

57 Daily	▲55 Daily	The Pioneer Limited 1 Daily	Afternoon Hiawatha 3 Daily	Morning Hiawatha 5 Daily	**Table A** *Central Time*	Morning Hiawatha 6 Daily	▲58 Daily	Afternoon Hiawatha ●2 Daily	The Fast Mail 56 Daily	The Pioneer Limited 4 Daily
	PM	PM	PM	AM	*Union Station*	PM	PM	PM	AM	AM
Does not carry passengers (See Table 1)	11.30	10.30	12.35	10.30	Lv **Chicago** .... Ar	2.45	9.40	7.25	5.00	7.45
	....	① 10.55	① 12.56	① 10.52	Lv Glenview .... Ar	① 2.20	① 9.05	① 6.59	① 4.18	① 7.14
	1.20	12.14	1.58	12.01	Lv **Milwaukee** .... Ar	1.20	7.25	5.55	3.00	5.40
	2.20	② 1.05	2.40	12.54	Lv Watertown Lv	12.22	6.20	5.09	f 2.05	....
	2.42	② 1.25	2.59	1.15	Lv Columbus Lv	12.04	5.54	4.51	1.47	....
	3.45	2.05	3.25	1.47	Lv Portage Lv	11.39	5.20	4.27	1.15	4.00
	4.52	2.55	4.02	f 2.33	Lv New Lisbon Lv	....	3.52	3.47	....	3.05
	7.15	4.20	4.55	3.47	Lv La Crosse Lv	10.13	1.45	2.55	11.05	2.00
	8.00	4.55	5.26	4.21	Lv Winona Lv	9.39	12.35	2.20	10.10	1.12
	9.30	6.03	6.28	5.31	Lv Red Wing Lv	8.43	11.10	1.18	9.02	12.03
	10.40	7.00	7.15	6.25	Ar **St. Paul** Lv	8.05	10.10	12.40	8.15	11.20
	11.30	8.00	7.50	7.10	Ar **Minneapolis** Lv	7.30	9.20	12.15	7.25	10.40
	AM	AM	PM	PM	*Milwaukee Road Station*	AM	AM	PM	PM	PM

① Stops to take or leave revenue passengers for or from Milwaukee or beyond. Does not carry passengers locally Chicago to Glenview or from Glenview to Chicago. Consult suburban timetable for service between these stations.

② Stops to take or leave revenue passengers.
f Stops on signal to take or leave revenue passengers.
● Does not carry checked baggage or dogs.
▲ Does not carry checked baggage or dogs between Chicago and Milwaukee.

EQUIPMENT

All cars are air-conditioned
Super Dome Cars open to all passengers. No additional charge.

WESTBOUND

THE PIONEER LIMITED

No. 1

From Chicago-Milwaukee to St. Paul-Minneapolis
Pullman Sleeping Cars
Duplex Roomettes, Roomettes and Double Bedrooms
Dining Car Service
A la carte or club breakfast
Buffet Service and Beverages
Reclining Seat Lounge Coaches

Note: *Sleeping Cars ready for occupancy in Chicago at 9:30 pm. Coaches 10:00 pm.*

THE AFTERNOON HIAWATHA

No. 3

From Chicago to St. Paul-Minneapolis
Skytop Lounge Drawing Room Parlor Car
Dining Car
Super Dome Car with Cafe Lounge (*Beverage Service*)
Reclining Seat Lounge Coaches
Connecting Bus Columbus to Madison

THE MORNING HIAWATHA

No. 5

From Chicago to St. Paul-Minneapolis
Skytop Lounge Drawing Room Parlor Car
Buffeteria Dining Car (*Economy Meals*)
Super Dome Car with Cafe Lounge (*Beverage Service*)
Reclining Seat Lounge Coaches
Connecting Bus Columbus to Madison

No. 55

From Chicago to St. Paul-Minneapolis
Reclining Seat Lounge Coaches

EASTBOUND

THE AFTERNOON HIAWATHA

No. 2

From Minneapolis-St. Paul to Chicago
Skytop Lounge Drawing Room Parlor Car
Dining Car
Super Dome Car with Cafe Lounge (*Beverage Service*)
Reclining Seat Lounge Coaches
Connecting Bus Columbus to Madison
Note: Does not carry checked baggage or dogs.

THE PIONEER LIMITED

No. 4

From Minneapolis-St. Paul to Chicago
Pullman Sleeping Cars
Duplex Roomettes, Roomettes and Double Bedrooms
Dining Car Service
A la carte or club breakfast
Buffet Service and Beverages
Reclining Seat Lounge Coaches

Note: *Sleeping Cars ready for occupancy in Minneapolis 9:30 pm.*

THE MORNING HIAWATHA

No. 6

From Minneapolis-St. Paul to Chicago
Skytop Lounge Drawing Room Parlor Car
Buffeteria Dining Car (*Economy Meals*)
Super Dome Car with Cafe Lounge (*Beverage Service*)
Reclining Seat Lounge Coaches
Connecting bus Columbus to Madison

No. 56

From Minneapolis-St. Paul to Chicago
Reclining Seat Lounge Coaches

No. 58

From Minneapolis-St. Paul to Milwaukee
Reclining Seat Lounge Coaches
From Milwaukee to Chicago
Reclining Seat Lounge Coaches

Source: Milwaukee Road Time Table
April 28, 1968

CHAPTER 14

The Canadian Pacific Scenic Domes

In late 1954, the Canadian Pacific Railway purchased 36 Vista Domes (The CPR designated them Scenic Domes.) from the Budd Company. Half of the cars are Coffee Shop-Coaches and the others are Dome Lounge Observation Sleeping cars named in the Park Series. Initially the equipment was assigned to both the Canadian and the Dominion. Each set of equipment for both trains carried one Dome Coffee Shop and one Dome Sleeper between Montreal and Vancouver. The Toronto section carried a Dome Coffee Shop-Coach between Toronto and Sudbury. This operation has continued on the Canadian through 1972. The Canadian has been called the California Zephyr of Canada, and it certainly is one of the most beautiful trains, inside and out, on the North American continent.

The Dominion carried Domes between Montreal, Toronto and Vancouver on a year around basis until the early 1960's. At that time, through Sleeping Car, Dining and Dome Car service was discontinued during the off season between Toronto, Montreal and the West Coast. The off season Dominion carried a Dome Coffee Shop-Coach between Montreal and Winnipeg, but simply operated a Buffet Coach west of Winnipeg. The spare Dome Cars were placed in service on the Frontenac and the Viger between Montreal and Quebec City. The Dome Sleeper Observation Lounges were operated as Parlor Cars. Such equipment was also in Parlor Car service on the Rideau between Montreal and Ottawa. At the same time, the Atlantic Limited received a Dome Coffee Shop-Coach between Montreal and St. John. During the Summer Months, the Dominion operated a full complement of Domes, Sleepers and Dining cars. This Summer and off season operation on the various trains mentioned above continued until 1966 when the Dominion was finally withdrawn from service.

One other train benefited from the Dominion's Domes, and that was the Soo Line's St. Paul – Vancouver train the Soo–Dominion and the Summer Season train, the Mountaineer. The Soo Line train carried through coaches and sleepers which were switched in to or out of the CP's Dominion at Moose Jaw, depending upon direction. Since the late 1950's, this became a May through September operation only and continued through the season of 1965. However, from 1963 on, the train operated via Winnipeg instead of Portal and was combined with the Winnipeger between St. Paul and Winnipeg.

With the Fall 1965 timetable, the CPR began operating Domes on two new trains between Montreal and Toronto, the Royal York, No. 21; and the Le Chateau Champlain, No. 22. Each train carried a Dome Sleeper as a Parlor Car and Dome Coffee Shop Coach. Effective with October, 1965 timetable, the Rideau continued to carry its Domes, but the Frontenac and the Viger lost their Domes to the new service. The Atlantic Limited continued to carry its Dome Coffee Shop Coach and did so through 1972.

Effective with the April, 1966 timetable the Montreal – Toronto service was discontinued.

TRAIN NO. 11, THE CANADIAN, departs Toronto with 10 cars for Sudbury, Ontario where it will be combined with train No. 1 for its transcontinental journey to Vancouver, British Columbia. (David B. Hanna)

THE

ROYAL YORK and LE CHATEAU CHAMPLAIN

Scenic Dome Stainless Steel Streamliners

ALL SPACE RESERVED—NO EXTRA FARE

For your added convenience, seats may be reserved for dinner in the deluxe Dining Room Car.

MONTREAL — OTTAWA — TORONTO

RDC Service Ottawa—Smiths Falls

THE ROYAL YORK 21 Daily	Miles	TABLE 20	LE CHÂTEAU CHAMPLAIN 22 Daily
5.00 PM	0.0	Lv...... MONTREAL Ⓜ ......Ar	10.45 PM
5.15 PM	4.7	.... Montreal West	10.30 PM
5.21 PM	9.6	.... Dorval	10.25 PM
6.56 PM	128.5	Ar...... Smiths Falls Ⓜ Lv	8.46 PM
♥ 261			♥ 262
5.30 PM	0.0	Lv...... Ottawa ......Ar	10.10 PM
5.37 PM	1.6	.... Hull	10.02 PM
5.40 PM	2.3	.... Hull West	9.57 PM
5.44 PM	3.9	.... Ottawa West	9.51 PM
6.01 PM	18.1	.... Stittville	9.31 PM
6.17 PM	31.6	.... Carleton Place	9.16 PM
6.20 PM	31.6	.... Carleton Place	9.15 PM
6.40 PM	48.7	Ar...... Smiths Falls Lv	8.55 PM
7.00 PM	128.5	Lv...... Smiths Falls ......Ar	8.43 PM
10.30 PM	334.5	.... Leaside	5.10 PM
10.45 PM	340.0	Ar...... TORONTO Ⓜ ......Lv Royal York Hotel	5.00 PM

Source: CPR Time Table Oct. 31, 1965

The Canadian

CP Rail

Scenic Dome Stainless Steel Streamliner
Voitures Modernes En Acier Inoxydable à Dôme Panoramique

All Space Reserved — No Extra Fare
Toutes Places Réservées Sans Frais Additionnels

For your added convenience, seats may be reserved for dinner in the deluxe Dining Room car.

Montréal to | à Vancouver 71 hrs. 30 min.
Toronto to | à Vancouver 68 hrs. 15 min.

Pour plus de commodité, vous pouvez réserver vos sièges pour le dîner dans la voiture-restaurant.

Vancouver to | à Montréal 70 hrs. 50 min.
Vancouver to | à Toronto 67 hrs. 10 min.

Westward / Vers l'ouest							***Eastward / Vers l'est***		
The Canadian Daily Quotidien	Example Exemple	Miles Milles	Altitude	***1***			Miles Milles	***The Canadian*** Daily Quotidien	Example Exemple
No. 1									
14 15	Fri. Ven.	0.0	110	Dp.........	Montréal	ET/HE....Ar	2878.5	19 50	Mon. Lun.
z 14 21	"	2.0	152	Dp.........	Westmount	........Ar	2876.5	z 19 43	"
z 14 27	"	4.7	157	Dp.........	Montreal West	........Ar	2873.8	z 19 35	"
z 14 33	"	9.5	89	Dp.........	Dorval	........Ar	2868.9	z 19 25	"
16 20	"	109.0	214	Ar.........	Ottawa	........Ar	2769.5	17 25	"
x 17 20	"	140.2	450	Ar.........	Carleton Place	........Ar	2738.3	x 16 40	"
x 17 47	"	163.6	300	Ar.........	Arnprior	........Ar	2714.9	x 16 12	"
x 18 12	"	181.9	416	Ar.........	Renfrew	........Ar	2696.6	x 15 45	"
x 18 57	"	216.6	380	Ar.........	Pembroke	........Ar	2661.9	x 15 08	"
19 35	"	238.4	523	Ar.........	Chalk River	........Ar	2640.1	14 35	"
22 12	"	355.7	662	Ar.........	North Bay	........Ar	2522.8	11 40	"
00 01	Sat. Sam.	434.7	857	Ar.........	Sudbury	........Dp	2443.8	10 05	"
No. 11								No. 12	
17 30	Fri. Ven.	0.0	254	Dp.........	Toronto	........Ar	2703.6	16 10	Mon. Lun.
z 17 45	"	4.5	393	Dp.........	West Toronto	........Ar	2699.1	z 15 50	"
20 38	"	131.4	790	Ar.........	MacTier	........Ar	2572.2	13 10	"
21 14	"	154.5	686	Ar.........	Parry Sound	........Ar	2549.1	12 31	"
23 40	Fri. Ven.	259.7	857	Ar.........	Sudbury	........Dp	2443.8	10 10	"
No. 1								No 2	
00 50	Sat. Sam.	434.7	857	Dp.........	Sudbury	........Ar	2443.8	09 25	"
01 40	"	468.7	1378	Ar.........	Cartier	........Ar	2409.8	08 35	"
04 50	"	605.1	1412	Ar.........	Chapleau	........Ar	2273.4	05 05	"
x 06 42	"	663.0	1097	Ar.........	Missanabie	........Ar	2215.5	x 03 30	"
08 20	"	735.0	1225	Ar.........	White River	........Ar	2143.5	01 37	"
x 08 56	"	756.2	1200	Ar.........	Regan	........Ar	2122.3	x 01 00	Mon. Lun.
09 50	"	798.0	703	Ar.........	Marathon	........Ar	2080.5	x 23 59	Sun. Dim.
x 11 12	"	844.9	896	Ar.........	Terrace Bay	........Ar	2033.3	x 22 47	"
11 28	"	853.3	996	Ar.........	Schreiber	........Ar	2025.2	22 20	"
x 13 00	"	916.6	682	Ar.........	Nipigon	........Ar	1961.9	x 20 55	"
x 13 09	"	921.6	642	Ar.........	Red Rock	........Ar	1956.9	x 20 47	"
14 30	"	981.4	614	Ar.........	Port Arthur ✢	........Ar	1896.7	19 30	"
14 50	"	985.8	617	Ar.........	Fort William ✢	ET/HE....Ar	1892.3	19 00	"
16 55	"	1133.0	1486	Ar.........	Ignace	CT/HC...Ar	1745.1	15 02	"
18 10	"	1196.7	1224	Ar.........	Dryden	........Ar	1681.8	13 51	"
19 54	"	1279.2	1091	Ar.........	Kenora	........Ar	1598.9	12 00	"
22 25	"	1404.9	772	Ar.........	Winnipeg	........Ar	1473.2	09 05	"
23 59	Sat. Sam.	1460.5	858	Ar.........	Portage la Prairie	........Ar	1417.6	07 55	"
x 01 18	Sun. Dim.	1526.7	1225	Ar.........	Douglas (Base Shilo)	......Ar	1351.4	x 06 48	"
01 37	"	1538.0	1204	Ar.........	Brandon	........Ar	1340.1	06 25	"
x 02 23	"	1585.2	1451	Ar.........	Virden	........Ar	1292.9	x 05 30	"
04 15	"	1668.9	1968	Ar.........	Broadview	........Ar	1209.2	04 00	"
06 00	"	1762.4	1896	Ar.........	Regina	........Ar	1116.8	01 50	"
07 02	"	1797.2	1779	Ar.........	Moose Jaw	........Ar	1075.2	00 51	Sun. Dim.
09 17	"	1914.4	2432	Ar.........	Swift Current	CT/HC...Ar	964.8	22 50	Sat. Sam.
11 00	"	2061.8	2181	Ar.........	Medicine Hat	MT/HR..Ar	817.4	18 45	"
14 30	"	2237.6	3439	Ar.........	Calgary	........Ar	641.6	15 10	"
17 05	"	2319.5	4534	Ar.........	Banff	........Ar	559.7	13 05	"
18 05	"	2354.2	5044	Ar.........	Lake Louise	........Ar	525.0	12 18	"
18 00	"	2374.2	4072	Ar.........	Field	PT/HP....Ar	505.0	10 15	"
19 27	"	2409.2	2583	Ar.........	Golden	........Ar	470.0	08 55	"
22 40	Sun. Dim.	2499.9	1494	Ar.........	Revelstoke	........Ar	379.3	05 35	"
00 49	Mon. Lun.	2563.1	1157	Ar.........	Salmon Arm	........Ar	315.9	03 38	"
02 45	"	2628.2	1159	Ar.........	Kamloops	........Ar	250.5	01 40	Sat. Sam.
06 50	"	2749.7	493	Ar.........	North Bend	........Ar	129.0	21 45	Fri. Ven.
08 51	"	2808.6	59	Ar.........	Agassiz	........Ar	70.1	19 50	"
09 29	"	2837.0	26	Ar.........	Mission City	........Ar	41.7	19 10	"
10 05	"	2861.6	39	Ar.........	Coquitlam (New Westminster)	........Ar	16.5	18 32	"
10 45	"	2878.7	18	Ar.........	Vancouver	PT/HP. .Dp	0.0	18 00	Fri. Ven.

Explanation of signs—Explication des symboles page 2

Equipment

Regularly assigned cars all AIR-CONDITIONED

Scenic-Dome Lounge Slee with Drawing Room and Bedrooms.

Scenic-Dome Coffee Shop.

Standard Sleeping Cars wit Drawing Rooms, Compartm Bedrooms, Roomettes, Duplex Roomettes, Berths.

Coaches with reserved seat

Dining Room Car.

Matériel

Les voitures régulières entièrement CLIMATISÉ

Voiture-dôme avec salon-li et chambres.

Voiture-dôme restaurant.

Voitures-lits avec salon-lits, compartiments, chambres, chambrettes, chambrettes duplex, lits ordinaires.

Voitures-coach avec sièges réservés.

Voiture-restaurant.

Printed in Canada
Imprimé au Canada

Source: Canadian Pacific Time Ta
October 26, 1969

CHAPTER 15

The Canadian National Sceneramic Domes

The Canadian National Railways purchased six Milwaukee Road Domes series 50 thru 54 and 56 in 1964. The cars were then refurbished, renumbered 2400 thru 2405 and named. The equipment initially went into service westbound on the Super Continental between Jasper and Vancouver, and eastbound from Vancouver to Edmonton. On the Panorama, the westbound operation was from Edmonton to Vancouver and eastbound from Vancouver to Jasper. The Sceneramic Domes remained in this method of operation except during the Summers, when because of the two section operation of the Super Continental, the Domes ran only between Vancouver and Jasper.

In October of 1965, the Sceneramic Domes were operated from Winnipeg to Edmonton and from Saskatoon to Winnipeg on the Super Continental. The Panorama's Dome ran from Edmonton to Vancouver westbound and from Vancouver to Saskatoon eastbound. During the Summer of 1966, the Domes again resumed their Jasper-Edmonton-Vancouver operation as described in the first paragraph of this chapter.

During the Winter Season schedule from October, 1966 to April, 1967 some changes were placed in the operation of the Dome Cars. First of all, the Sceneramic Domes were removed from the Super Continental and operated on the Panorama only between Winnipeg and Vancouver in both directions. The Super Continental was still a Domeliner with the addition of the B&O Sleeper Dome between Edmonton and Vancouver in both directions. The Summer of 1967 saw the Sceneramic Domes operating between Edmonton and Vancouver on the Montreal section of the Super Continental and between the same points on the Panorama. The B&O Sleeper Dome operated on the Toronto Section of the Super Continental between Edmonton and Vancouver in both directions.

The Winter of 1967-1968 saw the removal of both types of Domes from the Super Continental, and the Panorama became the exclusive Domeliner of the CNR with the Sceneramic Domes operating on a daily basis between Winnipeg and Vancouver. However, the Summer 1968 timetable brought about another equipment change. This time, both sections of the Super Continental carried the Scenaramic Domes between Edmonton and Vancouver. The B&O Dome Sleepers did not operate that Summer and went back east. The Panorama was no longer a Domeliner. The 1969 timetable showed the former Super Domes operating on both trains between Edmonton and Vancouver only.

January, 1970 brought about the discontinuance of the Panorama, and a new operating procedure (according to the public timetables) was set up by the CNR for the Sceneramic Domes. From January 7 through June 16 and from September 10 until the end of the year, the Dome Cars operated between Edmonton and Vancouver. However, from June 17 through

September 9, the Domes operated on the Toronto Section of the Super Continental. The operation in 1971 was similar to the 1970 procedure.

The Domes were purchased because of the Canadian National's never-ending effort to lure passengers back to the rails. Although the CNR lured passengers from the V-8 and the Jet by the thousands, the Road was unable to secure a profit picture. As of the present time, the Domes are still operating and as long as the Super Continental remains a popular train, they will probably remain in service to provide thousands of passengers with spectacular mountain scenery.

THE CANADIAN NATIONAL purchased six Super Domes from the Milwaukee Road in 1964. The six cars were completely refurbished inside and out and many of the dome seats were replaced with a club lounge section. (Canadian National)

THE EASTBOUND SUPER CONTINENTAL with the dome car "Jasper" rolls through a rock cut near Jasper, Alberta on the Canadian National main line. (Canadian National)

THE EASTBOUND SUPER CONTINENTAL near Hope, British Columbia. Notice the mixed consist of streamlined and standard passenger equipment in this transcontinental domeliner. (Canadian National)

THE INTERIOR OF THE former Milwaukee Road dome lounge has been modified extensively by the Canadian National. Many of the former coach type seats have been replaced with easy chairs, sofas and table seating for more extensive club lounge service. Interior colors are varied and the new arrangement in very attractive and restful. (Canadian National)

THE SHASTA Daylight rolls out of Martinez, California, in the early morning mist past oil refineries and toward a date with Portland, Oregon. No. 10's consist of this particular morning includes both Daylight colors and the two tone grey schemes. The single dome lounge will provide the ultimate in viewing as the train glides through the Cascades and other mountain ranges, not to mention the majestic "Mount Shasta." (Dick Steinheimer)

COAST LINE

SAN FRANCISCO — OAKLAND — SAN JOSE — SALINAS — SANTA BARBARA — VENTURA — LOS ANGELES

Elev	SOUTHBOUND Read Down Del Monte No. 126 Daily	Lark No. 76 Daily	Coast Daylight No. 98 Daily	No. 112 Daily	Mls.		NORTHBOUND Read Up Coast Daylight No. 99 Daily	No. 153 Daily	Lark No. 75 Daily	Del Monte No. 141 Daily
9	....	**8 30**	7 45	....	0	Lv Oakland (16th St.) ⊕	**7 30**	....	9 05	....
13	....	**8 50**	8 15	....	6	Ar San Francisco (3rd St.) ⊕	**7 10**	....	8 40	....
13	**4 50**	**9 00**	8 25	7 15	0	Lv SAN FRANCISCO (3rd St.) ....Ar	**7 00**	**8 40**	8 30	11 25
27	**5 17**	**9 28**	....	7 39	16	Lv Burlingame Lv	....	**8 09**	7 59	10 54
23	....	....	....	7 42	18	Lv San Mateo Lv	....	**8 06**	....	10 50
11	....	....	....	7 56	25	Lv Redwood City Lv	....	**7 51**	....	10 35
61	**5 39**	**9 57**	9 02	8 05	30	Lv Palo Alto Lv	**6 19**	**7 42**	7 37	10 23
99	**6 05**	**10 15**	9 19	8 35	47	Ar San Jose Lv	**5 59**	**7 20**	7 13	9 55
99	**6 10**	**10 28**	9 26 ↩		47	Lv SAN JOSE ....Ar	**5 53**	↩	6 55	9 44
193	**6 41**	....	....		77	Lv Gilroy Lv	....		....	9 12
22	**7 07**	**11 29**	....		97	Ar Watsonville Jct. Lv	....		5 48	8 46
22	**7 08**	**11 35**	....		97	Lv Watsonville Jct. ....Ar	....		5 40	8 44
21	**7 22**	....	....		107	Ar Castroville Lv	....		....	8 33
91	*f*7 39	↓	↓		0	Lv ORD (Fort Ord) .Lv	↑	↑	↑	*f*8 14
19	*f*				4	Lv Seaside Lv				*f*
9	*f*				6	Lv Del Monte Lv				*f*
6	**8 00**				7	Ar Monterey Lv				8 00
47	**8 10**				9	Ar Pacific Grove△ .Lv				7 45
21	**‡9▲19**	....	....		107	Lv Castroville ....Ar			....	†8▲08
45	**‡9▲35**	12 05	10 49		114	Ar SALINAS Lv	**4 36**		5 19	†7▲53
724	....	1 46	....		212	Lv Paso Robles Lv	....		3 29	....
240	....	3 08	**1 30**		248	Ar San Luis Obispo Lv	**1 56**		2 25	....
240	....	3 18	**1 38**		248	Lv SAN LUIS OBISPO Ar	**1 48**		2 15	....
82	....	*f*3 50	....		273	Lv Guadalupe Lv	....		*f*1 28	....
50	....	*f*4 20	....		299	Lv Surf Lv	....		12*f*55	....
15	....	5 36	**3 46**		367	Ar Santa Barbara Lv	11 34		**11 44**	....
15	....	5 43	**3 51**		367	Lv SANTA BARBARA Ar	11 30		**11 34**	....
51	....	6 26	....		394	Lv Ventura Lv	....		**10 45**	....
53	....	6 41	**4 37**		404	Lv Oxnard Lv	10 38		**10 23**	....
432	....	8 05	**5 45**		464	Lv Glendale Lv	9 35		**9 20**	....
297	....	8 30	**6 15**		470	Ar LOS ANGELES Lv	9 15		**9 00**	....

FREQUENT COMMUTATION SERVICE IS PROVIDED BETWEEN SAN FRANCISCO, SAN JOSE AND INTERMEDIATE STATIONS

NOTE A—For California intrastate passengers, Reserved Seat Charge of $1.00 is made for each chair car seat occupied by adult or child of any age between San Francisco and Los Angeles; proportionate charges to and from intermediate points.

All P.M. time in dark faced figures.

⊕-Bus service between San Francisco 3rd Street Station, and Oakland 16th St. Terminal via the Bay Bridge, affording a panoramic view of the San Francisco Bay area.

▲-Western Greyhound Lines Bus.

†—S. P. Station.

‡—W.G.L. Station.—Passengers to make their own arrangements between the W. G. L. and S. P. Depots.

△-Taxi Service furnished between Monterey and Pacific Grove, 216 Grand Avenue.

f—Flag stop to entrain or detrain passengers.

XS—Daily except Saturday.

XSH—Daily except Sunday and Holidays.

TRAINS 98-99 STREAMLINER COAST DAYLIGHT

Chair Cars: San Francisco-Los Angeles. Porter service.
For California Intrastate Passengers only Chair Car Seats May be Reserved Nominal Charge. See Note A.
Meal and Beverage Service: San Francisco-Los Angeles.
(Coffee Shop and Dome-Lounge service during summer season.)
Parlor Car: San Francisco-Los Angeles. (Railroad owned.) Reservations required.
Baggage: No checked service to or from intermediate points.

TRAINS 75-76 STREAMLINER LARK

Sleeping Cars: San Francisco-Los Angeles. (Roomettes, Bedrooms.)
Meal and Beverage Service: San Francisco-Los Angeles. (Free Continental Breakfa[st] for Pullman Passengers.)
Chair Cars: San Francisco-Los Angeles.
For California Intrastate Passengers only Chair Car Seats May be Reserved Nominal Charge. See Note A.
Pillow service available at nominal charge.
Baggage: No checked service to or from Paso Robles, San Luis Obispo, Guadalupe, Surf.

TRAINS 126-141 DEL MONTE

Parlor Snack Lounge Car. (Reserved Seats). **Chair Cars.** No baggage service.

LOS ANGELES—SAN DIEGO—A. T. & S. F. Ry. Daily.

	74	76	78
Lv Los Angeles	7 30	11 00	**7 45**
Ar San Diego	10 25	**1 55**	**10 40**

	73	75	77
Lv San Diego	7 00	11 30	**4 00**
Ar Los Angeles	9 55	**2 25**	**6 55**

SALINAS—SANTA CRUZ—MONTEREY—PACIFIC GROVE
Western Greyhound Lines Bus (Daily)

7 53	**5 58**	Lv Salinas (S.P. Depot) ....Ar	9 37	‡9
8 32	**6 32**	Ar Watsonville (W. G. L. Sta.) Lv	9 01	8
9 10	**7 10**	Ar Santa Cruz (W. G. L. Sta.) Lv	8 30	8

‡4 50	‡8 00	10 55	**4 45**	Lv Salinas (S.P. Depot) ....Ar	‡7 45	10 20	**4 15**	‡7
5 15	8 25	....	....	Ar Ord (Fort Ord) Lv	7 20	....	....	7
5 30	8 45	....	....	Ar Seaside Lv	7 00	....	....	7
5 35	8 50	†11 30	**†5 25**	Ar Monterey Lv	6 55	†9 38	**†3 33**	7
‡5 45	‡9 00	11 43	**5 40**	Ar Pacific Grove Lv	6 45	9 30	**3 25**	6

MONTEREY—CARMEL

(**Bay Rapid Transit Co. Daily**) Purchase rail tickets to Monterey only.
15 minutes running time. Lv Monterey and Carmel approximately every hour betwe[en] 7:00 A.M. and 5:00 P.M. Sun. thru Thurs.; 7:00 A.M. and 10:00 P.M. Fri. and Sat.

OAKLAND-SAN JOSE BUS VIA SAN LEANDRO

Peerless Stages, Oakland Depot 20th and San Pablo. Rail Tickets honored.

Daily	XS	Daily	XSH		Daily	Daily	Daily
7 00	**6 30**	8 20	7 15	Lv OAKLAND (20th-San Pablo) ....Ar	10 20	7 15	**11 15**
....	**6 46**	8 30	7 30	Lv Fruitvale Lv	....	....	*f*
....	**7 01**	....	7 45	Lv San Leandro Lv	....	**6 52**	*f*
7 25	**7 15**	8 45	8 02	Lv Hayward Lv	9 55	**6 37**	**10 30**
....	**7 36**	....	8 23	Lv Centerville Lv	....	**6 12**	**10 00**
8 00	**8 15**	9 30	9 15	Ar SAN JOSE (W.G.L.) Lv	9 20	**5 30**	**9 30**

Source: Southern Pacific Time Tabl[e]
October 1, 1967

SAN JOAQUIN VALLEY

SAN FRANCISCO — SACRAMENTO — FRESNO — LOS ANGELES

SOUTHBOUND Read Down					NORTHBOUND Read Up		
Elev.		S. P. San Joaquin Daylight No. 52	Mls.	For connections to and from Shasta Route points see Shasta Route page.	S. P. San Joaquin Daylight No. 51		
6	....	8 00	0	Lv SAN FRANCISCO, SP 3rd St. St.⊕. Ar	7 05	....	......
10	....	8 30	6	Lv OAKLAND, S.P. 16th St. Station⊕... Ar	•6 35	....	......
18	....	8 39	9	Lv Berkeley........................ Ar	6 16	....	......
41	....	8 48	15	Lv Richmond........................ Ar	6 05	....	......
14	....	9 06	29	Lv Crockett........................ Lv	5 44	....	......
10	....	•9 22	35	Lv Martinez........................ Lv	5 34	....	......
31	....	9 38	49	Lv Pittsburg....................... Lv	5 13	....	......
64	....	10 16	82	Lv Tracy........................... Lv	4 40	....	......
42	....	8 50	0	Lv SACRAMENTO (Trains #54-53).. Ar	5 55	....	......
52	....	9 35	36	Lv Lodi............................ Lv	5 11	....	......
19	....	9 55	48	Lv Stockton........................ Lv	4 50	....	......
26	....	10 10	58	Ar Lathrop......................... Lv	4 30	....	......
26	....	10 26	93	Lv Lathrop......................... Lv	4 24	....	......
91	....	10 59	113	Lv Modesto......................... Lv	3 48	....	......
107	....	11 13	126	Lv Turlock......................... Lv	3 30	....	......
171	....	11 39	150	Lv Merced (To Yosemite)............ Lv	3 08	....	......
278	....	11 58	184	Lv Madera.......................... Lv	2 24	....	......
290	....	12 24	205	Ar Fresno.......................... Lv	1 59	....	......
290	....	12 32	205	Lv FRESNO.......................... Ar	1 52	....	......
282	....	1 22	250	Lv Tulare.......................... Lv	1 02	....	......
312	....	2 01	281	Lv Delano.......................... Lv	12 28	....	......
414	....	2 34	313	Ar Bakersfield..................... Lv	12 01	....	......
414	....	2 44	313	Lv BAKERSFIELD ♦................... Ar	11 50	....	......
3967	....	4 14	360	Lv Tehachapi....................... Lv	10 19	....	......
2751	....	4 47	380	Lv Mojave.......................... Lv	9 45	....	......
2352	....	5 17	405	Lv Lancaster....................... Lv	9 17	....	......
1165	....	f6 36	450	Lv Saugus.......................... Lv	f8 01	....	......
425	....	7 15	477	Lv Glendale........................ Lv	7 20	....	......
293	....	7 50	482	Ar LOS ANGELES, Union Pass. Term. 800 North Alameda Street....... Lv	7 00	....	......

YOSEMITE TRANSPORTATION SYSTEM (Daily)

3 30	1 00	0	Lv Merced (Via El Portal) (S.P. Station)............ Ar	11 05	1 55
6 10	3 40	82	Ar Yosemite Valley.............................. Lv	8 30	11 30

♦ORANGE BELT BUS (Daily) — Bakersfield-Barstow (Rail tickets honored)

2 15	Lv Bakersfield.......................... (S.P. Station).................	Ar	10 30
3 15	Lv Tehachapi...	Lv	9 30
3 40	Lv Mojave..	Lv	9 05
5 15	Ar Barstow............................ (AT&SF Station)...............	Lv	7 45

TICKETS HONORED—All rail tickets reading between San Francisco and Bakersfield and intermediate stations are optionally honored either via Southern Pacific or Santa Fe Ry.

•—Connection between San Joaquin Daylight and Cascade is made at Oakland for Northbound passengers and at Martinez for Southbound passengers. See Shasta Route page.

FOR FOOTNOTES COMMON TO ALL SOUTHERN PACIFIC SCHEDULES SEE SUNSET ROUTE PAGE.

TRAINS 51-53 — 52-54 STREAMLINER SAN JOAQUIN AND SACRAMENTO DAYLIGHTS

Subject to special "Daylight" charge for interstate travel (Consult agent for exceptions).

Chair Cars: San Francisco–Los Angeles.
Chair Cars: Sacramento–Los Angeles. (Passengers transfer at Lathrop.)

Seat Reservations: See Note A Sunset Route Page.

Automatic Buffet Car: San Francisco–Los Angeles.

Lounge Car: San Francisco–Los Angeles. (During Summer Season.)

Porter Service.

Baggage: Only California Intrastate checked baggage handled to and from scheduled stops, except Richmond. No remains to or from Glendale, Lancaster, Tehachapi, Delano, Tulare. See general notes on Sunset Route page.

All schedules subject to change without notice.

Source: Southern Pacific Time Table
June 22, 1969

CHAPTER 17

The Rio Grande's Royal Gorge

Besides operating the World Famous California Zephyr, the Denver Zephyr and the Colorado Eagle, The D&RGW operated four other trains over its lines that included Dome Cars – in this case the ex-Chessie Coach Lounge Dome Observations.

In September, 1949, the D&GRW purchased the three Coach Lounge Dome Observation cars built for the Chessie and placed them in service on the Royal Gorge between Denver and Salt Lake City. This train traveled by way of the famous Royal Gorge (The Canyon of the Arkansas River) and Tennessee Pass and treated its passengers to a 10 minute stop at the Hanging Bridge. On Feb. 11, 1950, Numbers 1 and 2 were combined with the Prospector (trains 7 and 8 which provided overnight service between Denver and Salt Lake City) between Grand Junction and Salt Lake City. Thus the Prospector became a Domeliner on the west end of its run. The running time for the Royal Gorge was nearly 24 hours for the 745.1 mile run. The train left Denver around 9:00 AM (also handling the Colorado Springs section of the Denver Zephyr) and arrived at Grand Junction around 10:30 PM. The westbound Prospector arrived at Grand Junction at about 2:00 AM. Number 1's equipment was then switched into No. 7 and the train rolled into Salt Lake City at about 9:00 AM. Eastbound No. 8 handled No. 2's equipment to Grand Junction where the trains were separated. Number 2 departed the Junction around 2:40 AM and arrived at Denver at 3:00 PM. The train also picked up the eastbound section of the DZ at Colorado Springs. The Royal Gorge also carried a Grill Lounge Car between Denver and Grand Junction.

between Denver and Grand Junction.

On November 5, 1964, the Royal Gorge was discontinued west of Salida, Colorado. The train also lost its Grill Lounge car at that time. In July, 1967, the Royal Gorge was discontinued altogether. The Colorade Springs section of the Denver Zephyr had been discontinued on January 1, 1967. Gone too was the Prospector. The only train service remaining besides the CZ was the Yampa Valley Mail, trains 9 and 10. The Yampa Valley Mail operated between Denver and Craig via the Moffat Tunnel Route. The Dome cars from old No. 1 and 2 were transferred to service on to 9 and 10 in 1966. The cars remained in operation until Sunday, April 7, 1968 when the Yampa Valley became a part of history. The three Dome cars were then sold by the Rio Grande to a firm in Omaha, who in turn sold one of the cars to a Florida Company and another was placed in Rock Island Railroad service. (See Chapter 20)

As of today (1972), the Rio Grande continues to operate a tri-weekly Domeliner, known as the Rio Grange Zephyr, between Denver and Salt Lake City. The Rio Grande did not join AMTRAK and continues to operate 17 and 18 as a connection train to the California Zephyr, (now San Francisco Zephyr) which operates over the OVERLAND ROUTE.

The ex-Chessie Dome Cars were a welcome addition to the Rio Grande trains that traveled through the rugged and beautiful Colorado Rockies. Few Dome passengers anywhere can (or could) be treated to the scenery that was traversed by Rio Grande Domeliner trains 1, 2, 7, 8, 9, 10, 17 and 18.

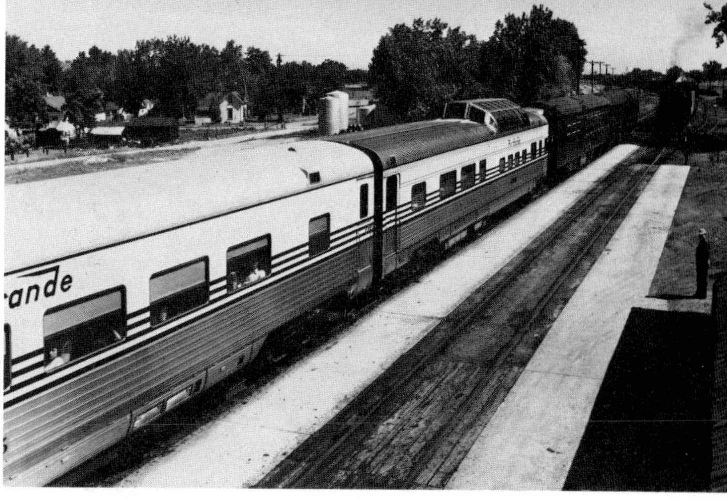

IN 1949 THE RIO GRANDE purchased the three dome observation lounge coaches built for the Chessie from the C&O. The D&RGW modified them for use on the Royal Gorge and numbered the cars 1248, 1249 and 1250. The cars were removed from regular service in 1968 and were very colorful in their Rio Grande color scheme. (Louis A. Marre & Gordon B. Mott)

ONE OF THE major modifications on the ex-C&O dome cars was the conversion of the cars for mid-train operation. The equipment as originally built had a tear drop end. The D&RGW built a short extension on the tear drop and added a diaphram. The cars could then be operated mid-train as shown here on the Royal Gorge with a standard dining car and chair car coupled on to the rear of the dome car. (State Historical Society of Colorado)

D&RGW TRAINS 1 AND 2, the Royal Gorge, each stopped for 10 minutes at the Hanging Bridge in the Royal Gorge of the Arkansas River so that passengers could take time to just "look" at God's work in the great State of Colorado. The ex-C&O dome cars were assigned to trains 1 and 2 between Denver and Salt Lake City. This photo shows the Royal Gorge behind 4 FT's with eight cars including one dome coach. (State Historical Society of Colorado)

THE STREAMLINED Prospector, trains 7 and 8, became domeliners on the west end of their runs between Grand Junction and Salt Lake City. This photo shows an 11 car consist with the Royal Gorge section cut in near the head-end of the train. The Prospector was an overnight run between Denver and Salt Lake City via the Moffat Tunnel Route. (State Historical Society of Colorado)

RIO GRANDE TRAIN NO. 1, the combined Royal Gorge and Denver Zephyr at Littleton, Colorado, in August, 1966. The first three cars make up the consist of the Royal Gorge section. The last five cars include two sleepers, one slumber-coach, one flat top coach and one dome coach for the Burlington Route's Colorado Springs section of the Denver Zephyr. (J. W. Swanberg)

THE YAMPA VALLEY MAIL with three cars including one dome coach at Plainview, Colorado, in a bright and sunny day in August, 1966. (J. W. Swanberg)

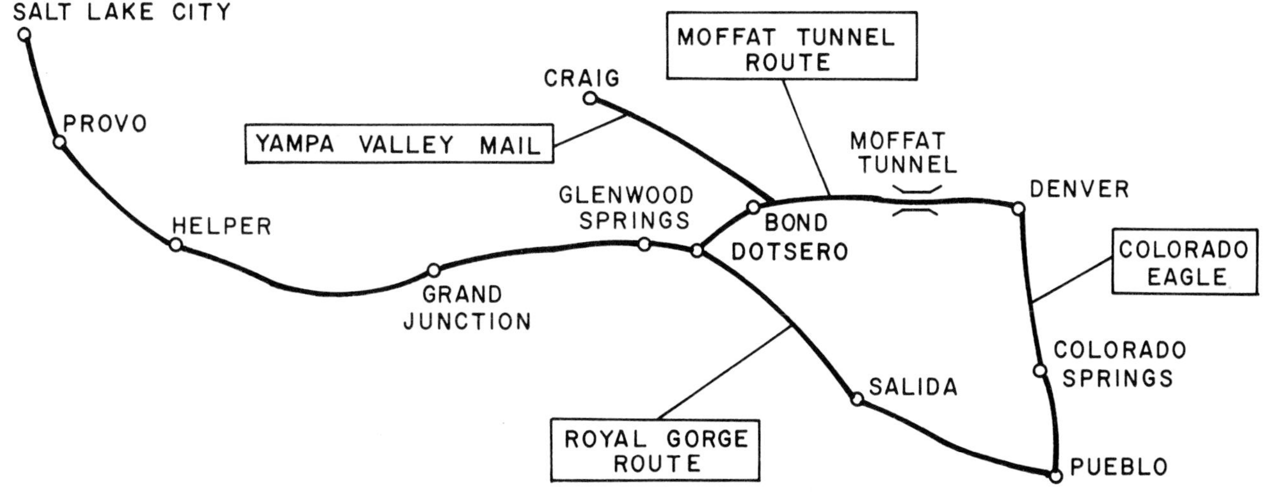

DENVER & RIO GRANDE WESTERN RAILROAD

Drawn By: Sy Dykhouse III

THE RIO GRANDE WAS ONE OF SIX RAILROADS that originally elected not to join AMTRAK and therefore, the California Zephyr (now the San Francisco Zephyr) was re-routed over the Union Pacific west of Denver. In place of the CZ, according to the law, the D&RGW operated the Rio Grande Zephyr on a tri-weekly basis between Denver and Salt Lake City. Here the Zephyr rolls out of Tunnel No. 1 near Plainview, Colorado with a consist that includes four ex-California Zephyr cars with the magnificent dome observation car on the rear end. The ex-CZ cars have been refurbished and do not carry the railroad's name on the letter board, but only D&RGW sub lettering in the corners. Despite the short consist compared to the CZ of old, the silver domeliner still makes a nice looking train. The photo was taken by Ronald C. Hill on October 23, 1971. (Carl Smith, Denver & Rio Grande Western Railroad Company)

ROUTE OF THE *Vista-Dome*

ROYAL GORGE

BETWEEN

DENVER • COLORADO SPRINGS • PUEBLO
GLENWOOD SPRINGS • GRAND JUNCTION
PROVO • SALT LAKE CITY

READ DOWN **See Page 9 for Equipment** READ UP

No. 1 Daily	Miles from Denver	Mountain Standard Time	No. 2 Daily
9 00 AM	0	Lv Denver, Colo. Ar	**3 00 PM**
10 50 "	75	Lv Colorado Springs, Colo. Lv	**1 10 "**
11 50 "	119	Ar Pueblo, Colo. Lv	**12 05 "**
12 15 PM	119	Lv Pueblo, Colo. Ar	11 45 AM
1 23 "	160	Lv Canon City, Colo. Lv	10 40 "
1 36 "	166	Ar Royal Gorge, Colo. Lv	10 27 "
Ten minute stop to view America's best loved travel wonder. Here is located Hanging Bridge, suspended between sheer canyon walls, just 30 feet apart. Above may be seen the World's Highest Bridge, across the Royal Gorge, 1,053 feet above the railroad tracks.			
1 46 PM	166	Lv Royal Gorge, Colo. Ar	10 17 AM
3 25 "	215	Lv Salida, Colo. Lv	9 00 "
f **5 15 "**	281	Lv Tennessee Pass, Colo. Lv	f 7 11 "
Cross the Continental Divide at Tennessee Pass, highest main-line standard gauge railroad in the United States.			
8 00 PM	360	Lv Glenwood Springs, Colo. Lv	4 40 AM
2 15 AM	450	Lv Grand Junction, Colo. Lv	2 40 "
5 34 "	619	Lv Price, Utah Lv	**8 42 PM**
7 59 "	701	Lv Provo, Utah Lv	**6 10 "**
8 55 "	745	Ar Salt Lake City, Utah Lv	**5 15 "**

EQUIPMENT

(All equipment is air-conditioned)

Nos. 1 and 2—THE ROYAL GORGE

(Diesel Power)

Grill-Lounge between Denver and Grand Junction. (Diner-Lounge between Grand Junction and Salt Lake City in Trains 7 and 8)

Vista Dome Chair Car between Denver and Salt Lake City. (In Trains 7 and 8 west of Grand Junction)

Denver Zephyr Connection

Standard Sleeper between Colorado Springs and Chicago (DZ-4) 10 Roomettes, 6 Double Bedrooms.

Slumbercoach between Colorado Springs and Chicago (CS-7) 24 Single Rooms, 8 Double Rooms.

Vista Dome Chair Car between Colorado Springs and Chicago (DZ-10) (In C. B. & Q. R.R. Denver Zephyr between Denver and Chicago)

Source: D&RGW Time Table October 16, 1960

ISSUED JUNE 14, 1971

TIME TABLES

DENVER • GLENWOOD SPRINGS • GRAND JUNCTION
SALT LAKE CITY • OGDEN

READ DOWN — READ UP

No. 17 Monday Thursday Saturday	Miles	RIO GRANDE ZEPHYR TRI-WEEKLY (Mountain Time)	No. 18 Tuesday Friday Sunday
7:30 AM	0	Lv. Denver, Colo. Ar.	9:00 PM
10:00 AM	75	Lv. Granby ◆ Lv.	6:35 PM
11:30 AM	129	Lv. Bond ◆ Lv.	5:00 PM
1:05 PM	185	Lv. Glenwood Springs Lv.	3:25 PM
1:40 PM	212	Lv. Rifle ◆ Lv.	2:50 PM
3:05 PM	275	Ar. Grand Junction Lv.	1:30 PM
3:20 PM	275	Lv. Grand Junction Ar.	1:15 PM
4:40 PM	353	Lv. Thompson, Utah ◆ Lv.	11:55 AM
x 5:05 PM	380	Lv. Green River ◆ Lv.	x11:25 AM
6:15 PM	444	Lv. Price ◆ Lv.	10:20 AM
6:30 PM	451	Lv. Helper ◆ Lv.	10:05 AM
8:30 PM	526	Lv. Provo ◆ Lv.	7:55 AM
9:30 PM	570	Ar. Salt Lake City Lv.	7:00 AM
9:40 PM	570	Lv. Salt Lake City (Note A) Ar.	6:50 AM
10:30 PM	607	Ar. Ogden, Utah (Note A) ◆ Lv.	6:00 AM

Note A: Limousine between Salt Lake City and Ogden for revenue passengers from or to points east of Salt Lake City, and revenue passengers arriving or departing Ogden on Amtrak train to or from Salt Lake City or east. No local passengers handled between Salt Lake City and Ogden.

◆ No checked baggage handled at this station.

x Stops on flag to discharge revenue passengers, also to receive revenue passengers holding advance reservations on notification to Agent, Thompson, Price or Helper, Utah.

EQUIPMENT
Reservations Required

Vista Dome Chair Car, Chair Car, Vista Dome Lounge, Dining Car, between Denver and Salt Lake City.

GLENWOOD SPRINGS — ASPEN
Glenwood-Aspen Stages
Rail Tickets Not Honored

Bus	Miles	Mountain Time	Bus
Note B	0 41	Lv. Glenwood Springs Ar. Ar. Aspen Lv.	Note B

Note B: Consult Agent for Bus Schedules.

For Additional Information See Other Side

CHAPTER 20

The Rock Island Railroad

It can be said that the Rock Island Railroad was the last major passenger railroad in the western United States to join the ranks of Dome Car operators. In 1971, the Company acquired a Dome Parlor Buffet Lounge Car from the Auto-Liner Corporation in Omaha. This particular car was one of the original three Dome Observation cars constructed for the C&O's Chessie. After trains 9 and 10 were discontinued on the Rio Grande, the Company placed the cars up for sale – and eventually made their way eastward.

The Rock Island's car is presently assigned to trains 5 and 6 operating between Chicago and Rock Island, Illinois on a daily basis. The car was placed in operation in an effort to improve the quality of both service and equipment on the 181 mile long distance commuter run. The car has been re-named the "Big Ben".

The Chicago, Rock Island and Pacific Railroad was one of six companies that did not join AMTRAK on May 1, 1971. Therefore, the Rock Island service to Peoria and to the Quad Cities Area via Joliet will be around for awhile by virtue of the law. Let us hope that the new dome car service, and the other new innovations such as the Ladies' Day Excursion Fares will draw passengers in sufficient amounts to insure continued "Domeliner Rocket" service on the Rock Island Line.

EX-CHESSIE, ex-Rio Grande dome parlor lounge "Big Ben" brings up the rear of the five car Rock Island passenger train, the Quad Cities Rocket. (Rock Island Railroad)

ROCK ISLAND train No. 5, the Quad Cities Rocket domeliner, waits for its departure time from the La Salle Street Station in Chicago. Movement to the right indicates that a Rock Island commuter streamliner is departing the station for its express run to Joliet. (Patrick C. Dorin)

THE EASTBOUND Quad Cities Rocket departs Joliet with a six car train including the dome parlor lounge Big Ben. The diner and three coaches are former "Golden State" equipment. (John H. Kuehl)

THE REAR ROOM parlor seats face inward, as is usually the case, but are comfortable and can be moved around. On the day this photo was taken, the headcovers on the seats were lettered "Golden State Route." (John H. Kuehl)

THE FRONT section of the dome car "Big Ben" contains table and lounge seating. Meals and beverages for parlor car passengers are served here if the passenger desires. Otherwise, there is the club diner just ahead for luxury dining for both coach and parlor car passengers. Note the mat on the floor which is used for servicing and cleaning to insure that the luxurious carpeting is not damaged in any way. (John H. Kuehl)

THE FRONT section of "Big Ben" also contains a small stand up bar or buffet (left rear of photo). All windows of the car include drapes and window shades, and the car leaves the rider with the desire to ride the car again – a crucial point in retaining business. (John H. Kuehl)

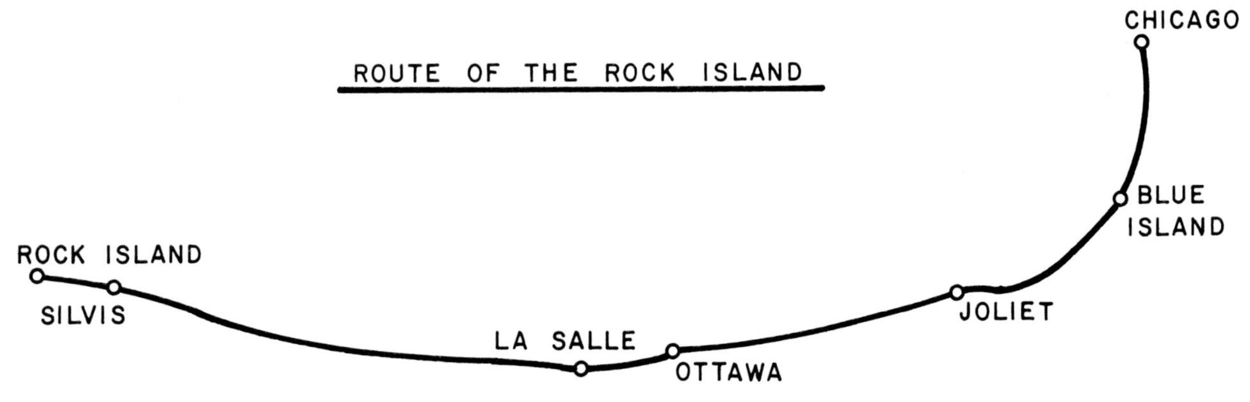

CHAPTER 21

AMTRAK

The Passenger Train has been at best an enigma for the railroad industry ever since the event of the automobile. It can be said that not a single train since that time has been a substantial money maker for any longer that just a few years. Many people claim that the railroads themselves caused the situation as it developed. Others claim that it was the public that deserted the railroads. At any rate, no one can deny that the passenger train was a financial loser. But then so were the airlines in 1970.

As we look at the American Passenger Transportation picture, it is easy to see we do not have a balanced system. We have over extended ourselves in airline service, and our highways are hopelessly unable to handle the volume of passenger traffic. Two cases in point: On May 28th, 1971, a Friday night, Interstate Highway # 75 (Detroit to Sault Ste. Marie, Michigan) contained a 14 mile long traffic jam west of Bay City and near Flint. This was the highway that was supposed to whisk drivers and their families from Detroit to Mackinaw City in four hours. Recently, an executive friend of this writer, who is employed by a Chicago firm, was scheduled to attend a meeting in New York City along with other members of his department. For some reason, he decided to travel to New York City on the Broadway Limited. His collegues chose to fly as was usually the case. They left Chicago early in the morning on a commuter flight that should have brought them to New York City in time for the 11:00 AM meeting. The jet was caught in an air traffic jam and they did not arrive in downtown New York City until 3:00 PM, just in time to see the end of the meeting.

Unfortunately, the above cases are becoming more typical every day. It is obvious that we need a safety valve for our expanding travel habits, and that safety valve could well be our railroad passenger system. It appears that this is what Congress had in mind when they created the National Railroad Passenger Corporation (now known as AMTRAK) in 1970. Although it is not what everyone thought it would be, it does provide some basis for hope that the United States Government is finally taking steps for a balanced transportation system in this great Nation.

AMTRAK began operating on May 1, 1971. On that date nearly all railroad passenger service was discontinued, except for the operations of the Georgia, Southern, Rock Island, Reading, Chicago, South Shore & South Bend Railroad and the Rio Grande who did not join the new system. All trains authorized by AMTRAK were then placed into service immediately. The corporation took over about 1500 passenger cars of the 3300 that were in operation in the USA at the time. This equipment was placed in service on the 184 daily passenger trains AMTRAK would initially be operating. As might be expected, a number of the cars were dome cars of most types that were in operation prior to May 1, 1971.

As of the Summer of 1971, AMTRAK operated 6 domeliners not including the Turbo trains of Penn Central. All of these were

THE COMBINED DENVER Zephyr/California Zephyr departs Chicago in mid-May, 1971 with 17 cars including four short domes and one Southern Pacific dome lounge. (John H. Kuehl)

TRAIN NO. 5, the combined Denver Zephyr/City of San Francisco (later renamed the San Francisco Zephyr) departs Chicago with 11 cars including a dome coach and dome lounge. The date is November 14, 1971. (John H. Kuehl)

THE inbound AMTRAK combined Super Chief/El Capitan arrives at Chicago with Penn Central's 12th Street Coach yard in the background. The train consists of 13 cars including a Hi-level lounge car and a dome lounge car. (John H. Kuehl)

operating in the west except for one Florida train. Except for some modifications, the trains were basically the same as they were prior to May 1st. The initial AMTRAK domeliners included the South Wind, Super Chief-El Capitan, Empire Builder, Denver Zephyr, California Zephyr and the Texas Chief.

However after the summer of 1971, some real dynamic changes began to take place and the number of domeliners in the USA expanded.

As time goes on, the routes will probably be changed somewhat and the dome cars reassigned until the problems with re-building the American Passenger Train are completed. AMTRAK is making a valiant effort with the passenger train. From this author's view point, they are making progress; but not as fast as many critics would like to see. (However, Rome was not built in one day either.) By the time this book is in print, it is hoped that many of the problems will be solved – and AMTRAK will be well on the way to providing the transportation safety valve for our crowded highways and airways.

UNLESS YOU look very carefully, you are not likely to notice the GP–20 at the end of the inbound "Texas Chief" pulling the train units and all back to the AT&SF coach yard. By the time of this photo, the Big Dome Lounges were sold to Auto-Train and replaced by flat top lounge cars; but the train retained its domeliner status by acquiring an almost daily dome coach from the former California Zephyr. On this rainy November 13, 1971 morning, the dome coach is ex-CB&Q "Silver Lariat." (John H. Kuehl)

THE MILWAUKEE Road – AMTRAK train No. 31 (later No. 7), the Empire Builder, departs Milwaukee on its first trip, May 1, 1971. The units are 9810, 9811, 9809 and 9812 (all F-9's) and cars visible are: 1205 baggage dormitory, ex-Twin Cities Zephyr dome coaches Silver Glade and Silver Wave, CB&Q flat top coach No. 1211, Ranch Car "Crossley Lake," and GN dome coach 1324. A twelve car train altogether and all Big Sky Blue except for the diesels and the Zephyr coaches and slumber-coach. (Jim Scribbins)

TRAIN No. 9, the combined Twin Cities/North Coast Hiawatha clumps across the Chicago & North Western diamonds at Western Avenue Tower on the west side of Chicago. (John H. Kuehl)

AMTRAK'S westbound Twin Cities Hiawatha picks up speed as she departs Chicago for Minnesota with a seven car consist including three dome cars. (John H. Kuehl)

THE eastbound North Coast Hiawatha, train No. 10, pauses at Livingston, Montana for a brief servicing and to load passengers for eastern points. The consist on this April 6, 1972 is 3 "F" units, one baggage car, two flat top coaches, one ex-GN dome coach, one former North Coast Limited dining car, a California Zephyr 10 roomette, 6 double bedroom sleeping car and finally a CZ dome observation lounge sleeper. (James Morin)

THE southbound South Wind behind two SCL units passes the legendary Pullman Car Company (on the right) at 111th Street in Chicago on October 20, 1971. Note the ex-B&O dome sleeper third car from the rear of the eight car domeliner. (John H. Kuehl)

THE TIME is early November, 1971, and it will not be long before these two trains: the South Wind and the City of New Orleans are replaced by the Floridian and Panama Limited. The new schedules will be evening departures instead of early morning and this scene will not be duplicated again. (John H. Kuehl)

AMTRAK (ex-PRR) E-8A No. 4316 and Baltimore and Ohio E-8A No. 1453 arrive at Chicago with the domeliner Floridian on a bright and sunny Saturday morning in February, 1972. With the coming of AMTRAK, this train operated out of the IC's Central Station in Chicago. On January 23, 1972, the train was returned to the Chicago Union Station. The eight car train includes two ex-Northern Pacific dome cars. (John H. Kuehl)

MOVING OUT behind B&O units 1439 and 1457, train No. 50, the George Washington, departs Chicago with five cars including a B&O dome coach. The photo was taken the first day the "George" carried a dome, November 1, 1971. (John H. Kuehl)

THE DATE is November 14, 1971 and the first run of the domeliner Prairie State, en route from Milwaukee to St. Louis, passes through Chicago with Milwaukee Road power, UP cafe lounge, ex-CB&Q dome coach and three flat top coaches. (John H. Kuehl)

OFFICIALLY, the GM&O E-7, with its headlight moved up to the mars light position and regular lens blanked with sheet metal, is heading up a Milwaukee Road—AMTRAK train. It is train No. 321 which has just arrived in Milwaukee on the first run of the day from Chicago. In consecutive order are ex-CB&Q Denver Zephyr dome parlor lounge, ex-SP Pride of Texas coffee shop car, ex-CB&Q dome coach, two flat top coaches and baggage car. With a fresh engine on the opposite end, this equipment will depart to St. Louis in the afternoon as the Abraham Lincoln. (Jim Scribbins)

TRAIN No. 302, the domeliner Abraham Lincoln, arrives at Chicago with a baggage car, two flat top coaches, ex-Northern Pacific dome coach, ex-SP coffee shop and last but not least, the ex-CB&Q Denver Zephyr dome parlor lounge car. No. 302 will make a 15 minute stop before continuing on as train No. 323 over Milwaukee Road trackage to Milwaukee. In 1972, the only through Chicago trains were the Milwaukee—St. Louis domeliner services. (John H. Kuehl)

THE northbound Abraham Lincoln at Joliet, Illinois en route to Milwaukee on a chilly January 8, 1972. Two GM&O E-7's lead a Santa Fe baggage car, Union Pacific coach, Burlington dome coach, Great Northern coach, dining car and the ex-Denver Zephyr dome parlor car on this particular day. (John H. Kuehl)

INTERCITY RAILROAD PASSENGER ROUTES

National Railroad Passenger Corporation

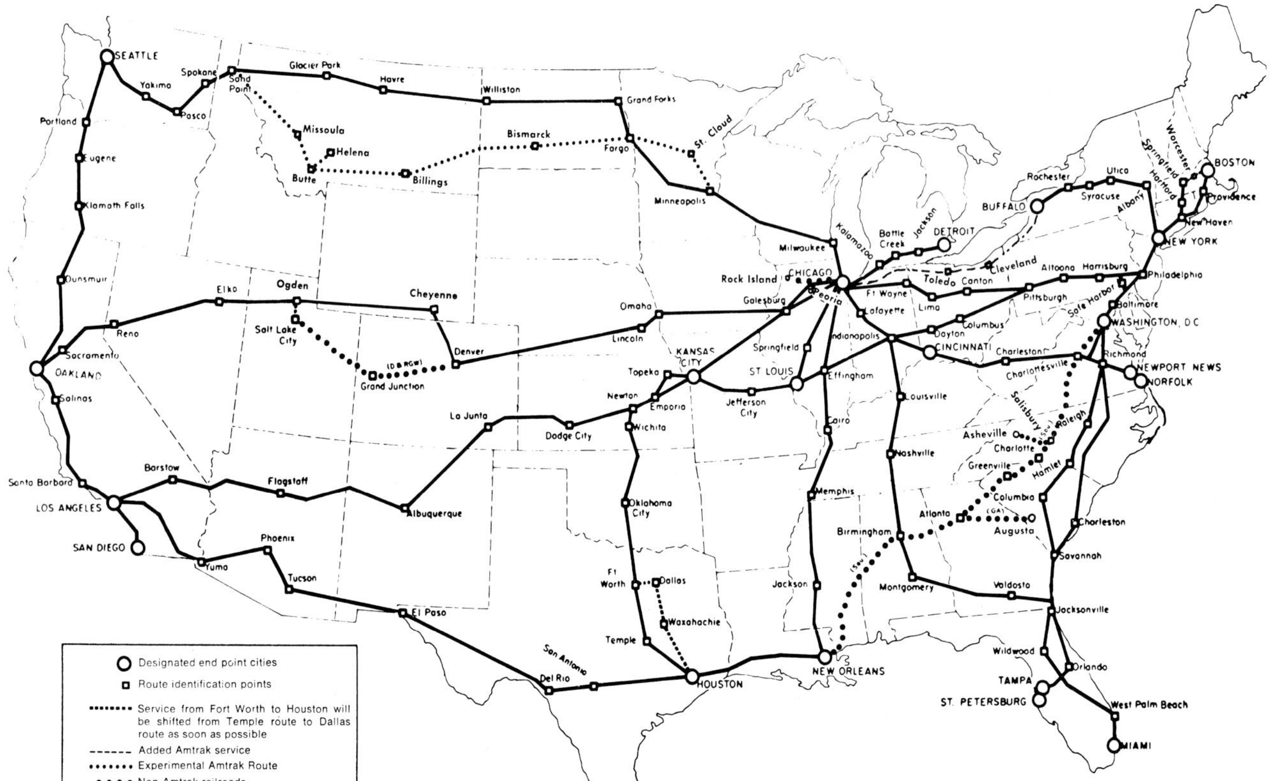

○ Designated end point cities
□ Route identification points
•••••••• Service from Fort Worth to Houston will be shifted from Temple route to Dallas route as soon as possible
– – – – – Added Amtrak service
•••••••• Experimental Amtrak Route
● ● ● ● Non-Amtrak railroads

Equipment

Train Number	Train Name	Sleepers	Slumbercoach	Parlor	Parlor with Food Service	Dining	Cafe Coach	Domes	Reserved Coaches	Checked Luggage	Notes
1-2	Sunset	•				•			•	•	
3-4	Super Chief/El Capitan	•	•			•		•	•	•	
5-6	Denver Zephyr	•	•			•		•	•	•	
	City of San Francisco	•				•		•	•	•	
7-8	Empire Builder	•	•			•		•	•	•	
9-10	Twin Cities Hiawatha					•		•		•	
	North Coast Hiawatha	•				•		•	•	•	
11-12-13-14	Coast Daylight					•		•		•	
	Coast Starlight	•				•		•		•	
15-16	Texas Chief	•				•		•		•	
30-31	National Ltd	•				•			•	•	Hand luggage only between Washington and Harrisburg
40-41	Broadway Ltd	•	•			•			•	•	
42-43	Keystone						•				
50-51	Geo. Wash/JW Riley	•				•		•		•	Hand luggage only
52-53	Floridian	•				•		•	•	•	
58-59	Panama Ltd	•				•		•	•	•	
70-71-72-73-74-75	(New York-Buffalo ser.)						•				
80-81	Silver Star	•				•			•		
82-83	Silver Meteor	•	•			•			•	•	
84-85	Champion	•	•			•			•	•	
86-87	Florida Special	•	•			•			•		
100 thru 127	Metroliners				•		•		•		
except: 101-106-113-118	Metroliners						•		•		
All other "100" series trains					•		•				
except: 150-151	(Boston-New York-Washington service)						•	•	•		
176-51				•		•				•	Dining car on 51 only
132-135							•				
170-171-172-177-180-181					•	•					
195-196	Puget Sound						•	•			
198-199	Mount Rainier						•	•			
200 series	(See Note)										Many 200 series trains have parlor and food and/or Snack service. See pages 52-53
301/320-304/329	Prairie State					•		•			
303/326-302/323	Abraham Lincoln			•		•		•		•	
321-328	(Chicago-Milwaukee service)			•		•		•			
322-325							•				
324-327							•	•			
347-348	Illinois Zephyr						•				
360-361	Wolverine						•			•	Checked luggage #361 only
362-363	St. Clair						•			•	Checked luggage #362 only
380 thru 387	(New York-Albany service)						•				
391-392	Shawnee						•				
390-393	Illini						•				
394-395	Campus						•				
400 series	(New Haven-Springfield)										(Coach only)
600 series	(Philadelphia-Harrisburg)										(Coach only)
640-641-642-643	West Virginian					•					
775-776-777-778	San Diegans						•	•			Dome on 775, 776 only

A dot shows the type of equipment provided on the train indicated.

CHAPTER 22

The TurboTrain

The newest concept in domeliners, and indeed in the passenger train itself, is the TURBO. The TurboTrains have been in daily train service between New York City and Boston since April, 1969. The train was designed and developed by the United Aircraft Corporation and is a program within the Surface Transportation Systems sub-division of the firm's Sikorsky Aircraft Division, Stratford, Conn.

Special Features

The TurboTrain has a number of advanced technical features. For example, there is the utilization of an aircraft type gas turbine engine for power and a pendulous banking suspension system.

The layout and decor of the interior were designed for maximum passenger comfort. There are carpeting and draperies, soft indirect lighting, individually controlled reading lights over each seat, fold down tables, reclining seats with head rests, and carry-on luggage racks at the doors. For fast, efficient food service, the unique "domeliner" is equipped with a compact but fully furnished galley.

Electric heat and air conditioning add to the passenger's comfort; and the cars are slightly pressurized to keep out dust and to reduce the noise level.

The train is powered by a gas turbine powerplant which is so small and compact that it can be located under the passenger domes. This arrangement permits complete utilization of the train's interior. The dome power cars are located at each end of the train to give bi-directional capability.

A major advance in the Turbo is its pendulous banking suspension system. The trains are suspended from near the top of the cars, above the center of gravity, on an A-frame type of assembly. The suspension system is located between cars, except in the power dome cars. In that case, it is located beneath the domes. The suspension system causes the train to bank inward around curves under the influence of centrifugal force, as opposed to the outward motion experienced by conventional trains. This enables the train to round curves with passenger comfort and safety at speeds 30 to 40 per cent faster than conventional trains. This feature, plus faster acceleration and higher cruising speeds, permits reduction of running times between terminals compared with conventional trains.

Ecological Considerations

According to United Aircraft, the TurboTrain is inherently favorable to ecology when compared to other systems. There are several reasons for this. First, since it is made of lightweight aluminum and other design features to reduce weight – for example, the Turbo has but two wheels between cars compared with four at the end of conventional cars – it requires a small amount of horsepower for its high speed and fast acceleration. A seven car Turbo using 2,000 horsepower, can carry the same number of passengers downtown-to-downtown as 150 auto-

THE UNITED AIRCRAFT TURBOTRAIN is in service on the AMTRAK route between New York City and Boston as part of the U.S. Department of Transportation's Northeast Corridor high speed ground transportation demonstration project. The train is powered by gas turbine engines and has a pendulous banking system which enables it to round curves with passenger comfort and safety at speeds 30 to 40 per cent faster then regular trains. The train has been operated at a speed of 170 miles per hour, hits more than 100 miles per hour in operational service on some stretches of the Penn Central's New Haven line. (Sikorsky Aircraft Division of United Aircraft Corporation)

mobiles (using an average of two passengers per auto). These autos would have a total of approximately 30,000 horsepower. Additionally, because of the high efficiency of the gas turbine, its effluents are only about 25% of those of an internal combustion engine of equal horsepower.

Another reason the Turbo causes less damage to the environment than other systems – both present and proposed – is that it requires no new rights-of-way. This means no additional housing need be destroyed nor nature disturbed to make way for the "Domeliner" TurboTrain.

Operations

As stated previously, the Turbo is presently being operated in the United States between Boston and New York City. Originally two 3 car trains and 5 seven car trains were built for the U.S. Department of Transportation and the Canadian National Railways respectively. As of early 1972, the CNR trains were still experiencing technical difficulties, but the DOT trains have been successful. Although only one train has been used in round trip service, patronage has been such that Sikorsky Aircraft built four additional cars, two for each train, which increased the capacity of each train from 144 seats to 240. The cars were inserted into the trains in 1972.

While one set of equipment has been in regular service, the other train has not been exactly wasting time. Technical research has been conducted extensively, including a 12,000 mile tour in 31 states during a 30 day period. This tour was conducted during August and September, 1971.

The data gathering on the trip was not simply an operational technical study, although such information was not to be ignored during the tour. AMTRAK and the DOT conducted a marketing study of the passengers using the train during the tour.

LARGE PARLOR car type seats are featured in the dome power cars of the United Aircraft TurboTrain. Big tinted windows on the sides and back of the dome enable passengers to view the scenery from any direction. In the front part of the dome, passengers can look over the operator's shoulder and see the track ahead. (Sikorsky Aircraft Division of United Aircraft Corporation)

FOLD DOWN tables provide passengers with convenient places for eating, playing cards, writing letters or the many other activities that a passenger can use a table for. The tables fold down from the seat ahead, but do not restrict in any way the reclining operation of the seat. (Sikorsky Aircraft Division of United Aircraft Corporation)

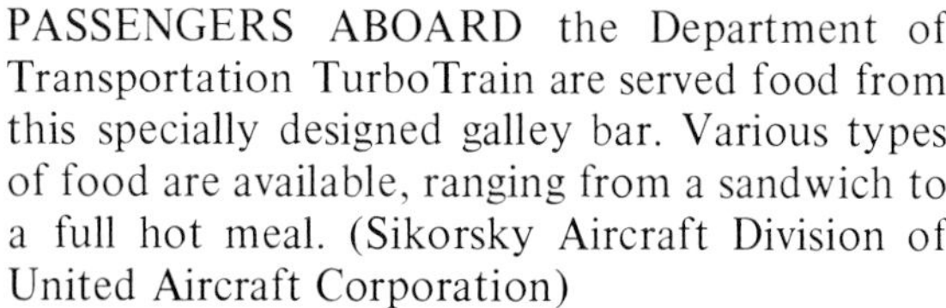

PASSENGERS ABOARD the Department of Transportation TurboTrain are served food from this specially designed galley bar. Various types of food are available, ranging from a sandwich to a full hot meal. (Sikorsky Aircraft Division of United Aircraft Corporation)

CARPETING, DRAPERIES, indirect lighting, fold down tables, reclining seats with head rests are featured in the luxurious interior of United Aircraft's high speed TurboTrain. (Sikorsky Aircraft Division of United Aircraft Corporation)

THE PENN CENTRAL – DOT'S domeliner TurboTrain approaches New London, Connecticut on its westbound trip from Boston to New York City. (W. Frank Clodfelter)

The technical and marketing data gathered from the tour was still being evaluated at the time of this writing, which was February, 1972. In the author's opinion, the words that can sum up the situation are "Cautiously Optimistic", if for no other reason then the accute need for a balanced transportation system in the United States and Canada.

The Department of Transportation has this to say in regard to that critical need:

> Over the past four years increased use of the private automobile, bus and airplane have created a serious imbalance in the nation's transportation network, precipitating a gradual decline in rail passenger traffic and a steady erosion of rail equipment and service.
>
> Today airway and highway systems face serious problems of their own. Traffic congestion in our central cities and suburbs, together with problems of noise and air pollution, excessive land use and dislocation of people, unrestricted expansion of these facilities expensive, and to a degree, impractical.
>
> While improvements can well be made in highway and airport facilities, it is clear that they cannot be relied upon exclusively to meet future intercity travel needs. They simply cannot do it alone.
>
> By the year 2000, the population of the United States will have increased by 100 million persons. To handle this influx, highways and airlines must be supplemented by swift, efficient rail passenger service.
>
> A revival of this service is now considered necessary to a balanced handling of intercity travel demands of the 70's and beyond.
>
> Upgraded and modernized, the train has unique capabilities for relieving intercity traffic congestion, particularly on short haul routes through high population density corridors and also on medium and long distance routes where it can provide a unique, distinctive, relaxed mode of travel.
>
> Source: *Tour of the Turbo*, Department of Transportation, Washington, D.C., Summer-1971, Pages 1 and 2.

With this critical need at our doorsteps, it can only be hoped that the unique domeliner TURBO, and the domeliner AUTO-TRAIN covered in the next chapter, will provide us with the practical answer for solving this great problem.

THE EASTBOUND TURBO approaches Stamford, Connecticut on its run to Boston on April 30, 1969. (W. Frank Clodfelter)

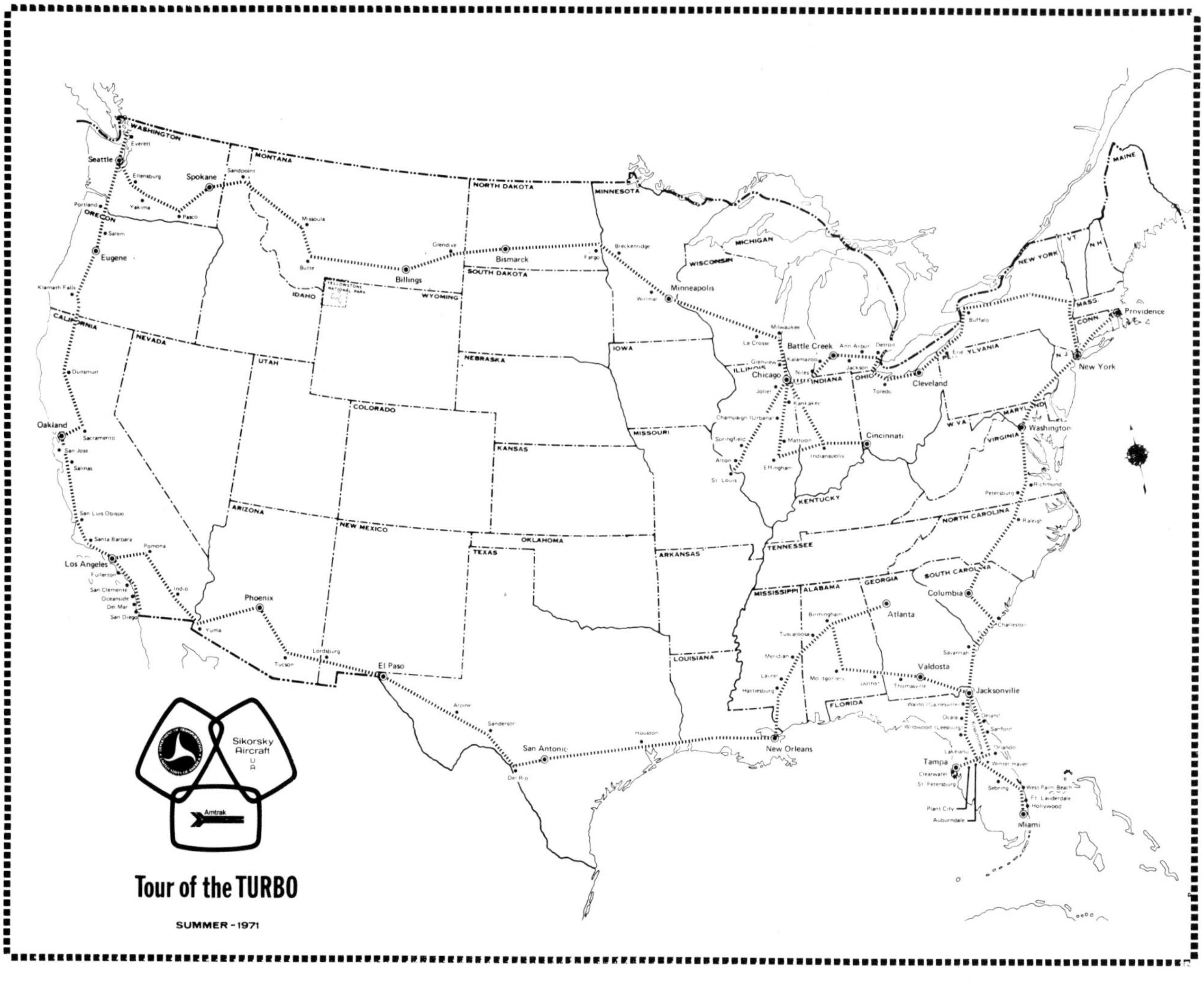

Sikorsky Aircraft

Amtrak

Tour of the TURBO

SUMMER - 1971

THE WESTBOUND TURBOTRAIN whips through Cos Cob, Connecticut under overhead wire on its run to New York City over the New Haven Region of the Penn Central. (W. Frank Clodfelter)

Miles	Eastward	Turbo Yankee Clipper 150 Except Sat&Sun
		PM
.0	Lv **Washington, D. C.**	▪ 1.00
10.0	" Capital Beltway, Md.	c 1▪10
40.1	" **Baltimore, Md.** (Penn Central Sta.)	▪ 1.36
108.5	" Wilmington, Del.	▪ 2.21
	Lv **Philadelphia, Pa.**	
------	" Penn Central Sta. (30th Street)	▪ 2.47
140.7	" North Philadelphia	------
168.5	" Trenton, N. J.	------
202 0	" Metropark, N. J.	------
216.6	" Newark, N. J.	▪ 3d48
226.6	Ar **New York, N. Y.** Penna. Station	▪ 4.00
226.6	Lv **New York, N. Y., Penna. Station**	4.15
------	" " " **Grand Cent. Term.**	------
------	" " " 125th Street♦	------
253.4	" Rye, N. Y.	------
262.6	Ar Stamford, Conn.	------
270.1	" Norwalk & South Norwalk	------
285.1	" Bridgeport, Conn.	------
301.6	Ar **New Haven, Conn.** (See Note 3)	5.32
	Connecting Train ⟶	Turboservice See Note 1 (Advance ticket purchase required)
301.6	Lv **New Haven, Conn.**	
314.1	" Wallingford, Conn.	
320.1	Ar Meriden, Conn.	
327.6	" Berlin, Conn.	
338.1	" Hartford, Conn.	
338.1	Lv Hartford, Conn.	
344.6	" Windsor, Conn. ⊕	
350.1	" Windsor Locks, Conn. ⊕	
355.6	" Thompsonville, Conn.	
363.6	Ar **Springfield, Mass.**	
417.6	" Worcester, Mass.	------
440.6	" Framingham, Mass. ⊕	------
446.6	" Wellesley	------
453.6	Ar Newtonville	------
301.6	Lv New Haven, Conn.	5.32
334.6	Ar Old Saybrook, Conn.	------
352.6	" New London, Conn.	6.24
362.1	" Mystic, Conn.	------
370.6	" Westerly, R. I.	------
387.6	" Kingston, R. I.	------
414.6	" **Providence, R. I.**	7.15
446.6	" Route 128, Mass.	d 7.45
------	Ar **Boston, Mass.** Back Bay Station	d 7.57
458.6	Ar **Boston, Mass.** South Station	8.00
		PM

No. **150**.—TURBO YANKEE CLIPPER.
See Note 1.
(Advance Ticket Purchase Required.)
Metroclub Car... Washington to New York (Meals and Beverages served at seats).
Metro Snack Bar Coach.. Washington to New York.
Turbo Coaches (Dome).. New York to Boston (Food and Beverage service).

RAILROAD AND PARLOR CAR FARES (Subject to change)

Between	ONE-WAY RAIL FARES (Double for round-trip) In Parlor Cars	In Coaches	TURBOSERVICE—METROLINER		Seat in Parlor Car ★
Boston and Route 128			Turbo Service		
Providence	① $3.50	① $2.50	① $3.50		$2.37
	② 2.75	② 2.00	② 3.00		2.37
New London	8.00	6.00	7.00		2.37
New Haven	11.75	8.75	10.00		2.37
New York (Pa. Sta.)	17.00	12.75	15.65		2.37
			•Metroclub	▲Metroliner Coach	
Trenton	23.40	17.15	24.55	21.15	3.03
Philadelphia	26.15	18.90	27.30	22.90	3.52
Wilmington	28.65	20.15	30.15	24.15	3.80
Baltimore	34.90	24.40	39.30	30.40	4.57
Washington	38.15	26.65	43.05	32.65	5.12
Providence and			Turbo Service		
New London	4.75	3.50	4.50		2.37
New Haven	8.50	6.50	7.50		2.37
New York (Pa. Sta.)	13.75	10.25	13.15		2.37
			•Metroclub	▲Metroliner Coach	
Trenton	20.15	14.65	22.05	18.65	3.03
Philadelphia	22.90	16.40	24.80	20.40	3.52
Wilmington	25.40	17.65	27.65	21.65	3.80
Baltimore	31.65	21.90	36.80	27.90	4.57
Washington	34.90	24.15	40.55	30.15	5.06
New London and			Turbo Service		
New Haven	3.69	2.72	4.00		2.37
New York (Pa. Sta.)	9.25	7.00	8.90		2.37
			•Metroclub	▲Metroliner Coach	
Trenton	15.65	11.40	17.80	14.40	2.37
Philadelphia	18.40	13.15	20.55	16.15	2.75
Wilmington	20.90	14.40	23.40	17.40	2.92
Baltimore	27.15	18.65	32.55	23.65	3.69
Washington	30.40	20.90	36.30	25.90	4.07
New Haven and			•Metroclub	▲Metroliner Coach	
New York (Pa. Sta.)	6.48	5.05	9.80	Ⓣ 6.00	2.37
Trenton	11.43	8.17	16.75	11.12	2.37
Philadelphia	14.18	9.92	19.50	12.87	2.37
Wilmington	16.68	11.17	22.00	14.12	2.37
Baltimore	22.93	15.42	31.02	20.37	3.14
Washington	26.18	17.67	34.71	22.62	3.58
Springfield and					
Trenton	16.40	11.90			2.37
Philadelphia	19.15	13.65			2.75
Wilmington	21.65	14.90			3.03
Baltimore	27.90	19.15			3.69
Washington	31.15	21.40			4.13
Hartford					
Trenton	14.65	10.65			2.37
Philadelphia	17.40	12.40			2.37
Wilmington	19.90	13.65			2.75
Baltimore	26.15	17.90			3.52
Washington	29.40	20.15			3.85

① From Boston.
② From Route 128.
• Includes Parlor Car Seat and Metroliner Service Charge.
▲ Includes Metroliner Service Charge.
★ For the use of rooms in parlor cars, the following minimum number of adult tickets is required:
Ⓣ Also applies on Turbo Service.

	Rail passage tickets	Seat tickets
Drawing room (seat service).....	2	2

Source: AMTRAK Time Table
Form 76
January 13, 1972

CHAPTER 24

The Alaska Railroad

The latest railroad by mid–1972 to become a domeliner operator was from the U.S.A.'s most northern state, the Alaska Railroad. The railroad, in late 1971, purchased 4 dome coaches from the Union Pacific Railroad. The equipment, along with several other ex–UP passenger cars, was refurbished and placed in operation on trains 5 and 6, the Aurora, in May, 1972. The Aurora is the road's daylight passenger train that operates on a daily basis between Anchorage and Fairbanks during the summers. (It runs twice weekly from about September 10th to May 21st.) No. 5 is scheduled for 11 hours and 15 minutes for the southbound trip, while No. 6 makes the trip in eleven and one half hours. The distance from Fairbanks to Anchorage is 356 miles.

Each train is equipped with three diesel units, 2 baggage cars, 2 flat top coaches, 2 dome coaches and 1 diner. This is the normal consist of the train, which is often expanded with extra traffic, including tours to Mt. McKinley National Park.

Motive power for the blue and yellow domeliner comes in the form of Electro-Motive Division (of General Motors) FP-7 units, 1500 horse power units. During the winter, the trains are also equipped with a power car, either the P-4 or P-5. The power cars are used as a supplementary power and additional hear source for the passenger train. The P-4 and P-5 are each equipped with two steam generators and a diesel electric generator. As would be expected, the passenger locomotives are also equipped with steam generators.

With the daylight schedule of the train, the domes are put to good use as the train passes through some of North America's most spectacular scenery. As No. 6 departs Anchorage, its southern terminal, she rolls through the following scenic areas:

Eagle River Canyon
Peters Creek
Willow Creek Gold Area
Little Susitna River
Willow Creek
Susitna River
Sheep Creek
Indian River
Chultina River
Summit Lake
Hurricane Gulch (Bridge with tracks 256 feet above streambed.)
Continental Divide
Cantwell River
Panorama Mountain
Carlo Creek
Mt. McKinley (Highest in North America)
Nenana River
Tanana River
Gold Stream Creek

and literally thousands of other lakes and streams along the world famous Alaska Railroad, which is most appropriately named "The Mount McKinley National Park Route." Coincidently, there is a flag stop along the domeliner's route by the name of "Dome," 14 miles south of Fairbanks.

THE SCENERY along the Alaska Railroad has always dictated the use of some type of observation cars – from the old heavy weight arch window cars operated on the Matanuska Valley Special to the dome cars run on today's Aurora. (Rail Photo Service)

THE AURORA crosses the Hurricane Bridge, which is 296 feet above the streambed. (Alaska Railroad)

BEFORE THE DOME cars went into service, the Alaska Railroad assembled a special train for the company photographer. The baggage cars and the flat top coaches on the head-end were also purchased from the Union Pacific Railroad. (Alaska Railroad)

THE CONSIST OF THE SPECIAL also included a business car on the rear of the seven car domeliner. (Alaska Railroad)

Alaska is often referred to as the land of the mid-night Sun. So in the summer despite the fairly late arrival times at Fairbanks and Anchorage (8:30 and 8:15 PM respectively) dusk is a long way off and passengers have daylight viewing from one end of the railroad to the other.

Conversely, during the winter time, most of the trip is in darkness with a few hours of daylight especially at the Anchorage end of the line. However, riding in the dome cars during this time of the year can still be an unforgettable experience. In this Northland there are frequent displays of the Aurora Borealis. What greater travel experience could one have than riding the domeliner "Aurora" through the Winter day in Alaska with the Northern Lights in full regalia?

The addition of the ex-Union Pacific dome coaches to the "Aurora" have made traveling through and viewing that famous scenery finer and easier than ever before. The Alaska Railroad is to be congratulated for taking these steps to operate dome cars through one of the World's most beautiful areas – GOD'S COUNTRY.

ROUTE OF THE AURORA

ALASKA RAILROAD

Drawn By: Sy Dykhouse III

THE READER WILL NOTE THAT DOME COACH NO. 7014 has a color scheme opposite the scheme shown in the previous photographs. In both cases the trucks are silver and the roof is an off grey. (Alaska Railroad)

Epilogue

The passenger train, including the Domeliner, is basically a vehicle for moving people from point A to point B. Man has developed several different types of vehicles since he has invented the wheel to move people and goods from one place to another. It is a known fact that there is a direct correlation between the development and efficiency of the transportation system and the development of a nation. Russia and Australia are very much aware of this and have been working very diligently to expand and improve their rail systems.

In America, we have used four basic methods of transporting people: the automobile, the bus, the airplane and the train. In modern times, two of the methods have become over loaded. The train has nearly, but not quite, gone out of existence.

Because of America's dependence on the automobile and the airplane for moving people, we have slowly moved into a situation that is causing a break down and a drastic loss of efficiency in our transportation system. The airlines in their zest for competition have over expanded and have purchased too many new airplanes. Now we have over crowded skies and the companies are racing toward a financial crisis. Despite increased partonage from year to year, operating problems and increasing costs have placed the airlines in the economic phase of diminishing returns.

The automobile is also causing us problems. It seems almost incredible that this vehicle which carries over 90% of the inter city passenger traffic could be headed for real trouble. Yet it is. Americans have been madly in love with this creature. It can lay claim to more accomplishments and more death and destruction than any other single machine that Man has invented. It has changed our life style. It took people from the city to the country to live. It helped build suburbia, it has saved time going to and from work and it is (usually) comfortable to ride in and warm in winter. But it also kills us at the rate of more than 50,000 people per year in the United States. And it has been doing this for years. As of lately, American traffic jams have increased not only in size but in duration. They give out a fantastic amount of pollution although this problem appears to be solvable. However, this is only part of the problem, and we are now about to face a bigger one.

Although it is now only mentioned on the back pages of the newspapers, it is generally agreed by the experts that we will soon face a fuel shortage. American automobiles are really very inefficient. They consume millions of gallons of gasoline as if the supply will always be there. The fact of the matter is that the supply is running low, even with the Alaska North Slope. This means that if we are going to make our reserves last, we are going to have to cut down on the use of the automobile and the airplane, and turn to the passenger train which can move far greater numbers of people with far less fuel than either the plane or the car. Again, as this writer pointed out in *Commuter Railroads*, we must work toward a balanced transportation system where air is used for long distance travel with some cruise type trains (such as the Empire Builder, etc.), trains and planes for the intermediate distant travel ranges up to 1000 miles, and rail for the short distances. Buses could be used for feeder services and the automobiles for pleasure and in areas where public transportation is impractical. This is contingent of course as to how the USA will have to solve its fuel shortage problem which will soon be approaching the critical stage.

Our ever increasing dependence on the airplane and highway has caused us some other problems too. Despite all the technological advances made by the air and highway transport systems, they are still subject to the weather. There are areas of the US where winter weather literally closes the air and highway services,

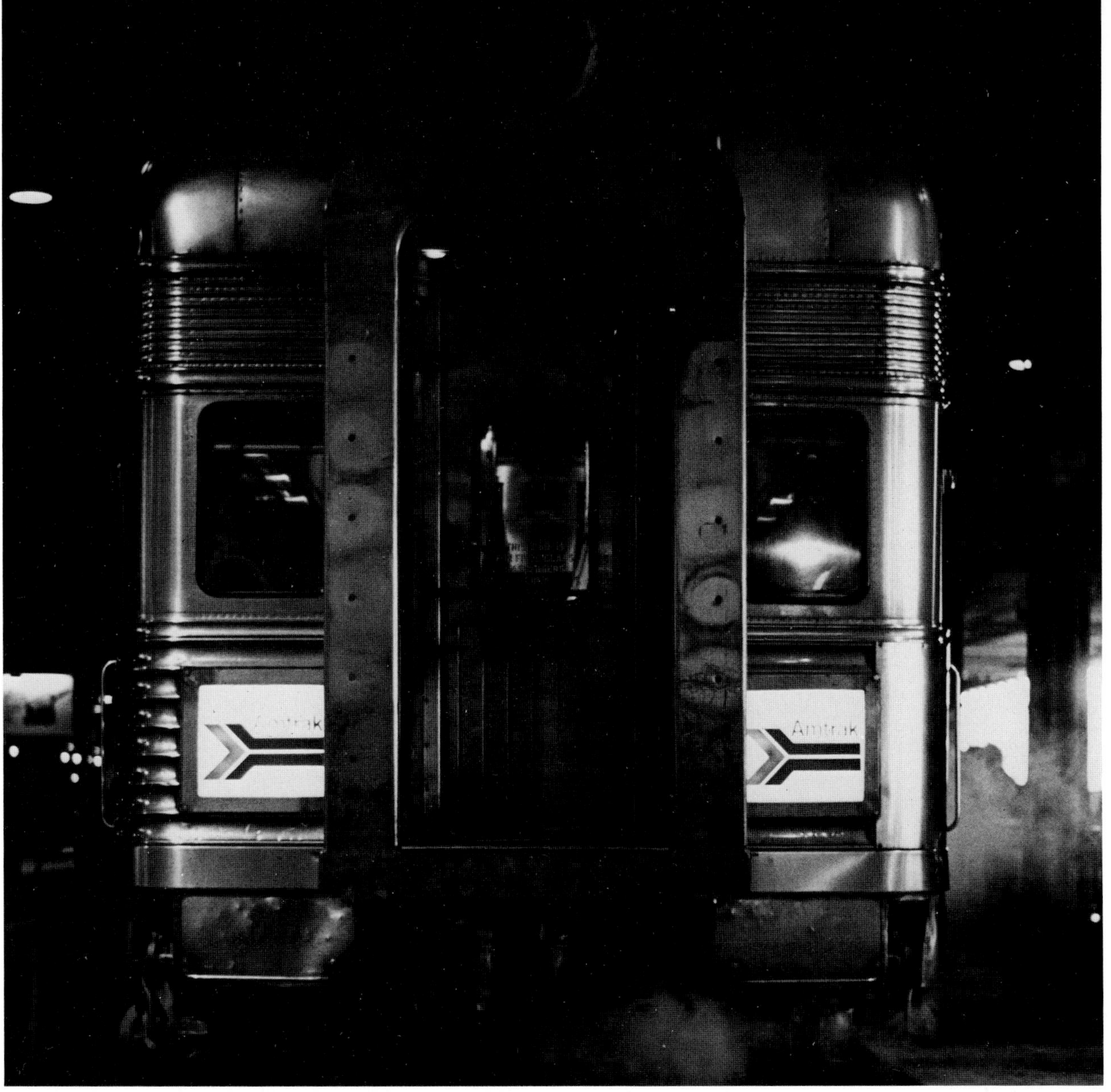

THE LAST CAR OF A ST. LOUIS – MILWAUKEE "Domeliner" proudly displays the AMTRAK logo for all passengers to see as they board the train in Chicago. AMTRAK represents America's last efficient (or shall we say least costly) chance for the development of a sound, safe and *balanced* transportation system. If AMTRAK fails, it will not be because of too few passengers or potential passengers. (Note AMTRAK's increase in patronage from 1971 to 1972 of over 12%.) The failure will be because not enough people understood the economy and the total transportation system and failed to realize the consequences of our present imbalanced transportation. Our highways and airways cannot hope to handle our transportation needs in the future – it is impossible. If AMTRAK fails, the passenger train will eventually have to be re-invented and that will be a costly job. Much more expensive than if we really worked to solve the problem now. This writer urges the reader not to sit back and criticize AMTRAK and the railroads for their short comings, but to write to their congressmen expressing the need for a balanced transportation system. AMTRAK has a big job to do, it cannot be done in a year or two, and it needs our support. (Photo by John Kuehl)

sometimes for days at a time. Consequently, entire sections of various states (Northern Wisconsin, Minnesota, Michigan, Maine, North Dakota, South Dakota to name only a few) are literally cut off from the outside world because there is no all-weather mail and passenger service operating. This is just one more reason why we should concentrate on the re-development of rail transport services.

One may now be asking what does this have to do with domeliner passenger trains? First of all, domes have a definite place in the cruise type passenger trains (or auto-train) which travel cross country. Secondly, can anyone mention any mode of travel that could whisk you from Chicago to St. Paul in a little over six hours that was more pleasant than a Vista Dome Zephyr or a Super Dome Hiawatha? One could relax and gather his thoughts during the interlude. It was speed without fighting highway traffic to the airport both at Chicago and at the Twin Cities. When one rides on a train, the world literally leaves you alone.

America has a giant problem to face. We have a vast rail system to help us solve this problem with a minimum of cost. The train is the only transport system that can give us a variable capacity according to need with a giant edge in safety and efficiency coupled with all-weather operation. If Americans really sit down and think about this problem, the railroad system is the only way we can go.

APPENDIX

Roster of Dome Cars

Burlington Route

Type	Numbers and/or names		Built	Original Service	Sub-sequent Service
Coffee Shop Lounge Dorm.	250	Silver Club	1948	CZ	Pool
	251	Silver Lounge	1948	CZ	Pool
	252	Silver Roundup	1948	CZ	Pool
Coffee Shop Lunch Count. Dormitory	253	Silver Cup	1956	DZ	
	254	Silver Kettle	1956	DZ	
Coach	4709	Silver Castle	1945	TCZ	Pool
	4714	Silver Dome	1945	TCZ	Pool
Coach	4716	Silver Bridle	1948	CZ	Pool
	4717	Silver Lodge	1948	CZ	Pool
	4718	Silver Lariat	1948	CZ	Pool
	4719	Silver Ranch	1948	CZ	Pool
	4720	Silver Rifle	1948	CZ	Pool
	4721	Silver Saddle	1948	CZ	Pool
	4722	Silver Stirrup	1948	CZ	Pool
	4723	Silver Bluff	1947	TCZ	Pool
	4724	Silver Glade	1947	TCZ	Pool
	4725	Silver Island	1947	TCZ	Pool
	4726	Silver River	1947	TCZ	Pool
	4727	Silver Stream	1947	TCZ	Pool
	4728	Silver Wave	1947	TCZ	Pool
	4729	Silver Scene	1947	TCZ	Pool
	4730	Silver Vision	1947	TCZ	Pool
	4735	Silver Buckle	1956	DZ	
	4736	Silver Brand	1956	DZ	
Parlor Buffet Lounge	235	Silver Chateau	1956	DZ	
	236	Silver Vernada	1956	DZ	
Coach Buffet Lounge	320	Silver Garden	1952	ARZ	Pool
	321	Silver Patio	1952	ARZ	Pool
Parlor Observation	360	Silver View	1947	TCZ	
	361	Silver Vista	1947	TCZ	
	365	Silver Terrance	1952	KCZ	TCZ
	366	Silver Tower	1952	KCZ	TCZ
Sleeper Observation	375	Silver Horizon	1948	CZ	
	376	Silver Penthouse	1948	CZ	
	377	Silver Solarium	1948	CZ	
	378	Silver Lookout	1952	CZ	
Coach	1333		1955	EB	
	1334				
	1335				
Lounge	1395	River View	1955	EB	
Sleeper	304		1954	NCL	
	305		1954	NCL	
Coach	557		1954	NCL	
	558		1954	NCL	
Slpr–Lnge	380	(Ex–CB&Q 304)	1967	NCL	

Remarks: All CB&Q dome cars were built by the Budd Company.

The following number series operated by AMTRAK:
4709
4714
4716 thru 4730
4735
4736

375 thru 378

250 thru 254

320
321
235
236
360
361
365
366
1333 thru 1335, 1395
557 thru 558
305
380

Type	Numbers and/or names	Built	Original Service	Subsequent Service
	Denver & Rio Grande Western			
Coach	1105 Silver Bronco	1948	CZ	RGZ
	1106 Silver Colt	1948	CZ	RGZ
	1107 Silver Mustang	1948	CZ	RGZ
	1108 Silver Pony	1948	CZ	RGZ
Coach (Purchased from C&O)	1248	1947	Royal Gorge	Yampa Valley
	1249	1947		
	1250	1947		
Coffee Shop Lounge Dorm.	1140 Silver Shop	1948	CZ	
Sleeper Observation	1145 Silvery Sky	1948	CZ	RGZ

Remarks: All D&RGW dome cars were built by the Budd Company.

Type	Numbers and/or names	Built	Original Service	Subsequent Service
	Western Pacific Railroad			
Coach	811 Silver Dollar	1948	CZ	
	812 Silver Feather	1948	CZ	
	813 Silver Palace	1948	CZ	
	814 Silver Sage	1948	CZ	
	815 Silver Schooner	1948	CZ	
	816 Silver Scout	1948	CZ	
	817 Silver Thistle	1948	CZ	
Coffee Shop Lounge Dorm.	831 Silver Chalet	1948	CZ	
	832 Silver Hostel	1948	CZ	
Sleeper Observation	881 Silver Crescent	1948	CZ	
	882 Silver Planet	1948	CZ	

Remarks: All WP dome cars were built by the Budd Company. Series 811 thru 817 purchased by Auto–Train in 1971.

Type	Numbers and/or names	Built	Original Service	Subsequent Service
	Great Northern Railway			
Coach	1320 thru 1331	1955	EB	
Lounge	1390 Glacier View	1955	EB	
	1391 Ocean View	1955	EB	
	1392 Mountain View	1955	EB	
	1393 Lake View	1955	EB	
	1394 Prairie View	1955	EB	
	Northern Pacific Railway			
Coach	550 thru 556	1954	NCL	
	549	1957	NCL	
Sleeper	307 thru 313	1954	NCL	
	314	1957	NCL	
Sleeper Lounge	375 thru 379 (Ex NP cars 307, 308, 311, 312 and 314)	1967	NCL	
	Spokane, Portland and Seattle Railway			
Coach	559	1954	NCL	
	1332	1955	EB	
Sleeper	306	1954	NCL	

Remarks: All GN, NP and SP&S dome cars were built by the Budd Company.

The following BN (ex GN, NP and SP&S) number series operated by AMTRAK:

1320 thru 1331
1390 thru 1394
549 thru 556
306
309
310
313
375 thru 379
1332

Type	Numbers and/or names	Built	Original Service	Subsequent Service
	Union Pacific Railroad			
Coach	7000 thru 7009	1955	Cities	
	7010	1946	GN–NP–UP Pool	
	7011 thru 7015	1959	Cities	
Dining Car	8000 thru 8009	1955	Cities	
	8010	1946	GN–NP–UP Pool	
Lounge	9000 thru 9014	1955	Cities	
	9015	1946	GN–NP–UP Pool	
Sleeper	Dream Cloud	1946	GN–NP–UP Pool	

Remarks: The following dome cars were built by Pullman–Standard:

7010, 7011 thru 7015
8010
9015
Dream Cloud

Cars 7010, 8010, 9015 and Dream Cloud made up the consist of the "Train of Tomorrow".

All other cars constructed by ACF Industries.

Following number series sold to Alaska Railroad:

7004, 7008, 7013 and 7014

Following number series sold to Auto–Train Corp. in May, 1972:

7000 thru 7003, 7005, 7007, 7009, 7011, 7012 and 7015.

8000 thru 8009 except 8003, which was donated to the National Railroad Museum at Green Bay, Wisconsin in September, 1971.

9000 thru 9003, 9005 thru 9014.

Following dome cars retained by the Union Pacific:

7006, 9004

Train of Tomorrow cars were scrapped during the time period 1961 through 1965.

Type	Numbers and/or names	Built	Original Service	Subsequent Service
	Santa Fe Railway			
Lounge	500 thru 505	1950	Super Chief	
Big Dome Lounge Dorm.	550 thru 555	1954	San Fran. Chief	Texas Chief
Big Dome Lounge	506 thru 513	1954	El Cap. Trains 9, 11 and 12.	Chief
Hi-level Lounge	575 thru 580	1956	El Capitan	

Remarks: All dome cars were built by the Budd Company except series 500 thru 505 which were constructed by Pullman.

The following number series operated by AMTRAK:

500 thru 505
575 thru 580

The following number series sold to Auto–Train Corp.:

507 thru 513
550 thru 555

Big Dome Lounge No. 506 was retained by the Santa Fe.

Missouri Pacific Railroad

Type	Numbers and/or names	Built	Original Service	Subsequent Service
Coach	590 thru 592 (Ex-890 thru 892)	1948	Eagles	
	593 (Ex-893)	1952	Eagles	
	594 thru 596 (Ex-894 thru 896)	1952	Eagles	

Remarks: Series 590 thru 592 were constructed by the Budd Company.
Series 593 thru 596 were constructed by Pullman Standard.
Series 590 thru 594 and 596 sold to the Illinois Central in 1967.
Dome car No. 595 retired and scrapped in 1967.

Texas and Pacific Railway

Type	Numbers and/or names	Built	Original Service	Subsequent Service
Coach	597 (ex T&P No. 200)	1952	Eagles	Trains 21 and 22.

Remarks: Retired in 1967.

Illinois Central Railroad

Type	Numbers and/or names	Built	Original Service	Subsequent Service
Coach	2200 thru 2202 2210 thru 2212	1948 1952	Cities Cities	
Sleepers	Various numbers leased from Northern Pacific and Burlington Route		City of Miami Panama Limited	

Remarks: All Illinois Central domes were purchased from the Missouri Pacific in 1967. Series 2200 thru 2202 were constructed by the Budd Company, series 2210 thru 2212 by Pullman Standard.

All dome cars were retired in February, 1971.

Southern Railway

Type	Numbers and/or names	Built	Original Service	Subsequent Service
Coach	1613	1959	Trains 3 and 4	
Parlor	1602	1952	Southern Crescent	

Remarks: Dome coach No. 1613 was acquired from the Central of Georgia Railroad on May 1, 1971.

Dome parlor No. 1602 was acquired from the C of G in 1970.

Central of Georgia Railroad

Type	Numbers and/or names	Built	Original Service	Subsequent Service
Parlor	1602	1952	Nancy Hanks II	
Coach	1613	1959	Nancy Hanks II	

Remarks: Dome parlor No. 1602 was acquired from the Norfolk and Western Railway in January, 1968.

Dome coach No. 1613 was acquired from the N&W in 1970.

Pennsylvania Railraod

Type	Numbers and/or names	Built	Original Service	Subsequent Service
Sleeper	Various numbers leased from the Northern Pacific for winter season service.		South Wind	

Louisville & Nashville Railroad

Type	Numbers and/or names	Built	Original Service	Subsequent Service
Sleeper	(See Pennsylvania Railroad)		South Wind	

Seaboard Coast Line Railroad

Type	Numbers and/or names	Built	Original Service	Subsequent Service
Sleepers	Moonlight Dome Starlight Dome Sunlight Dome	1948	Florida Special	

Remarks: First leased and operated by the Atlantic Coast Line in 1965. These three cars are operated by AMTRAK.

The Milwaukee Road

Type	Numbers and/or names	Built	Original Service	Subsequent Service
Lounge	50 thru 59	1952	Hiawathas	City of Denver Challenger Various Chgo–Milw. Madison trains.

Remarks: Domes 50 thru 54 and 56 were sold to the Canadian National in 1964.

Milwaukee Road dome cars were constructed by Pullman Standard.

Canadian National Railways

Type	Numbers and/or names	Built	Original Service	Subsequent Service
Lounge	2400 Jasper 2401 Athabaska 2402 Yellowstone 2403 Fraser 2404 Qu'Appelle 2405 Columbia	1952	Super Continental Panorama	

Remarks: The CNR purchased the six Super Dome cars in 1964.

Canadian Pacific Railway

Type	Numbers and/or names	Built	Original Service	Subsequent Service
Coach–Coffee Shop	500 thru 517	1954	Dominion Canadian	Montreal & Toronto Pool
Sleeper Obs. Lounge	Algonquin Park Assiniboine Park Banff Park Evangeline Park Fundy Park Glacier Park Kokanee Park Kootenay Park Laurentide Park Prince Albert Park Revelstoke Park Riding Mountain Park Sibley Park Strathcona Park Tremblant Park Tweedsmuir Park Waterton Park Yoho Park	1954	Dominion Canadian	Montreal & Toronto Pool

Remarks: All CPR domes were constructed by the Budd Company.

Fundy Park was destroyed and is no longer on the Canadian Pacific roster.

Baltimore and Ohio Railroad

Type	Numbers and/or names	Built	Original Service	Subsequent Service
Coach	5550 High Dome 5551 Sky Dome	1949	Columbian	Capitol Limited Shenandoah
Sleepers	Moonlight Dome Starlight Dome Sunlight Dome	1948	Capitol Limited Shenandoah	

Remarks: Domes 5550 and 5551 were constructed by Pullman Standard. The sleeper domes were constructed by the Budd Company for the Chesapeake and Ohio Railway, and sold to the B&O in 1950.

Coaches 5550 and 5551 operated by AMTRAK.

Type	Numbers and/or names	Built	Original Service	Sub-sequent Service
Chesapeake and Ohio Railroad				
Sleeper	1850 thru 1852	1948	Chessie	Sportsman
Observation Lounge	1875 thru 1877	1948	Chessie	Pere Marquette

Remarks: Sleepers sold to Baltimore & Ohio Railroad in 1950.

Observation Lounge cars sold to the Denver & Rio Grande Western in 1949 and converted to coaches.

All domes were constructed by the Budd Company.

Type	Numbers and/or names	Built	Original Service	Sub-sequent Service
Southern Pacific Company				
Lounge	3600 thru 3606	1954	Daylights Over-land	City of San Fran-cisco

Remarks: All SP dome lounge cars were built by Southern Pacific.

AMTRAK operated SP dome lounge cars in the California Zephyr, and later on the City of San Francisco during 1971 and 1972.

Type	Numbers and/or names	Built	Original Service	Sub-sequent Service
Alaska Railroad				
Coach	7004, 7008, 7013 and 7014	1954 1959	Aurora	

Remarks: Purchased from the Union Pacific Railroad in 1971.

Type	Numbers and/or names	Built	Original Service	Sub-sequent Service
Rock Island Railroad				
Parlor–Lounge	Big Ben	1948	Quad Cities Rocket	

Remarks: Originally constructed by the Budd Company for the Chesapeake and Ohio Railroad.

Type	Numbers and/or names	Built	Original Service	Sub-sequent Service
TURBO				
3 CAR	Department of Trans – portation (Two sets/four domes)	1968	New York–Boston Washington–Parkersburg	
7 CAR	Canadian National (Five sets/ten domes)	1968	Montreal–Toronto	

Type	Numbers and/or names	Built	Original Service	Sub-sequent Service
Auto-Liner Corporation				
Coach–Lounge–Bar	200 Linoma	1948	Special Trains	

Remarks: Originally constructed for the C&O. This car now has 28 seats in the coach section, 11 seats in the observation lounge and 24 seats in the dome with six tables and dome dining service. The car is fitted for mid-train operation.

Type	Numbers and/or names	Built	Original Service	Sub-sequent Service
Auto-Train				
Coach Dorm–Bar	510 thru 515 (ex AT&SF 550 thru 555)	1954	Lorton–Sanford	
Coach Lounge Bar	520 thru 524 (ex AT&SF 507 thru 513)	1954	Lorton–Sanford	
Coach	460 to 463, 470 to 472 (ex WP 811 thru 817)	1948	Lorton–Sanford	
Lounge	540 and 541 (From AT&SF series 507 thru 513)	1954	Lorton–Sanford	

Type	Numbers and/or names	Built	Original Service	Sub-sequent Service
Norfolk and Western Railway/Wabash Railroad				
Coach	1610 thru 1612 (Ex-Wabash 200 – 202)	1950	Blue Bird	Banner Blue Pocahontas
Parlor Obs.	1601	1950	Blue Bird	Banner Blue
Parlor	1602 (Blue Bird Room)	1952	Blue Bird	
Coach	1613 (Ex-Wabash 203)	1959	City of St. Louis	

Remarks: Wabash series 1610 thru 1612 and 1601 were constructed by the Budd Company. Cars 1602 and 1613 were built by Pullman Standard. Coach No. 1613 was painted in The Union Pacific color scheme under both the Wabash and Norfolk and Western names.

Series 1610 thru 1612 and 1601 operated by AMTRAK.

INDEX